SEXUAL HARASSMENT
of
WOMEN at WORKPLACES

Thank you for choosing a SAGE product!
If you have any comment, observation or feedback,
I would like to personally hear from you.

Please write to me at **contactceo@sagepub.in**

Vivek Mehra, Managing Director and CEO, SAGE India.

SEXUAL HARASSMENT *of* WOMEN at WORKPLACES

Mental Health and Social Aspects

R. C. JILOHA

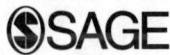

Los Angeles | London | New Delhi
Singapore | Washington DC | Melbourne

First published in 2021 by

SAGE Publications India Pvt Ltd
B1/I-1 Mohan Cooperative Industrial Area
Mathura Road, New Delhi 110 044, India
www.sagepub.in

SAGE Publications Inc
2455 Teller Road
Thousand Oaks, California 91320, USA

SAGE Publications Ltd
1 Oliver's Yard, 55 City Road
London EC1Y 1SP, United Kingdom

SAGE Publications Asia-Pacific Pte Ltd
18 Cross Street #10-10/11/12
China Square Central
Singapore 048423

Published by Vivek Mehra for SAGE Publications India Pvt Ltd. Typeset in 10.5/13 pt Adobe Caslon Pro by AG Infographics, Delhi.

Library of Congress Control Number: 2021934655

ISBN: 978-93-5388-423-9 (HB)   .

SAGE Team: Rajesh Dey, Ankit Verma, Aishna Bhatt and Anupama Krishnan

Contents

Foreword

With improved access to education and employment, millions of women are entering the workforce across the globe, the domain which was earlier monopolized by males. Similar gender equity has occurred in the distribution of men and women entering previously male-dominated professional schools, such as law and medicine. In addition, the proportion of women managers has risen manifold. Along with shifts in numbers have come shifts in women's attitudes and expectations regarding work outside the home.

Change in the demographic profile of the workplace and educational institutions has led to change in the interpersonal dynamics culminating into gender bias and gender discrimination. Sexual harassment is a form of gender discrimination which has emerged as a prominent feature of workplaces and educational institutions.

The issue of sexual harassment of women at workplace was addressed comprehensively by the Honourable Supreme Court in *Vishaka vs. the State of Rajasthan* in 1997. In the absence of legislation, the apex court, in the case under reference, issued 12 guidelines based on the basic framework laid down by Articles 11 and 24 of the Convention on the Elimination of Forms of Discrimination against Women. These guidelines became the law of the land till the enactment of legislation on the subject. The Sexual Harassment at Workplace (Prevention, Prohibition and Redressal) Act, after its enactment, came into force with effect from 9 December 2013.

Many women confront sexual harassment at the workplace almost every day, which not only adversely affects work productivity but even leads to detrimental health effects on the victim.

Although sexual harassment has received much attention both socially and legally in the last two decades, there is not much work on the clinical aspects of the problem. The cause and impact of sexual harassment in educational institutions, offices, factories and other places of work have not received much attention until recent times.

Professor Jiloha's book is one effort in this direction.

This book emphasizes that, more than anything else, sexual harassment affects the mindset of the women, leading to a wide range of mental health problems needing therapeutic and rehabilitative intervention in addition to the legal redressal. The book highlights the need for strong empirical evidence to establish an effective framework to deal with clinical aspects, including treatment, which is relatively scarce and limited at present. This book is the first attempt in the Indian context to investigate the profiles of harassers in terms of biological predispositions, conditioning and social learning experiences and the sociocultural contexts in which the sexual harassment behaviour unfolds. The diversity of factors which play a part in the aetiology and maintenance of sexually harassing behaviour have been well highlighted in the book. Professor Jiloha has tried to provide newer insights to understand sexual harassment from the psychosocial and mental health perspective.

Society often underestimates actions, words and gestures with sexual tint as trivial and terms them 'harmless flirtations' in an effort to shield the culprit in many reported cases. Sexual harassment of women at the workplace is a common occurrence in India that goes unspoken in most of the cases due to social stigma or fear of retribution. In many instances, women remain silent when they face abject experiences at the workplace because of ignorance of law and the lack of understanding of their rights or fear. Even the employers who are obligated under the Act to protect the rights of their employees often take no cognisance of such cases and do not facilitate redressal of complaints on the pretext that they would somehow get resolved on their own.

This book addresses the plea of victims and serves well as a valuable resource for raising awareness of their rights and as a guide to claim their legitimate share in social life. The book provides invaluable information for effective implementation of the Sexual Harassment at Workplace (Prevention, Prohibition and Redressal) Act, 2013.

Rekha Sharma
Chairperson,
National Commission for Women

Preface

Recently, Delhi High Court refused relief to a Delhi University professor who was compulsorily retired by the university authorities for sexually harassing a woman student. The court observed that a student harbouring an infatuation towards a teacher may be pardonable, but it is entirely unpardonable for the teacher to succumb to the infatuation and reciprocate. According to the court, students may be impressionable, but any reciprocation renders a teacher unfit to continue to teach in the institution. The observation made by the court speaks not only about the responsibility invested with those in authority, but it also directs the educational institutions to curb the incidents of sexual harassment. The teacher–student relationship is sacred, and slightest sexual tinge in this relationship on the part of the teacher indelibly tarnishes this relationship and consigns it to profligacy. Although sexual exploitation in a teacher–pupil relationship is common in educational institutions, it is no less common at other places where men and women work together. It is a pervasive phenomenon across cultures, and the power dynamics play a big role in almost all cases. It is so common at the workplace that one sexual harassment scandal comes after another with a similar shape and form wherein a powerful man exploits his junior colleague sexually for decades and goes unpunished until the victim picks up the courage to complain against him.

Society often trivializes women's experience of men with expressed or implied actions of sexual tint. Because of social taboo, women often tend to either avoid the harassers or ignore the harassment. Many of them do not want to enter into the complications of complaint procedure because of embarrassing interrogations, social scrutiny, criticism and mockery. Formal complaints, legal cases and survey reports show how the perpetrators, for their vicarious sexual gratification, target the vulnerable females. Mostly, the incidents are swept under the carpet, and the women suffer silently.

The recently launched #MeToo crusade against sexual coercion reveals the widespread prevalence of the problem at the workplace with most of the accused having quietly resumed work and climbed back to their social perches without being punished. An actor, accused of rape by several women, is even playing the role of an upright judge who cares about women's rights in a movie. A former minister and editor, against whom there are multiple testimonies, has slapped a case of defamation against a woman journalist continuing to sound off in prestigious publications and applauded by other men. In India, most of the sexual harassment victims who spoke out have been made to suffer for it. Women who joined hands to press their case have been out of work, and the men accused of crime have suffered no scratches on their career.

The feminist movement of recent times has created widespread awareness that the unwelcome sexual conduct of men not only erodes the human rights of the victims, but it also makes the environment hostile and thus adversely affects the work productivity of the organizations.

The traditional approach to deal with the cases of unwelcome sexual conduct, which include apprehending, charging, convicting and punishing the culprits by the criminal justice system, constituted only few offenders and the majority of criminals went unpunished.

However, with the advent of more rational and innovative measures, we may proceed well-equipped to deal with the problem.

One such innovative measure during the recent times has been the introduction of the Sexual Harassment of Women at Workplace (Prevention, Prohibition and Redressal) Act, 2013, meant to protect women from sexual harassment at their place of work.

Sexual harassment is a phenomenon limited not only to the legal aspects, important for the delivery of justice, but it also has wider ramifications in terms of health, social justice, financial difficulties and the stigma attached with it.

Human mind reacts cognitively to every incident and sexual harassment is no exception. Since sexual harassment involves the violation of the victim's integrity, her health is bound to get adversely affected, requiring therapeutic and rehabilitative intervention to restore normalcy in her life. Strong empirical evidence is required for a framework to describe clinical aspects, including treatment, which is relatively scarce and limited at present. The book seeks to address these issues in the light of available scientific data.

To begin with, book reviews the existing literature and traces the history of the evolution of legal environment against sexual harassment and then describes the Sexual Harassment of Women at Workplace (Prevention, Prohibition and Redressal) Act, 2013, followed by psychodynamics of gender-based crimes.

The book also discusses the characteristics and personality profile of the harassers, their psychopathology and the treatment they need. In an attempt to provide perspective on the harassers or the perpetrators, researchers have implicated biological factors, social learning experiences and sociocultural factors to develop therapies to help them to modify their behaviour.

The background information from various non-clinical disciplines has been incorporated in the book, but it is neither intended to make it an extensive legal document nor a summary of current research. It is to provide relevant information to allow clinicians to focus their attention on intrapsychic issues and the complex external environmental factors associated with the phenomenon. While providing psychological intervention, an active, flexible and eclectic approach should be adopted that focuses on both internal and external needs. This can be possible with an understanding of both the workplace and the individuals involved. Understanding of the dynamics of the workplace environment is necessary not only to know the negative psychological consequences of sexual harassment but also to know how victimized people recover from these adverse experiences in that particular environment. Structural and environmental conditions of workplace contribute to discriminatory events and can be clinically significant in several ways. Environmental conditions also help the victims to avoid internalization of guilt and shame. The therapist and the victim in a mutual collaboration formulate an effective and adaptive coping plan. This book elaborately describes all these mechanisms.

The book is both ahead of time and immensely late to reach the readership. It is ahead of time because the adverse health effects of sexual harassment and their treatment described in this book aim at a serious mental health problem, one which has been incompletely defined and unrecognised as a health problem by majority of professionals. Dealing with sexual harassment and its damaging health consequences, this book is immensely late as little has been described about the treatment interventions for the sexual harassers till date, even though women have been occupying significant space at the workplace which makes them vulnerable to various forms of sexual harassment and their harassers stay at large without any kind of behavioural intervention to correct their anti-social conduct.

The book is meant for all establishments for basic understanding of sexual harassment. Men and women with different backgrounds meeting at workplace may have different meaning for sexual harassment, but at a common platform, it is undesirable, unwelcome and, of course, a crime. For physicians, psychiatrists and psychologists, it is a clinical condition to study, provide relief and develop strategies for prevention. The book will help professionals in diagnostic understanding and treatment planning. It will also be of help to other associated professionals, such as administrators and managers, in understanding sexual harassment and dealing with it.

Acknowledgements

Behind the writing of this book, there is an investment of the hard work and dedication of several friends and colleagues, whose names may not be possible to mention here. I gratefully acknowledge their help in bringing this book to its current shape, which, I believe, will be highly useful for the readers.

Warm appreciation and thanks are extended to Professor Dinesh Kataria of Lady Hardinge Medical College, New Delhi, for his assistance in procuring rare research literature on the subject and to Dr Meely Panda of Hamdard Institute of Medical Sciences and Research, New Delhi, for her valuable research inputs. I sincerely thank Surender Mahi, Executive Director, Indian Railways, for critically reviewing the manuscript. Thanks to all concerned for contributing clinical and theoretical expertise. Greatest appreciation is extended to my daughter, Raahath, and my wife, Krishana, who generously supported me through this lengthy project.

CHAPTER 1

Introduction and Overview

Millions of women across the globe experience violence and live under its shadow on a daily basis.[1] Throughout the history of mankind, women have remained the victims of men's high-handedness, often accepted by society, and condoned and even approved by the law.[2] In older times, Roman law permitted men to inflict cruelty on their wives, even to the extent of killing them; burning of alleged witches in Europe during the mediaeval period was accepted by both, the church and the state.[3], [4] In India, *satee*, the practice of burning of widowed women alive with their dead husbands, was considered an act of merit for a faithful, pious and devout wife. The cases of honour killing are not a rare occurrence in modern Indian society with its roots in ancient religious scriptures.[5] Whether it was Sita's fire-trial or Draupadi's disrobing act, there have been countless instances depicting women's victimization across world's history and geography speaking volumes on the atrocities men caused on women simply because they have been women. There has been no society in the past where women's freedom from violence has been secured,[6] their harassment is a phenomenon since times immemorial and continues even today with almost the same vigour.

Women's experience of pervasive sexual intimidation and outright abuse is a consequence of social pathology which makes regular headlines of daily newspapers. It includes rape, violence by intimate partners, sexual harassment by non-intimate partners and strangers and so on.[7] The violence against women is closely related to the traditional view of women as men's property with a subservience social role. The likely perpetrators are in-laws, spouses, partners, other family members, professional colleagues and the seniors, wielding power or influence. At the places of work, sexual harassment of women is often overlooked by the employers to minimize its intensity and allow it to continue without cognizance; it is almost universally underreported.[8]

Women who are able to raise their voice against it are few considering the enormity of what actually happens in reality at workplaces and in the educational institutions.[9] Gender discrimination in the labour force maintains and perpetuates women's disadvantaged position leading to persistent gender inequalities. Right to gender equality for women is often violated, and their life and liberty are put at risk by men who wish to control them sexually or otherwise making the work environment insecure and hostile for them. It discourages women from participating in work and decision making and adversely affects their economic empowerment and partnership in inclusive growth and productivity.

Traditionally, outdoor work has remained a male domain since ages to support and sustain families, leaving women to stay at home to cook food and bring up children. During the period of industrialization, in Europe, White workers and employers monopolized the running of industry, marginalized outsiders—the enslaved Blacks, denied them training and consigned poorest paying jobs. Women remained among the worst of the sufferers of exclusion and marginalization. They were not only the subjects of deprivation and discrimination, but they were also sexually exploited for the favour of securing jobs and job-related benefits. Objectification of women, therefore, is not a new phenomenon; discrimination and sexual coercion can be traced to colonial times.[10]

Despite long-standing historical evidence, sexual harassment has remained an unimportant element of the workplace and academic institutions. Although it is prevalent in all human societies, it remained obscured from view for various reasons. It remained ignored by the powerful and unexamined of scientific scrutiny by the civil society for long. It was only after the political initiative of the Civil Rights Movement in the USA during the 1960s that a meaningful definition of gender discrimination and sexual harassment as a specific form of gender discrimination was provided. It was defined during the Women's Movement in the 1970s, focusing on various forms of sexual violence against women.[11]

Gradually, the subject of sexual harassment of women became the focus of academic interest in various educational institutions. Legal and social science scholars began academic exploration to theorize and explain the phenomenon in legal, social and psychological perspective[12] to carry out prevalent studies on sexual harassment from a broad spectrum of employment and academic settings as well as from the people who were the victims of this social menace. These studies revealed the prevalence of sexual harassment at workplace, often associated with adverse impact on both individuals and the establishments.[13]

Legal activities proliferated along with the management research which culminated into a documentation of certain observations classified into the following two broad categories:

- The nature of discriminatory actions the women were subjected to.
- The extent and liability of damages suffered by the individual victims and the organizations.

Subsequent studies focused on the characteristics of harasser–victim interaction resulting in negative psychological and other health effects on the aggrieved women or the victims. Public, in general, and most clinicians, in particular, regarded sexual harassment as a legal than a health issue, and the clinical aspect of the phenomenon remained overlooked for long. To pursue the significance of clinical aspects in the broader organizational, legal, socio-psychological and ethical domains, studies began to fully comprehend the nature of the problem in terms of public health concerns. For this purpose, the terms used in research need to be succinctly defined with regard to their evolving meaning in relation to psychological and health consequences. With the advent of a reasonably good understanding of the phenomenon, generally agreed definitions have emerged for the following terms which are often used in research studies:

1. Gender and sex
2. Gender bias
3. Gender/sex discrimination
4. Sexual harassment

For our understanding, research, legal application and to explore the health needs, these terms are defined as follows.

1.1. Gender and Sex

The term sex is described in relation to the biological distinction of males and females on the basis of anatomical and physiological differences. Gender means personal characteristics, abilities and interests that are culturally attributable and socially constructed differently between the two sexes. Sex and gender are intricately intertwined because gender characteristics are assigned based on whether one is born male or female—the anatomical assignment. According to Barrell and Hearn,[14] the framework for conceptualizing sexuality and gender is as follows:

1. Biological essences
2. Outcome of social roles
3. Fundamental political categories
4. Communication practices and discourses of powers

It is relevant to know the difference between sex and gender to understand some psychological consequences of discrimination and harassment, though these terms are often used interchangeably. However, there is a small percentage of people who have incompatibility in their biological sex and gender; they feel distressed with their biological attributes and have a strong desire to change to the opposite sex. They are the transgenders and are referred to as third sex.

1.2. Gender Bias

Gender bias occurs when importance is given to one gender over the other. It is the conscious or subtle like or dislike of one gender over the other. Under certain situations, some aspects of work or educational experiences differ on the basis of the sex of employees or students. Very commonly perceived behaviour on account of one's gender is the core feature of gender bias, which is often levelled against men for their differential treatment. Gender equality forms the basis of laws which govern workplaces, family courts and even the voting booth in many countries. Although most counties in the world do not observe gender bias, many legal and political scholars argue that complete gender parity is a difficult proposition.

The differential approach of favouring one sex over the other may lead to a positive or negative impact, or there may be no impact at all; bias is likely to lead to discrimination. Birth of a daughter in a traditional Indian family is generally not welcome, and preference is given to a male child. This attitude of the family leads to inequality in bringing up children. Although the gender disparity has dwindled to a great extent since the mid-20th century, pay equality between the male and female employees has still remained a debatable issue at several places. Men receiving more money than women for the same work is illogical and unjust and speaks of gender bias. Those who oppose women's equal pay with men argue that women work less over their lives, instead making a choice to remain at home and raise children. Those who support pay equality believe that the argument of those who oppose equality is the overall gender bias.

1.3. Gender or Sex Discrimination

Gender or sex discrimination includes gender biases with negative impact. Theoretically, gender or sex discrimination often presents in the following forms.

1. **Unequal rewards:** Men and women receive different rewards for the same work at the workplace or in academic institutions. This unequal distribution of rewards is based not on their work

performance but on their gender. In the process, one sex is discriminated against another, leading to unequal rewards.

2. **Limited access:** Gender discrimination limits an individual to avail an opportunity or a resource because of his/her sex or may face harassment for availing the opportunity or the resource. Women are often denied certain jobs, but when they manage to get these jobs, they are harassed in various ways, including sexual harassment.

3. **Inhibiting individuals:** Social forces that inhibit individual from fully seeking appropriate, lawful and educational work experience outside those that are culturally defined as appropriate for their sex, operate vigorously in certain communities and societies.

The legal definition of sex discrimination is more limited than the theoretical framework. The legal definition of sex discrimination qualifies if the pervasive patterns of disparate treatment or disparate impact or creation of a hostile environment have a negative impact on the student or the employee of one sex as compared to the other. Some employees are treated unfavourably and thus directly discriminated while some others are assumed to be incapable. Discrimination of the employees on the basis of sex may include the following examples:

- Preferring males for certain jobs despite females being equally qualified and competent.
- For the same job and equal number of working hours, there are different rates of pay or benefits for men and women.
- Employer's assumption that a women employee is incapable of handling a senior position in the organization prevents promoting women to a senior position.
- Dividing up work tasks according to gender rather than seniority and competence.

1.4. Sexual Harassment

The terminology of sexual harassment has been developed fairly recently. Till the late 1970s or the early 1980s, there was no word or phrase defining specific behaviours or conducts that were sexually inappropriate in the context in which these behaviours occurred.[9] According to Barr,[15] the behaviour with sexual connotations that is unwelcome or uncalled for is sexual harassment. It is a simple definition, but the phrase 'sexual connotation' needs further explanation. MacKinnon[16] attempts to define sexual harassment as an imposition of sexual requirements, unwanted in the context of a relationship of unequal power. Uggen and Blackstone[17] explain the meaning of sexual harassment in the context of the age, gender, race, class and caste of the affected person.

It is a global problem affecting almost all societies; however, there is no common social definition to help its victims readily identify such behaviour.

Although sexual harassment is very common in prevalence and widely studied gender discrimination, it is still without a universally accepted definition. There is no generally agreed-upon operational terminology because it is the subjective experience of the victim that matters and complicates the issue as the interpretation of perception may differ with different people for the same experience in different sociocultural contexts. There could be many who disagree with the victim about the qualification of sexual experience as harassment. Fitzgerald and Schulman[18] divide sexual harassment behaviour into the following two broad categories.

1.4.1. Priori

Priori definition is derived from theoretical construct and is a commonly accepted description,[19] providing a standard for legal and institutional definitions and includes unsolicited sexual conduct, asking for sexual favours and or other verbal or physical behaviour with sexual connotation when:

1. A woman submits herself to such conduct to get employment.
2. Continuity of a woman in employment is subject to acceptance or refusal of such a conduct.
3. Performance at the workplace is substantially affected by such a conduct.

The first two situations refer to 'quid pro quo' type in which employment or academic opportunities or service benefits are exchanged for sexual compliance. It is demanding sexual favours in return for professional benefits such as promotion, higher salary and academic endorsements or recommendations. A woman is compelled to comply with the demand; her refusal to do so can result in retaliation in the form of termination of service, demotion, damaging memos to superiors, spoilt work record and unhealthy work conditions. The exchange is coercive when there is refusal to comply.

The third situation is about the damage created by a 'hostile environment'. Although it is very common, it not very clearly understood. This is a form of workplace sexual harassment which often involves work conditions or behaviour towards a woman that makes it unbearable for her to be even present there. In the hostile work environment, a woman is neither promised nor denied anything in her work context; she still faces sexual harassment because she is a woman.

1.4.2. Empirical

Empirical category pertains to the list of behaviours derived from the database. Psychometrically, the standardized empirical definition has five levels of harassing behaviour, which are listed as follows.

1. **Gender harassment:** This includes generalized sexual remarks and behaviours to communicate degrading or sexist attitude towards women.
2. **Seducing behaviour:** This behaviour includes inappropriate and offensive sexual advances to seduce a woman.
3. **Sexual bribery:** This is the behaviour that includes soliciting sexual activity for some benefit to the woman.
4. **Sexual coercion:** It includes a threat of punishment for non-compliance to sexual demands.
5. **Sexual imposition:** Sexual imposition includes attempts to touch, kiss, grab or actual sexual assault against the victim's wishes.

Empirical explanations emphasize the importance of perception of the victim. It is the victim's experience that matters, which may not necessarily be in agreement with the harasser.

The International Labour Organization defines sexual harassment as[20]:

> [A]ny behaviour of a sexual nature that affects the dignity of women and men, which is considered as unwanted, unacceptable, inappropriate and offensive to the recipient, and that creates an intimidating, hostile, unstable or offensive work environment.

All the above definitions suffer from limitations and may not correlate directly to psychological consequences. To improve upon these definitions, Fitzgerald[21] gives the following definition based on the combination of empirical and theoretical perspectives:

> Sexual harassment consists of sexualisation of an instrumental relationship through the introduction or imposition of sexual remarks, requests or requirements in the context of formal power differences. Harassment can also occur where no such power difference exists if the behaviour is unwanted or offensive to woman.

Sexual harassment can be categorized into four types according to the way it is expressed by the harasser. These four types are as follows:

- Verbal
- Non-verbal
- Visual
- Physical

'Verbal form' is expressed in words in the hearing range of the victim, particularly the sexual jokes, the most frequent experiences, go ignored in most cases. Comments about the figure, such as body make, is another 'verbal type' most commonly experienced, such as *moti* and *naati*. This form of sexual harassments has no precise statistical account available, but it is as common as sexual jokes. 'Non-verbal form' is in the form of facial expressions, gestures and actions such as staring, leering, making sexual gestures and whistling are also commonly experienced which are often tolerated silently by the victims without reporting. 'Visual' type of sexual harassment includes showing pornographic material, exhibiting genitals or becoming naked in front of the victim. The 'physical form' includes unsolicited physical contact, sexual imposition and may include inappropriate touching, fondling, molesting, grabbing, kissing or raping.[22] Depending upon the intensity and severity, sexual harassment can be measured from 'mild misbehaviour' to severe sexual crime like rape.[9]

Sexual harassment and sex-based harassment are two distinct entities, and sexual harassment is not necessarily about sexuality or sexual desire; rather, it can be an assertion of the power of one sex (as in maleness or femaleness) over the other.[23] The sexual behaviour based on mutual attraction, friendship, love and respect is not sexual harassment. A consensual interaction which is welcome, inviting and reciprocated is not sexual harassment.

1.5. The Magnitude of Sexual Harassment

Sexual harassment is often underreported, and in most cases, women remain silent and ignore certain forms of behaviour of men, passing it off as 'male behaviour'. These behaviours include eve-teasing, passing lewd comments or wolf-whistling which go unnoticed or passed off as usual male behaviour. The United States Merit Systems Protection Board[24] was the first to study sexual harassment on the federal workforce in 1980, 1987, 1994 and 2016. The behaviours classified as sexual harassment rose sharply from 1980 to 2016, and the percentage of men who believed pressuring a female coworker for sexual favours increased from 65 per cent in 1980 to 93 per cent in 1994 and further to 97 per cent in 2016. However, the lack of reporting was not due to respondents' inaccurately defining sexual harassment, but due to the reluctance of the victims to take formal action for various reasons.

The US military is another organization to study sexual harassment starting in 1995 and going to 2012 using a sequence format. The Defense Manpower Data Centre found the gender-harassing form the most prevalent type of sexually harassing behaviour.[25] In 2016, the Equal Employment Opportunity Commission (EEOC) found 25–85 per cent of women reporting experience of sexual harassment at their workplace though 75 per cent of all incidents go unreported.[19]

In 1998, the European Commission in the European Union found that one out of every two–three women experienced some form of sexual harassment or sexually unwanted behaviour at the workplace.[26] Similarly, 79 per cent of US women suffered from sexual harassment at their workplace; 51 per cent of them were harassed by their supervisors only. Sexual harassment occurs in a majority of professions—business, trade, banking, finance and the industries, where sexual harassment is quite common. In a 1982 study on sexual harassment in a university campus in the USA, 30 per cent female students reported unwanted sexual attention from male instructors.[11]

The wide variation, in prevalence, is because of underreporting in certain societies. In the male-dominated societies, women often do not report due to the fear of retaliation, disgrace and further harassment. However, the surveys conducted in confidentiality by various researchers come out with the data on the prevalence of sexual harassment, which reflects the true picture of the situation. To measure sexual harassment, a multidimensional index which includes sexist remarks, sexually crude or offensive behaviour, infantilization, work policing, and gender policing was developed by Leskinen and Cortina. This scale has been used in several epidemiological surveys to know the magnitude of the problem.[27] However, cultural variations do exist resulting in variation in prevalent figures, for example, rates of unsolicited physical contacts differ between countries and cultures, depending upon social acceptance and tolerability.[28]

Indian society, with its vast cultural diversity and social mannerism, expresses sexual harassment in a variety of local and global forms.[29] According to Satpodar,[30] India tops the Reuters with 26 per cent women reporting sexual harassment. In some traditional cultures and certain unorganized sectors of workplace, sexual promiscuity is an accepted norm; sexual jokes, gestures and even inappropriate touch are not considered bad by the men in general, and women tolerate such conducts of men as a part of their gender dominance despite the fact that, for most of these women, such conducts are unwelcome, unwanted and forced.[31] However, with the advent of education and increased awareness about the behaviours that constitute sexual harassment, women are becoming increasingly conscious of their legitimate rights to protest against any such violation. A similar change has been witnessed among men to refrain from behaviours that violate women's rights and dignity. The proportion of men considering unwanted sexual jokes and remarks as sexual harassment has also increased from 42 per cent in 1989 to 64 per cent in 1994.[32]

Most of the incidents of sexual harassment in India go unreported due to the lack of a centralized mechanism to collect the data. The data available reflects only the tip of the iceberg. According to Ghosh et al.,[33] out of 500 cases, only 50 are reported to the authorities. It poses a serious threat for assimilating women in organizations, offices and educational institutions.

Not only the cases of sexual harassment go unreported, but also the amount of work women do is not adequately reflected in official statistics. This has a direct link with their sexual harassment. Their work is not included in the official data, but if included, their overall work participation would be 86.2 per cent. Women's work participation rate is 25.3 per cent in rural settings and 14.7 per cent in the urban settings, but as per estimates, the women's workforce is huge.[34] Around 93 per cent of the women workers are employed in the unorganized sector without any protection by laws. With no laws or mechanisms to protect them, proactive measures are needed to make their workplaces safe.

In 2014, the National Commission for Women (NCW) reported a progressive increase in the cases of sexual harassment in the preceding three years. National Crime Records Bureau started collecting data under 'insult to the modesty of women (Indian Penal Code [IPC] Section 509) at office premises and other places related to work' since 2014 and reported a total of 526 cases of sexual harassment.[35], [36] A total of 337,922 cases of crime against women were reported in the year 2014 as against 309,546 in 2013, thus showing an increase of 9.2 per cent during the year 2014.[37] There is a significant rise in the cases as 72 per cent women are of the opinion that gender discrimination prevails at workplaces, and effective policies are needed to curb it.[38] The data provided by India's corporate affairs ministry[39] for the top 100 companies listed on the National Stock Exchange became double in the financial year 2014–2015 substantiates the need for an effective policy.

Research across the country reveals ongoing discrimination of women within both the organized and unorganized sectors of the workplace.[40] Studies from different service sectors provide figures on the prevalence of sexual harassment in government offices and educational institutions, including private organizations. Around 21.4 per cent of women civil servants believed sexual harassment to be on the rise in coveted government jobs like Indian Administrative Services,[41] 88 per cent women employees of information technology (IT) and back-office operations sector reported they were sexually harassed in some form or the other, and similar findings were reported in the health sector.[42] The Social and Rural Research Institute[43] from eight cities in the country found that 17 per cent women faced sexual harassment at the workplace, in both formal and informal sectors of the workplace.

Poonam Sahgal and Aastha Dang[40] in their research found that the women who are divorced or separated are at a greater risk of sexual harassment as they are deemed to be 'available'. The women running their own business are persistently harassed for returns in the form of 'favours' to get business leads or contracts. A new entrant in the job or a woman lower in the organizational hierarchy is more vulnerable to harassment. Single women and those from small towns working far from their homes and staying alone are more vulnerable as they do not have support systems in the bigger city and are perceived 'easy prey'. According to an organization working against sexual harassment reveals 80 per cent of women as victims of sexual harassment of which 53 per cent had no equal opportunities with men, and another 53 per cent were treated unfairly by the employers. Around 58 per cent of the women were not aware of any redressal mechanism available to approach.

Sexual harassment is a complex social issue that adversely affects individuals, organizations and society.[43], [44] In India, it is one of the most closeted forms of gender discrimination.[44] Although various laws and institutional measures have been promulgated,[45] research reveals that women continue to be discriminated everywhere in various ways.[40], [46]

Sexual harassment is violative of the fundamental right to gender equality and the right to life and liberty. IPC, 1860;[47] the Criminal Procedure Code, 1908;[48] the Criminal Procedure Code, 1973;[49] Indian Evidence Act, 1872,[50] along with many other special Acts and welfare legislation deal with this issue in one way or the other and provide specific protection of women against sexual harassment. International conventions to which India is a signatory are also a source of law,[51] but these provisions do not prove sufficient while handling commonly occurring cases.

Like everywhere in the world, a number of measures have been deployed in India to address the ubiquitous levels of workplace sexual harassment. In view of sexual harassment being violative of the fundamental right of women to equality, there were several landmark judicial pronouncements to fill up the vacuum till the enactment of 2013 legislation. The Vishaka Guidelines,[52] formulated by the Supreme Court of India in August 1997, was a landmark pronouncement. In this case, legally binding guidelines based on the right to equality and dignity accorded under the Indian Constitution and the United Nations Convention on the Elimination of All Forms of Discrimination against Women, were created by the court.[51]

Vishaka judgement[52] provided for international standards to expand the scope of India's constitutional guarantees and fill in the existing gaps. The apex court laid down the foundation and paved path for the legislation which came some 16 years later in 2013 as the Sexual Harassment of Women at Workplace (Prevention, Prohibition and Redressal) Act.[53] Initiated by the Vishaka Guidelines,[52] this Act has given critical visibility to India's innovative to tackle sexual harassment at workplace. Within this context, all the places of work including educational institutions are bound to ensure safe and secure spaces for women. With this, sexual harassment at the workplace is recognized as a criminal offence in the country. Through this legal exercise, a clear definition of sexual harassment has emerged as,

Any unwelcome, sexually determined physical, verbal or non-verbal conduct such as sexually suggestive remarks about women, demands for sexual favours and showing sexually offensive visuals in the workplace.

Women's disadvantaged position in their workplace and the threats relating to their employment decisions negatively affect their work profile. Employers have the responsibility to ensure safety and provide protection against a hostile work environment.

The Act provides a redressal mechanism in the form of complaints committees which are mandated to have a woman head, with at least half its members being women and an external member. The Act also has a provision of creating awareness among the employees through regular workshops and awareness programmes. According to the Act, it is mandatory for every establishment to have a written sexual harassment policy to guide its employees.

1.6. #MeToo Movement

#MeToo movement originated in the USA in October 2017 by the use of a hashtag with two words—#MeToo.[54] It was started by an actress Alyssa Milano to draw attention against sexual harassment and sexual assault. To begin with, it was confined to the cinema industry and soon spread to workplaces, in general. The actress managed to encourage women to express grievances of sexual harassment experienced at any point in their lives. Within 24 hours of its initiation, it was posted million times on Facebook showing the gravity of the problem. No doubt, the '#MeToo' was fronted by a famous White US woman, but it was founded by an African–American activist, Tarana Burke,[55] on behalf of women of colour from lower socio-economic backgrounds, to come forward, share their experiences and begin a process of redressing their grievances. The movement gradually expanded globally across various social media platforms. Burke's work is recognized but remained confined to the middle and upper classes of society having access to the Internet.

Gradually, many vulnerable groups of society became part of this movement, to express themselves and to have their voices heard by others across the world. Through this movement, people could expand their conversation, beyond celebrities, to involve common people— friends, neighbours, co-workers and family—openly discussing their experiences with sexual harassment. This movement has been disturbing for many and an eye-opener for most.

In India, the sexual harassment of staff nurses, air hostesses, women teachers and of research students[56] is an all-pervasive phenomenon. Some high-profile and controversial cases which have hit the headlines of media during the recent times,[57]-[61] speak volumes about the prevalence of the problem. These cases alert employers to take appropriate action to prevent economic burden and efficiency losses from sexual harassment.[59]-[61]

Domestic workers in India often don't speak about sexual harassment for many other reasons. Most of them are not aware of #MeToo movement according to the National Domestic Workers' Movement (NDWM).[62] Not only the domestic workers but also highly educated women with considerable economic leverage suffer from sexual harassment at the workplace[59] in the corporate world. Power is no protection against sexual harassment. From the actor to the magistrate, nobody is immune to sexual harassment.[63]

Despite several safeguard measures, significant numbers of women are routinely subjected to sexual harassment.[64] Alyssa Milano's[54] approach to reach the victims through #MeToo helps the society understand the magnitude of the problem and stand in solidarity to all those who have been hurt. The success of #MeToo will require men to take a stand against behaviour that objectifies women.

However, men have taken a stand against the republication of the same story of sexual harassment by several anonymous authors. Delhi High Court, in its recent judgement, ruled that the '#MeToo' campaign by continuously republishing articles based on sexual harassment complaints, where women remained anonymous, violates a man's right to privacy. The court said that if the republication is permitted to go on continuously, the plaintiff's right to privacy, of which the right to be forgotten and the right to be left alone are inherent aspects, would be jeopardized. The campaign also not ought to become an unbridled and unending complaint against an individual.[65]

On the one hand, we keep the strife for equality in gender roles and take the best foot forward in order to provide equal working options for our females,[53] but on the other hand, we somewhere lag behind in keeping the working environment protective. The provisions and their implementation need to go hand in hand for an effective result and progress. Last five years have seen majority of schools including or at least planning to include basic life courses in the student curriculum with a focus on bad touch and good touch, which is a welcome step. Child sexual abuse is not that rare in the community as it is thought to be 55 per cent of all children suffer from sexual abuse at some stage. A non-governmental organization (NGO), working for the children, 'Our Voix', has come out with a comic book to teach children about good and bad touch enabling young children to know about their rights.[66] However, those women who are already working, at present, also need some sort of training, which will act as a top up to boost their courage to act and know when to respond. A prepared mind knows when to act and where to stop.[67] In this direction, there have been some encouraging efforts like Delhi Police has taken an initiative to train 7,000 cops in which the male cops are sensitized about their behaviour with female colleagues, while the women personnel are made aware about the ways to deal with harassment by their male colleagues or those coming in contact with them while on duty. The training is imparted through e-learning portal, NIPUN, developed by Delhi Police.[68]

No doubt, legal and social aspects are very important, but the clinical aspect in terms of health effects and therapeutic interventions are no less important and need to be examined and addressed to restore the physical and mental health of the victimized women and also to explore the possibility of helping those who habitually indulge in harassment behaviour to refrain from such behaviour.

References

[1]   Word Health Organization. Multi-country Study on Women's Health and Domestic Violence against Women: Initial Results on Prevalence, Health Outcomes and Women's Responses. Available at: http://www.who.int/gender/violence/who_multicountry_study/en/index.html (accessed on 11 December 2020).

[2]   Wilson K, Faison R, Britton GM. Cultural aspects of male sex aggression. *Deviant Behavior*. 1983 Apr 1;4(3s–4): 241–255.

[3]   Herbermann CG. *Catholic Encyclopedia: An International Work of Reference on the Constitution, Doctrine, Discipline, and History of the Catholic Church*. New York, NY: Robert Appleton Company; 1913.

[4]   Goode E, Ben-Yehuda N. *Moral Panics: The Social Construct of Deviance.* Hoboken, NJ: John Wiley & Sons; 2010. p. 195.

[5]   Marriam Webster. Honour. Available at: https://www.merriam-webster. com/dictionary/honor (accessed on 11 December 2020).

[6]   Sanday PR. The socio-cultural context of rape: A cross-cultural study. *Journal of Social Issues.* 1981 Oct;37(4):5–27.

[7]   Watts C, Zimmerman C. Violence against women: Global scope and magnitude. *The Lancet.* 2002 Apr 6;359(9313):1232–1237.

[8]   United Nations Population Fund. Five Underreported Stories Kick off 16 Days of Activism against Gender-based Violence Campaign. 2007. Available at: https://www.unfpa.org/pcm/node/6565 (accessed on 11 December 2020).

[9]   Farrell M. *Engendering the Workplace: Gender Discrimination and Prevention of Sexual Harassment in Organisations.* New Delhi: Uppal Publishing House; 2014.

[10] Lenhart SA. *Clinical Aspects of Sexual Harassment and Gender-discrimination: Psychological Consequences and Treatment Interventions.* Abingdon: Routledge; 2004.

[11] Beito DT, Beito LR. *Black Maverick: T. R. M. Howard's Fight for Civil Rights and Economic Power.* Champaign, IL: University of Illinois Press; 2009. pp. 99–100.

[12] Wood JT. Telling our stories: Narrative as a basis of theorizing sexual harassment. *Journal of Applied Communication Research.* 1992 Nov;20(4):349–362.

[13] Fitzgerald LF, Hulin CL, Fritz D. The antecedents and consequences of sexual harassment in organizations: An integrated model. In: Keita G, Hurrell J, editors. *Job Stress in a Changing Workforce: Investigating Gender, Diversity, and Family Issues.* Washington DC, WA: American Psychological Association; 1994. pp. 55–73.

[14] Barrell G, Hearn J, Sheppard DL, Tancred P, editors. *The Sexuality of Organization.* London: SAGE; 1989.

[15] Barr PA. Perception of sexual harassment. *Sociological Inquiry.* 1993; 63(4):7–13.

[16] MacKinnon C. *Sexual Harassment of Working Women: A Case of Sex Discrimination.* New Haven, CT: Yale University Press; 1979.

[17] Christopher U, Blackstone A. Sexual harassment as gendered expression of power. *American Sociological Review.* 2004 Feb;69(1):64–92.

[18] Fitzgerald LF, Schulman SL. Sexual harassment: A research analysis and agenda for 1990s. Special issue: Sexual harassment in the workplace. *Journal of Vocational Behaviour.* 1993; 42(1):5–27.

[19] EEOC. Policy Guidance on Current Issues of Sexual Harassment. 1990. Available at: http://www.eeoc.gov/policy/docs/currentissues.html (accessed on 11 December 2020).

[20] International Labour Office. Sexual Harassment at Work. Declaration on Fundamental Principles and Rights at Work. 2015. Available at: https://

www.ilo.org/wcmsp5/groups/public/---ed_norm/---declaration/documents/ publication/wcms_decl_fs_96_en.pdf (accessed on 11 December 2020).

[21] Fitzgerald LF. Sexual harassment: The definition and measurement of as construct. In: Plaudi M, editor. *Ivory Power: Sexual Harassment on the Campus.* Albany, NY: State University of New York Press; 1990. pp 21–44.

[22] Farrell M. Sexual harassment in the Indian workplace: An exploratory study in civil society organisations. *Madhya Pradesh Journal of Social Sciences.* 2013 Jun 1;18(1). Available at: https://www.questia.com/library/ journal/1G1-412800303/sexual-harassment-in-the-indian-workplace-an-exploratory (accessed on 11 December 2020).

[23] Berdahl JL. Harassment based on sex: Protecting social status in the context of gender hierarchy. *Academy of Management Review.* 2007 Apr 1;32(2): 641–58.

[24] U.S. Merit System Protection Board. Sexual Harassment Trends in the Federal Workplace. 2017. Available at: https://www.mspb.gov/netsearch/ viewdocs.aspx?docnumber=253661&version=253948 (accessed on 11 December 2020).

[25] Kabat-Farr D, Cortina LM. Sex-based harassment in employment: New insights into gender and context. *Law and Human Behaviour.* 2014 Feb;38(1):58–72.

[26] European Commission. Sexual Harassment in the Workplace in the European Union.1998. Available at: https://www.un.org/womenwatch/ osagi/pdf/shworkpl.pdf (accessed on 11 December 2020).

[27] Leskinen EA, Cortina LM. Dimensions of disrespect: Mapping and measuring gender harassment in organizations. *Psychology of Women Quarterly.* 2013 Mar; 38(1):107–123.

[28] Ministry of Women and Child Development. Handbook on Sexual Harassment of Women at Workplace (Prevention, Prohibition and Redressal) Act 2013. Available at: https://www.iitk.ac.in/wc/data/ Handbook%20on%20Sexual%20Harassment%20of%20Women%20at%20 Workplace.pdf (accessed on 11 December 2020).

[29] Sharma K. Sexual harassment of women at workplace in India: An ubiquitous hazard. *IOSR Journal of Humanities and Social Science.* 2017 Sept;22(9):36–46. Available at: http://www.iosrjournals.org/iosr-jhss/ papers/Vol.%2022%20Issue9/Version-9/D2209093646.pdf (accessed on 11 December 2020).

[30] Satpodar A. Sexual harassment of women: Reflections on the private sector. *Economic and Political Weekly.* 2013 Oct; 48(40):18–22.

[31] Jiloha R.C. *The Native Indian: In Search of Identity.* New Delhi: Blumoon Books; 1994.

[32] The World Bank. Labour Force, Female (% of Total Labor Force). Available at: https://www.google.com/url?sa=t&rct=j&q=&esrc=s&sour ce=web&cd=2&cad=rja&uact=8&ved=2ahUKEwiiicfNxqXiAhUJfisKH Qw1C2UQFjABegQIAxAB&url=https%3A%2F%2Fdata.worldbank.

org%2Findicator%2FSL.TLF.TOTL.FE.ZS&usg=AOvVaw3FCt2p8zfy Wu5YN6OB8xrv (accessed on 11 December 2020).

[33] Ghosh A, Puri M, Dewan N. India Inc. Is Waking up to the Menace of Sexual Harassment. *The Economic Times*, 2010. Available at: https://economictimes.indiatimes.com/special-report/india-inc-is-waking-up-to-the-menace-of-sexual-harassment/articleshow/6389463.cms (accessed on 11 December 2020).

[34] Basu K. The economics and law of sexual harassment in the workplace. *Journal of Economic Perspectives*. 2003; 17:141–157.

[35] Press Information Bureau. Sexual Harassment of Women at Workplace. Government of India, Ministry of Women and Child Development. Available at: pib.nic.in/newsite.

[36] Crime against Women –National Crime Records Bureau. Available at: ncrb.nic.in/statPublication.

[37] Pandey P. Sexual Harassment Cases at Workplace More Than Double in 2014. *The Hindu*. 2015. Available at: https://www.thehindu.com/todays-paper/tp-business/sexual-harassment-cases-at-workplace-more-than-double-in-2014/article7925337.ece (accessed on 11 December 2020).

[38] *The Times of India*. Preventing and responding to sexual harassment at workplace. 2012. November 28. Available at: timesofindia.indiatimes.com.

[39] Sarpotdar A. Implementing or ignoring the law on sexual harassment? *Economic and Political Weekly*. 2016 Nov;51(44–45). Available at: https://www.epw.in/journal/2016/44-45/commentary/implementing-or-ignoring-law-sexual-harassment.html (accessed on 11 December 2020).

[40] Sahgal P, Dang A. Sexual harassment at workplace: Experiences of women managers and organizations. *Economic and Political Weekly*. 2017 June 3;52(22).

[41] Thakur S. Increasing Awareness for Change: A Survey of Gender and the Civil Services, Mussoorie: Lal Bahadur Shastri National Academy of Administration. 2004.

[42] Chaudhuri P. Sexual harassment at the workplace: Experiences with complaints committees. *Economic and Political Weekly*. 2008 Apr;43(17):99–106.

[43] Social and Rural Research Institute: Sexual Harassment at Workplace in India. A study supported by Oxfam India, Delhi: SRI.2012.

[44] Gelfand MJ, Louise FF, Drasgow F. The structure of sexual harassment: A confirmatory analysis across cultures and settings. *Journal of Vocational Behaviour*. 1995 Oct;47(2):164–177.

[45] O'Connell CE, Korabik K. Sexual harassment: The relationship of personal vulnerability, work context, perpetrator status, and type of harassment to outcomes. *Journal of Vocational Behaviour*. 2000;56:299–329.

[46] Shukla S. Indecent Proposal. *Business Today*, 2002. Available at: http://archives.digitaltoday.in/businesstoday/20020901/cover1.html (accessed on 11 December 2020).

[47] Wikipedia. The Indian Penal Code. Available at: https://en.wikipedia.org/wiki/Indian_Penal_Code (accessed on 11 December 2020).

[48] Menon NRM, Banerjea D, West Bengal National University of Juridical Sciences. *Criminal Justice India Series.* Ahmedabad: Allied Publishers; 2005. p. 229.

[49] Bharti D. *The Constitution and Criminal Justice Administration.* New Delhi: APH Publishing; 2005. p. 320.

[50] Wikipedia. Indian Evidence Act. Available at: https://en.wikipedia.org/wiki/Indian_Evidence_Act (accessed on 11 December 2020).

[51] United Nations General Assembly. Convention on Elimination of *all Forms of* Discrimination against Women *(*CEDAW*).* Treaty Series. 1979; 1249.

[52] Wikipedia. Vishaka and Others vs State of Rajasthan. Available at: https://en.wikipedia.org/wiki/Vishakha_and_others_v_State_of_Rajasthan (accessed on 11 December 2020).

[53] Press Information Bureau. The Sexual Harassment of Women at Workplace (Prevention, Prohibition, and Redressal) Act 2013, Published in The Gazette of India.

[54] CBS News. More than 12M 'Me Too' Facebook Posts, Comments, Reactions in 24 Hours. Available at: https://www.cbsnews.com/news/metoo-more-than-12-million-facebook-posts-comments-reactions-24-hours/ (accessed on 3 May 2019).

[55] Burke, T. #MeToo Was Started for Black and Brown Women and Girls. They're Still Being Ignored. *The Washington Post.* 2017. Available at: https://www.washingtonpost.com/news/post-nation/wp/2017/11/09/the-waitress-who-works-in-the-diner-needs-to-know-that-the-issue-of-sexual-harassment-is-about-her-too/ (accessed on 11 December 2020).

[56] Patel V. Crusade of University of Mumbai Against Sexual Harassment at Place of Work (Presented at a Seminar 'An Interdisciplinary Approach to the Unexplored Areas Related to Women'). University Grants Commission and Maniben Nanavati College for Women, Mumbai; 2004.

[57] Dalal S. Bias in the Boardroom. *The Sunday Express.* 2003, May 18.

[58] Menon NRM, Banerjee D. West Bengal National University of Juridical Sciences. *Criminal Justice India Series.* Chandigarh: Allied Publishers; 2005.

[59] The Times News Network. Disclosures: What Is Sexual Harassment? *The Times of India,* 2003, 15 June.

[60] *Business Today.* 2002, 1 September.

[61] *The Indian Express,* Mumbai Newsline, 2004, 21 October.

[62] Peggie S. Domestic worker mobilisations in India—Work like any other, work like no other. *Employee Rights and Employment Policy Journal.* 2011;51(157).

[63] Bhandare N. Even Judges Aren't Safe: Power Is No Protection against Sexual Harassment. *Business Standard.* 2017, November 20.

[64] Dalbir B. *The Constitution and Criminal Justice Administration.* Ahmedabad: APH Publishing; 2005. p. 320.

[65] Mahapatra D. 'Me Too' Can't Become a 'Sullying You Too' Campaign: Delhi High Court. *The Times of India.* 2019, May 17.

[66] Yadav P. Good Touch, Bad Touch: Comic Book to Teach City School Kids about Sexual Abuse. *The Times of India.* 2019, August 11.

[67] O'Donohue W, Downs K, Yeater EA. Sexual harassment: A review of the literature. *Aggression and Violent Behavior.* 1998;3(2):111–112.

[68] TNN. 7,000 Cops Undergo Sexual Harassment Training Online. *The Times of India.* 2019, April 12.

CHAPTER 2

Evolution of Legal Environment

It is a matter of common observation that those in power have the prerogative to define the world from their own perspective and, thus, both consciously and unconsciously exclude the experiences of their subordinates. Those in power at the workplace often ignore the feelings of their juniors to impose what they feel is right and convenient. It leads to exploitation of the vulnerable in various ways including sexual harassment which has a long history and continues to remain endemic, deep-rooted in relationships with the gendered assumption that women's implied responsibility is to stay at home and bring up the children.

Till recently, the phenomenon of sexual harassment remained insignificant, unexamined and unnamed in most of the societies. Only the recent developments have brought the phenomenon to legal and academic scrutiny.

2.1. Global Trends

Historically, employers' supervisors at a workplace in the industrialized world exploited the widely prevalent gender bias in the workforce. This attitude reinforced the mechanisms of exclusion.[1]

The civil rights movement of the USA[2] in the 1960s high-lighted the discrimination against employees at the workplace by the employment agencies and labour organizations.[3] As a result, EEOC[4] was appointed by the US Congress to interpret and adjudicate cases and develop guidelines to eliminate gender bias in employment. State departments of health and human services received complaints related to sex, race, ethnicity, religious affiliation, national origin, age, pregnancy, veteran status, disabilities, gender identity and even political affiliations. The court cases[1] began to pile up from the ranks of the labour force and repercussions of which led to the development of various provisions in the legal system. In these cases, the courts recognized[5] discrimination in the following two forms which led to the development of the definition of sexual harassment:

2.1.1. Quid Pro Quo

In the industrial world, it was a common practice to get a job for sexual favours, and those in desperate need of work submitted themselves silently to the predators' demand. Against this practice, the first case to reach a US District Court was *Williams v. Saxbe*. Diane Williams, an African–American, a federal employee of the US Justice Department, was dismissed from her job for refusing to provide sexual services to her boss, Harvey Brinson. Her refusal to accept his demand for sexual favours infuriated her boss. To punish her, he withheld some important work-related information and then dismissed her for not satisfying job requirements. In 1972, Diane Williams sued her employer to get her job back. The court observed, 'She would have been treated differently had she been a male. Brinson discriminated against her because she was a female.' The court judgement came in 1976.

Quid pro quo, in this case, was continuing with employment in exchange for sexual favours. Quid pro quo is anything like advancement in academic assignments, salary hikes, other perks or punishment for refusal for sex—losing job, demotion, lesser marks in examination, etc. All these conditions of quid pro quo come under the civil rights violations.

2.1.2. The Hostile Environment

Hostile work environment, like discriminatory behaviours, was also included in the definition of sexual harassment by the court. Mechelle Vinson, an employee of the federal government and an African–American woman, lost her job after she rejected her employer Richard L. Taylor's sexual advances at Meritor Savings Bank in 1975. She held that he fondled and humiliated her in front of others and had raped her more than 40 times at the workplace and outside. She claimed that she had submitted to Taylor's demands, but always unwillingly, fearing dismissal if she refused. The court initially rejected that she had suffered gender-based discrimination; however, a federal court reversed the decision, calling the demand for such favours 'a discrimination, based on sex'. The 'hostile environment' encountered by her at work amounted to sexual harassment. Taylor's unwelcome sexual behaviour affected her capacity to perform at her job. His behaviour had created a hostile environment at the workplace that made it difficult for the complainant to work efficiently.

2.2. Defining Sexual Harassment

As a specific form of gender discrimination, sexual harassment was defined during the 1970s in the USA when such cases began to appear in the courts. The first case in the UK, in which sexual harassment was argued to be a form of sex discrimination, came in 1986 under the Employment Protection Act.[6] The term, however, remained unknown outside academic and legal circles.

In the subsequent years, sexual harassment became a topic of debate as there was no consensus on a generally agreed definition among the academicians and the legal experts. More cases followed, and in the coming years, sexual harassment became a legally prohibited form of discriminatory behaviour that limited women's opportunities restricting their options in the workplace and the academic institutions.

EEOC[1][4] gave an explicit description of sexual harassment at the workplace as a discriminatory behaviour violating Title VII of the

---

[1] https://en.wikipedia.org/wiki/Equal_Employment_Opportunity_Commission

Civil Rights Act of 1964. In 1984, Title VII was expanded to include educational institutions. The original intention of the Civil Rights Act of 1964 was to end discrimination in the workplace, which is clarified in Titles VII and Title IX, a 1972 amendment for schools. The EEOC defines sexual harassment as:

Unwelcome sexual advances, requests for sexual favours or other verbal or physical conduct of a sexual nature when

1. A woman's continuing into job depended on her submission to such conduct
2. Decision regarding continuing in employment depended on acceptance or refusal of such conduct by an individual
3. The purpose or effect of such conduct created a hostile work environment

No doubt, the primary responsibility is of the person who sexually harasses a co-worker, but the organization is also responsible for the conduct of its employees, agents and contractors unless it is demonstrated that adequate measures were taken by the organization to prevent the incidents of sexual harassment. The following points are observed to note:

- Most countries have laws to hold employers vicariously liable for acts of harassment committed by anyone within their organizations.
- It is the responsibility of employers to prevent sexual harassment at their establishments. Employers become liable when a case of sexual harassment is brought to their notice, and no action is taken by them.

In the UK, sexual harassment was not specifically covered by any law until 1 October 2005, although it was referred to in the Sex Discrimination Act, 1975, as unlawful discrimination based on sex.[6] The change in European Equal Treatment Directive, 2002, required the UK to specifically outlaw sexual harassment, and in response to this, the Act was amended to Sex Discrimination Act 1975 (Amendment) Regulations, 2008, which became effective from the 6 April 2008.[7] The Act made it illegal for an employer to avoid taking action for the safety of an employee from sexual harassment when the employer knows about such harassment in advance.[8]

All over the world, similar provisions are available to deal with the problem, but the attitude of assigning women a subservient role in the society creates hurdles in the implementation of the legal provisions favouring them. This attitude percolates to workplaces as well, causing inequality there like inequality in the society at large.[9]

2.3. Violation of Human Rights

In view of prevailing normative assumptions based on cultural beliefs and social sanctions, the UN[10] acknowledges gender equality in multiple spheres. It underlines that the universal principle of equality of rights is violated by discrimination against women and attacks on their dignity.

Specific attention has been drawn by the International Labour Organization[11] to domestic workers, who have a right to 'enjoy effective protection against all forms of abuse, harassment and violence.' They belong to an unorganized sector of work, often ignored for their protection against sexual harassment; they are more vulnerable to exploitation than others due to the nature of their work and generally have no protection by any labour union.

International law and policy frameworks should make sexual harassment a fundamental human rights and equality issue and not just a problem to be solved using labour or employment laws as suggested by the Platform for Action to take strategic action on violence against women—specifically, sexual harassment in the workplace.[12]

2.4. Legal Provisions in India

Sexual harassment of women at the workplace has remained a matter of concern for the women's movement in India since the early 1980s.[13] The efforts of Forum Against Oppression of Women in Mumbai which took up the cause of nurses, air hostesses, teachers and students was not well received by the trade unions during the initial years,[14] but this trivialization of the issue by the trade unions did not deter the activists in taking systematic action against sexual harassment.[15] Several women's groups came forward, collectively as well as individually, to fight for their rights.[16] Several controversial cases of sexual harassment of women hitting the headlines in the newspapers and bringing implication of various legal provisions were taken up by these groups of women.[17]-[19]

Before the Vishakha Guidelines came in 1997 to provide relief to working women, Section 354 of IPC[20] was the only provision to deal with the criminal cases amounting to outrage women's modesty. Section 509 punishes the guilty for using a 'word, gesture or act intended to insult the modesty of a woman'. Moreover, the interpretation of these provisions on 'outraging women's modesty' was largely left to the investigating police officer.

Supreme Court's judgement in the Vishakha case laid down guidelines for the establishments for the complaints about sexual harassment to be implemented for the time until legislation was passed to deal with the cases of sexual harassment.[21]

In compliance with the apex court's directive, the bill was drafted keeping all developments in consideration.[10], [22] However, the bill took several years to become an Act after suitable modifications in 2013. During the course of time, several legislative measures were adopted, which are discussed as follows:

2.4.1. The Criminal Law (Amendment) Act, 2013

The city of Delhi witnessed a shameful act of gangrape of a physiotherapy intern on 16 December 2012, which generated international concern. United Nations condemned the incident and called upon to ensure justice.[2][23] On 22 December 2012, a judicial committee was constituted to suggest amendments to the existing criminal law on a sexual assault[3] which submitted its report on 23 January 2013

---

[2] https://en.wikipedia.org/wiki/Criminal_Law_(Amendment)_Act,_2013#cite_note-7

[3] https://en.wikipedia.org/wiki/Sexual_abuse

indicating government's failure behind crimes against women in the country. The committee made certain recommendations which were incorporated in the Criminal Law (Amendment) Ordinance, 2013. The ordinance recognized certain acts as offences which were dealt under related laws.[24]

Section 370 of IPC[20] is substituted with new Sections—370 and 370A—dealing with trafficking of a person[4] for exploitation, including prostitution, slavery, forced organ removal and so on, and made punishable with imprisonment ranging from at least seven years to imprisonment for life.

The definition of rape[5] under IPC Section 375 has been extended to include the following acts in addition to vaginal penetration: the penetration of the penis[6] into the urethra, anus or mouth or the penetration of any object or any part of the body to any extent into the vagina[7], urethra[8] or anus of a woman, or making another person do so. Applying mouth to or touching the private parts[9] of a woman by a man is also an offence of sexual assault, according to the ordinance. It has also been clarified in the section that penetration implies 'penetration to any extent', and whether or not physical resistance was offered is immaterial for ascertaining whether an offence was committed. With the exception of certain aggravated situations, the punishment will be imprisonment, of not less than seven years but which may extend to imprisonment for life, and the offender shall also be liable to be fined.

Section, 376A is a new addition. It deals with a person committing the offence of sexual assault: '… inflicts an injury causing death of the victim or a persistent vegetative state'.[10] Such a person shall be punished with rigorous imprisonment for a term of 20 years extendable to imprisonment for life, which shall mean the remainder

---

[4] https://en.wikipedia.org/wiki/Human_trafficking
[5] https://en.wikipedia.org/wiki/Rape
[6] https://en.wikipedia.org/wiki/Penis
[7] https://en.wikipedia.org/wiki/Vagina
[8] https://en.wikipedia.org/wiki/Urethra
[9] https://en.wikipedia.org/wiki/Groping
[10] https://en.wikipedia.org/wiki/Persistent_vegetative_state

of that person's natural life.[11][25] In the case of 'gang rape', persons involved regardless of their gender shall be punished with rigorous imprisonment for 20 years extendable to imprisonment for life. Such persons shall also pay compensation to the victim, which shall be reasonable enough to meet the medical treatment and rehabilitation expenses of the victim. The age of consent[12] in the country has been increased to 18 years. This means any sexual activity with a woman below the age of 18, whether or not consent was given, will constitute statutory rape.[13]

2.4.1.2. Sexual Harassment at Workplace in India

Sexual harassment and gender discrimination have their roots in the social fabric of patriarchal society of Indian subcontinent. The general perception that men are superior to women and that some forms of violence against women are acceptable and justified is deeply ingrained in the psyche of people. Traditional Indian societies where the language of religion, nurturance, obedience and subordination—instilled in children from a young age—frames the normative boundaries of behaviour. In the caste-ridden traditional society extracting free labour and sexual services from the women of underprivileged sections of the society was not only a common phenomenon, but it was also the part of the cultural norms.[7] Socially defined traditional role of women served to label them as a homemaker in a subservient capacity. The ideology of the home served to regulate workforce participation, and women stayed at home to perform a subordinate role of cooking food and rearing children, while men worked outdoors to earn a livelihood for the family.

Thus, women's role was traditionally limited within the four walls of their household, and their subservient role of looking after the domestic chores and upbringing of the children rendered them inferior. This apparent inferiority reduced them to the level of lesser

---

[11] https://en.wikipedia.org/wiki/Criminal_Law_(Amendment)_Act,_2013#cite_note-17

[12] https://en.wikipedia.org/wiki/Age_of_consent

[13] https://en.wikipedia.org/wiki/Statutory_rape

members in the domestic and social life and made them vulnerable to discrimination and exploitation.

Globalization has brought a radical change in the status of women worldwide. With the spread of education among the women and for other socio-economic reasons, the demography of the workplace in India is changing fast; today, women work in almost all spheres of the work domain. With this change, women have replaced men as chief human resources officers in 60 per cent companies across the country.[8] With the larger influx of women in the mainstream workforce, sexual harassment at the workplace in India has assumed greater dimensions. In view of the traditionally held attitude towards women, their changing role has brought the women in a vulnerable situation to become victims of sexual harassment. Women work with men, interact with a wide range of male colleagues, juniors and bosses, supervisors and employers, stay together to work at odd hours and at times in secluded environment. Work situations expose women to become easy prey of the predators, particularly at the places where male workers are in majority. Sexual exploitation by the male co-workers ranges from trivial incidents often ignored by the women workers as 'natural' male behaviour to serious sexual harm and assault, which is not uncommon.

Sexual harassment, which violates a woman's fundamental right to equality and right to life, guaranteed under Articles 14, 15 and 21 of the Constitution of India, is a common phenomenon at the workplace in India. It is not only an infringement of the fundamental rights of a woman, under Article 19 of the Constitution 'to practice any profession or to carry out any occupation, trade or business', but it also erodes equality and puts the dignity and the physical and psychological well-being of the working women at risk. As a consequence, there is poor productivity, frequent absenteeism, disturbed interpersonal relations and an overall negative impact on the organization. In fact, it is a mirror reflection of male power over the women and sustains patriarchal relations leading to altered efficiency in work performance, unique in Indian society. In the recent times, workplace sexual harassment in India is increasingly recognized as a violation of women's rights and a form of violence against women despite the fact the traditional social construct of male privileges in society continues to justify violence against women in the private and public sphere.

2.4.1.3. Women's Legal Safeguard in IPC

As already described sexual harassment clearly violates the fundamental rights of a woman to equality under Article 14(2) and 15(3), her rig/ht to life under Article 21(4) and her right to practise any profession and carry on any occupation, trade or business, which includes a Right to a safe environment free from sexual harassment.

There are certain specific provisions in IPC[10] relevant to protect women against sexual violence and for the safety of the women from the perpetrators. Sections 354, 375 and 509 of IPC cover the remedial measures against sexual crime. These new offences such as an acid attack, sexual harassment, voyeurism, stalking have been incorporated into IPC.

The process of recording the victim's statement has been made more victim-friendly and easy by bringing in specific changes in the Criminal Procedure Code[26] and the Indian Evidence Act.[27] Two critical changes are:

- The character of the victim must not be considered relevant in any way.
- 'No consent' must be presumed in a case where sexual intercourse is proved, and the victim states in the court that she did not consent to such intercourse.

The ordinance expressly recognized certain acts as offences, which were dealt with under related laws. These new offences such as an acid attack, sexual harassment, voyeurism and stalking have been incorporated into IPC. These are discussed as follows.

1. **Outraging the modesty of a woman:** Outraging the modesty of a woman is covered under Section 354, which concerns assault or use of criminal force to commit the crime:

   Whoever assaults or uses criminal force to any woman, intend-ing to outrage or knowing it to be likely that he will thereby outrage her modesty, shall be punished with imprisonment of either description for a term which shall not be less than one year but which may extend to five years, and shall also be liable to fine.

2. **Sexual harassment by a man:** Section 354A relates to sexual harassment and punishment for it.

   This Section defines the offence and the punishment for the men who indulge in the activity of sexual harassment with a woman (Table 2.1).

3. **Assault or use of criminal force to a woman with intent to disrobe:** Under 354B assault or use of criminal force with the intention of disrobing or compelling a woman to be naked is a punishable offence with simple or rigorous imprisonment for a term which shall not be less than three years but which may extend to seven years and fine.

4. **Voyeurism:** Under Section 354C, watching or capturing the image of a woman engaging in a private act in circumstances where she would usually have the expectation of not being observed either by the perpetrator or by any other person at the behest of the perpetrator or disseminates such image is a punishable offence. Punishment for the first conviction is simple or rigorous imprisonment for a term which shall not be less than one year but which may extend to three years and fine. For the second or subsequent conviction, the punishment shall be simple or rigorous imprisonment for a term which shall not be less than three years but which may extend to seven years and fine. It is a cognizable offence.

5. **Stalking:** It is a punishable offence to follow a woman and contacting or attempting to contact her to foster personal interaction repeatedly despite a clear indication of disinterest by her or monitoring the use by a woman of the internet, email or any other form of electronic communication under Section 354D. Punishment for the first conviction is simple or rigorous imprisonment for a term which may extend to three years and fine, and for the second or subsequent conviction, the punishment is simple or rigorous imprisonment for a term which may extend to five years and fine.

6. **Insulting the modesty of a woman:** Under Section 509, uttering any word, making any sound or gesture or exhibiting any object,

Table 2.1. *Criminal Law (Amendment) Ordinance, 2013*

Offence	IPC Section	Punishment	Gender Relation
Acid attack	326A	Imprisonment, not less than 10 years, may extend to life imprisonment & with fine to meet medical expenses & paid to the victim	Gender neutral
Attempt to acid attack	326B	Imprisonment, not less than five years, may extend to seven years, also be liable to fine	Gender neutral
Sexual harassment	354A	Rigorous imprisonment up to three years or with fine or with both	Protects women. Provisions are: 1. Physical contact and advances involving unwelcome and explicit sexual overtures 2. A demand or request for sexual favours 3. Forcibly showing pornography 4. Making sexually coloured remark or any other unwelcome physical, verbal or non-verbal conduct of sexual nature
Act with intent to disrobe a woman	354B	Imprisonment, not less than three years, may extend to seven years & with fine	Only protects women against 'assaults or use of criminal force or abets such act with the intention of disrobing or compelling her to be naked'

| Voyeurism[a] | 354C | Imprisonment, not less than one year, may extend to three years and liable to fine and be punished on a second or subsequent conviction, with imprisonment of either description for a term which shall not be less than three years, but which may extend to seven years, and shall also be liable to fine. | Only protects women. The prohibited action is defined thus: "Watching or capturing a woman in 'private act", which includes an act of watching carried out in a place which, in the circumstances, would reasonably be expected to provide privacy and where the victim's genitals, buttocks or breasts are exposed or covered only in underwear or the victim is using a lavatory or the person is doing a sexual act that is not of a kind ordinarily done in public.' |
| Stalking | 354D | Imprisonment not less than one year but which may extend to three years, and shall also be liable to fine | Only protects women from being stalked by men. The prohibited action is defined thus: 'To follow a woman and contact or attempt to contact such woman to foster personal interaction repeatedly despite a clear indication of disinterest by such woman or monitor the use by a woman of the internet, email or any other form of electronic communication. There are exceptions to this section which include such act being in course of preventing or detecting a crime authorized by State or in compliance of certain law or was reasonable and justified.' |

Note: https://en.wikipedia.org/wiki/Voyeurism

intending that such word or sound shall be heard or that such gesture or object shall be seen, by a woman, with an intention to insult her modesty or intruding upon the privacy of such woman is a punishable offence. Punishment is simple imprisonment for a term which may extend to three years and fine. Section 509 provides for the 'word, gesture or act intended to insult the modesty of a woman.'

> Whoever, intending to insult the modesty of any woman, utters any word, makes any sound or gesture, or exhibits any object, intending that such word or sound shall be heard, or that such gesture or object shall be seen, but such woman, or intrudes upon the privacy of such woman, shall be punished with simple imprisonment for a term which may extend to three years, and also with fine.

The Criminal Law (Amendment) Ordinance, 2013,[24] is strongly criticized for not including marital rape, reduction of age of consent and amending the Armed Forces (Special Powers) Act so that no sanction is needed for prosecuting a person accused in a crime against a woman even if he is part of the armed forces.[25], [28]

The ordinance was later replaced by a bill with a large number of changes, which was passed by the Lok Sabha on 19 March 2013 and by the Rajya Sabha on 21 March 2013 with certain changes done in the ordinance provisions.[29]-[31]

The bill received presidential assent on 2 April 2013 and became effective from 3 April 2013.[32] The changes made in the Act compared to the Ordinance are listed in Table 2.2.

Forced sexual intercourse by a man with his wife, if she is living separately, whether under a decree of separation or otherwise, was made a crime, punishable with at least a two-year prison term under Section 376B of the 2013 law.[33], [34]

Forced sex by a man on his wife may also be considered a prosecutable act of domestic violence under Sections 498A as well as the Protection of Women from Domestic Violence Act, 2005. The Protection of Children from Sexual Offences Act, 2012, further

Table 2.2. Criminal Law (Amendment) Act, 2013

Offence	Changes
Acid attack	Fine shall be just and reasonable to meet medical expenses for treatment of victim, while in the ordinance, it was fine up to Rupees 10 lakh.
Sexual harassment	'Clause (v) any other unwelcome physical, verbal or non-verbal conduct of sexual nature' has been removed. Punishment for offence under clause (i) and (ii) has been reduced from five years of imprisonment to three years. The offence is no longer gender-neutral, only a man can commit the offence on a woman.
Voyeurism	The offence is no longer gender-neutral, only a man can commit the offence on a woman.
Stalking	The offence is no longer gender-neutral, only a man can commit the offence on a woman. The definition has been rewarded and broken down into clauses. The exclusion clause and the following sentence has been removed 'or watches or spies on a person in a manner that results in a fear of violence or serious alarm or distress in the mind of such person, or interferes with the mental peace of such person, commits the offence of stalking.' Punishment for the offence has been changed; a man committing the offence of stalking would be liable for imprisonment up to three years for the first offence and shall also be liable to fine and for any subsequent conviction would be liable for imprisonment up to five years and with fine.
Trafficking of person	'Prostitution' has been removed from the explanation clause

outlined and described mandatory punishments for the crime of sexual assault on a child, that is, anyone below the age of 18 years.[35], [36]

All sexual acts between the members of the same sex, consensual or forced, previously constituted crimes under Section 377 of IPC, after the Criminal Law (Amendment) Act, 2013, with the same punishment as that of rape. However, the Supreme Court, in a landmark judgement of 6 September 2018, overturned this. It stated that consensual sexual acts between adults who satisfy the age of consent are not violative of Section 377. Hence, gay sex in India now stands decriminalized.[37] It was a revolutionary judgement in view of the sociocultural background of Indian society.

Recently, the Delhi High Court has affirmed the application of Section 354A of IPC (1860) to transgender (women) victims of sexual harassment. Now, transgenders can also pursue criminal case of sexual harassment against their perpetrators like women in general.[38] The Court, in an inclusive move, has ruled that Section 354A of IPC can now be used by transgender persons to register complaints of sexual harassment.

2.4.2. Industrial Employment (Standing Orders) Act, 1946

An employer is required to define and publish uniform service conditions of employment as standing orders in compliance with the Industrial Employment (Standing Orders) Act, 1946.[39] It should contain employment terms such as work hours, wage rates, shifts if any and timings thereof, norms for attendance and late coming and provisions for leaves/holidays and termination, suspension or dismissal of employees.

An industrial establishment with 100 or more employees is required to follow Model Standing Orders, which serve as guidelines for employers. If an employer has not framed and certified its own standing orders, the provisions of the Model Standing Orders shall apply. The Model Standing Orders under the Industrial Employment (Standing Orders) Central Rules, 1996, (standing orders rules) prescribe a list of acts constituting 'misconduct', and this list specifically includes sexual harassment. Sexual harassment is defined in line with the definition under the Vishaka Judgement in the Model Standing Orders along with the emphasis on the establishment of complaints committee for redressing grievances. However, sexual harassment has not been kept limited to women under the standing orders rules.

2.4.3. Genesis of Vishaka Guidelines

Sexual harassment infringes a woman's fundamental right to gender equality under Article 14 and her right to life and to live with dignity under Article 21 of the Constitution of India. This includes the right to a safe working environment free from sexual harassment. Several judgements of the Supreme Court in the interpretation of these

Articles have strongly emphasized the right to life with dignity as assured by Article 21 of the Constitution.

Acts like the Indecent Representation of Women (Prohibition) Act, 1987,[40] are insufficient to deal with sexual harassment situations. The cases of discrimination and workplace harassments come under provisions such as Article 15 and Article 19(1)(g) of the Indian Constitution. Article 15 for 'prohibition of discrimination on grounds of religion, race, caste, sex or place of birth' and Article 19(1)(g) for the right to freedom which upholds a woman's right 'to practice any profession or to carry on any occupation, trade or business'.

Until the mid-1990s the concept of sexual harassment at workplace was not recognized by the Indian courts, and such cases were dealt with in accordance with the existing provisions.[20], [24], [26], [40] Some relevant cases which deserve mentioning are as follows.

1. *Rupan Deol Bajaj vs. Kanwar Pal Singh Gill* (1995)[41]: This was a case in which the court interpreted the outraging of the modesty of a woman as including the outraging of the dignity of a woman. It recognized sexual harassment as a crime falling under Section 354 of IPC. Later in 1997, in its landmark judgement in *Vishaka vs. State of Rajasthan and Ors*[42] case, the Supreme Court, for the first time, provided a definition of workplace sexual harassment.

2. **Bhanwari Devi case**[42]: It relates to a rural Rajasthani woman who worked as a *saathin*, a grassroot community worker in the Women's Development Project run by the Rajasthan Government. She took up the cause of discouraging and preventing child marriages widely practised in the rural areas of the state despite being illegal.[43] During the course of her assigned work, she managed to prevent this practice at some places with police intervention. The villagers didn't like her meddling in their age-old customs and her playing with their sentiments. When she prevented a nine-month-old infant's marriage with the police help, she faced harassment from the family members of the infant and other village men. Her complaint to authorities went unheard, and five men from the village gang-raped her for challenging the age-old social order.

   Bhanwari Devi's case exemplifies the perennial prospect of sexual harm, irrespective of their location and social background.

It also reflects the extent to which the harm can expand if adequate measures are not taken to check the sexually offensive behaviour of the predatory males at the workplace or anywhere else within the scope of their work.

Public interest litigation was filed by Vishaka and some other woman groups. The PIL proposed that sexual harassment be recognized as a violation of the fundamental right to equality which women are entitled to and that the accountability and responsibility to uphold this right applies to all workplaces, establishments and institutions.

The Supreme Court in its judgement of *Vishaka vs the State of Rajasthan* 1997 [26] case created guidelines, making the right to equality and dignity as its basis and in compliance with the United Nations Convention on the Elimination of All Forms of Discrimination against Women.[10]

3. *Vishaka versus the State of Rajasthan and Ors*[44]: After this case, the Supreme Court, for the first time, provided a definition of workplace sexual harassment.

4. **Vishaka Guidelines:** The Supreme Court of India laid down Vishaka guidelines in 1997 which include

   a. Definition of sexual harassment
   b. Shifting of accountability from individuals to institutions
   c. Priority to prevention
   d. Provision of an innovative redressal mechanism

The apex court defined sexual harassment as 'any unwelcome, sexually determined physical, verbal, or non-verbal conduct, that is, sexually suggestive remarks about women, demands for sexual favours, and sexually offensive visuals in the workplace.' The definition also took into account situations where a woman could be placed in a situation of disadvantage in her workplace due to threats relating to employment decisions that could negatively affect her working life.[45]

It placed the onus on employers to ensure that women employees are not forced to work in a hostile environment. The court issued directions for establishing redressal mechanisms, in the form of complaints committees to inquire into allegations of sexual harassment of women at the workplace, headed by a woman employee with not less than half of its members being women and involvement of a third-party person or NGO expert on the board to prevent any undue pressure on the complainant. The guidelines are applicable to all variety of employment, from paid to voluntary, across the public and private sectors. The court observes, 'workplaces must be made safe for women and that it should be the responsibility of the employer to protect women employee at every step.'

International standards or laws were roped in to expand the scope of India's constitutional guarantees to make workplaces safe and ensure women worked in a secure environment. The court relied on the Convention on the Elimination of All Forms of Discrimination against Women,[10] adopted by the United Nations in 1979 and held that international treaties can be relied on to bridge the gap due to the absence of any law in the country and protect the human rights of people in India. India's innovative history in dealing with workplace sexual harassment, starting with the Vishaka Guidelines and the subsequent legislation, has given crucial visibility to the issue.

Having raised the levels of responsibility for workplaces, institutions and those in positions of responsibility, a clear obligation to uphold working women's fundamental right, the Supreme Court has given a path-breaking judgement. The following three key obligations were imposed on institutions to meet that standard:

- Prohibition
- Prevention
- Redress

These obligations were subsequently incorporated into the concerned Act, which came up in 2013.

2.4.4. Post-Vishaka Developments

After the Vishaka verdict, some other important judgements were delivered by the Supreme Court, some of which are as follows.

1. *Apparel Export Promotion Council vs A. K. Chopra*[46]: The Vishaka judgement opened an issue that was swept under the carpet for a long time. In the case of Apparel Export Promotion Council versus

A. K. Chopra, the Court upheld the dismissal of a superior officer of the Delhi based Apparel Export Promotion Council found guilty of sexually harassing a subordinate female employee at the workplace. The Court ruled that physical contact was not essential for an act of sexual harassment. If the behaviour of the accused fulfils other criteria of unwelcome sexual conduct for qualification as sexual harassment, the accused is guilty.

2. ***Medha Kotwal Lele and Ors vs Union of India and Ors***[45]: The Supreme Court undertook the monitoring of the implementation of Vishaka Guidelines on the basis of Medha Kotwal's letter which was supported by several sexual harassment complaints. The letter said that the Vishaka Guidelines were not effectively implemented by various organizations. State governments were directed by the court to file an affidavit on the steps taken by them to implement Vishaka Guidelines. The court observed that 'the implementation of the Vishaka Guidelines has to be not only in form but also in substance and spirit so as to make available safe and secure environment for women at workplace in every aspect and thereby enabling working women to discharge their duty with dignity, decency and due respect.' Expressing its dissatisfaction over the implementation of the Vishaka Guidelines, it directed states to put in place sufficient mechanisms to ensure effective implementation. In case of a non-compliance or non-adherence of the Vishaka Guidelines, the aggrieved persons are free to approach the respective high courts.

On the basis of the ongoing developments and the Vishaka Guidelines, the Sexual Harassment of Women at Workplace (Prevention, Prohibition and Redressal) Act, 2013,[47] was enacted by the Indian Parliament to ensure respect for women's right to equality of status and opportunity at the workplace by mandating safe workspaces and enabling work environments, free from sexual harassment, in compliance with the abovementioned requirements.

Although the Act is in place for many years now, it is observed that women often do not report their plight due to various reasons such as fear of reprisal from the harasser, losing their jobs, being stigmatized or suffering a loss of professional standing and personal reputation. It is more so in the educational institutions evident from various studies.[48]

The Act is women friendly to ensure full justice to them; however, the possibility of misuse of the Act cannot be ruled out. In a recent case of an army officer, the court has observed such a possibility. A serving major general, who played a key role in 2015 surgical strike, was dismissed from service on account of alleged sexual harassment of a junior army officer. The major general was found guilty under various laws, and a case of sexual harassment is said to have proved. For the genuine reasons, these laws are beneficial for the women; however, these can be easily misused by the women to implicate males in frivolous and false cases to 'teach a lesson' to some male with whom they wish to settle their scores.[49] Such a practice has already been observed with Section 498 A of IPC in dowry cases where many innocent people have been implicated in false cases. Suitable amendment in these laws for the safeguard of the innocent males has to be there. Law is a vital tool to contain society in order, and its misuse defeats the objective of natural justice.

References

[1] Lenhart SA. *Clinical Aspects of Sexual Harassment and Gender Discrimination: Psychological Consequences and Treatment Interventions.* Hove, NY: Brunner-Routledge; 2004.

[2] Constitutional Rights Foundation. A Brief History of Jim Crow. Civil Rights Act of 1957. Civil Rights Digital Library. Available at: https://www.crf-usa.org/black-history-month/a-brief-history-of-jim-crow (accessed on 16 December 2020).

[3] EEOC. Title VII of the Civil Rights Act of 1964. AAUW: Empowering Women Since 1881. Available at: https://www.eeoc.gov/statutes/title-vii-civil-rights-act-1964 (accessed on 16 December 2020).

[4] EEOC. Policy Guidance on Current Issues of Sexual Harassment. 1990. Available at: http://www.eeoc.gov/policy/docs/currentissues.html (accessed on 16 December 2020).

[5] Bloomberg. How Two Legal Cases Established Sexual Harassment as a Civil Rights Violation. 2019. Available at: https://www.bloomberg.com/news/articles/2014-12-04/sexual-harassment-naming-it-paved-the-way-to-legal-victories (accessed on 16 December 2020).

[6] Hodges A, Bimrose J. Sexual harassment in the workplace: An ethical dilemma for career guidance practice? *British Journal of Guidance and Counselling.* 2004;32(1): 109–121.

[7] UK Statutory Instruments. The Sex Discrimination Act 1975 (Amendment) Regulations 2008. No. 656. 2008. Available at: https://www.legislation.gov.uk/uksi/2008/656/introduction/made (accessed on 16 December 2020).

[8]   Crosthwaith, J. and Priest, G. The definition of sexual harassment. In: Lemoncheck L, Sterba JP, editors. *Sexual Harassment: Issues and Answers.* New York, NY: Oxford University Press; 2002. pp. 62–77.

[9]   Jiloha RC. *The Native Indian: In Search of Identity.* New Delhi: Blumoon Books; 1994.

[10] UN Women. Convention on the Elimination of All Forms of Discrimination against Women. 2008. Available at: https://www.un.org/womenwatch/daw/cedaw/ (accessed on 16 December 2020).

[11] International Labour Organization. Rights and Protection of Domestic Workers in India. 2016. Available at: https://www.ilo.org/newdelhi/info/public/vid/WCMS_522314/lang--en/index.htm (accessed on 16 December 2020).

[12] McGolgan A. Report on Sexual Harassment in the Workplace in EU Member States. The Irish Presidency of the European Union in association with Farrell Grant Sparks Consulting. Available at: http://www.justice.ie/en/JELR/SexualHrrsmtRpt.pdf/Files/SexualHrrsmtRpt.pdf (accessed on 16 December 2020).

[13] Patel V. *Women's Challenges of the New Millennium.* New Delhi: Gyan Publications; 2002.

[14] Patel V. Crusade of University of Mumbai Against Sexual Harassment at Place of Work. Presented at a Seminar 'An Interdisciplinary Approach to the Unexplored Areas Related to Women.' University Grants Commission by Maniben Nanavati College for Women, 2004.

[15] Forum Against Oppression of Women. Moving ... but Not Quite There: Evaluation Report of One Decade 1980–1990. 1991.

[16] Dalal S. Bias in the Boardroom. *The Sunday Express*, 2003. Available at: http://www.suchetadalal.com/?id=ee8b2392-6c9b-cd25-492e8bb636ee&base=sections&f (accessed on 16 December 2020).

[17] The Times News Network. Disclosures: What Is Sexual Harassment? *The Times of India*, 2003.

[18] *Business Today*, Indecent proposal. 1 September 2002.

[19] *The Indian Express*, Cover story. Latest Issue. Mumbai Newsline, 21 October 2004.

[20] Atul Chandra Patel. An historical introduction to the Indian Penal Code. *Journal of the Indian law Institute.* 1961;3(3):351-366.

[21] Mathew M. Sexual Harassment at Workplace. India Centre for Human Rights and Law, 2002.

[22] Chorine C, Desai M, Gonsalves C. *Women and Law (Vol. I and II).* Mumbai: Socio-legal Information Centre; 1992.

[23] Stenhammer AF. UN Women Condemns Gang Rape of Delhi Student. UN Women, 2012. Available at: https://www.unwomen.org/en/news/stories/2012/12/un-women-condemns-gang-rape-of-delhi-student (accessed on 16 December 2020).

[24] indianKanoon.org. Section 7 in the Criminal Law (Amendment) Ordinance, 2013. Available at: https://indiankanoon.org/doc/341214/ (accessed on 16 December 2020).

[25] NDTV. Ordinance vs Verma Committee Recommendations. NDTV, 2013. Available at: https://www.ndtv.com/india-news/read-ordinance-vs-verma-commission-recommendations-512121 (accessed on 16 December 2020).

[26] Bharti D. *The Constitution and Criminal Justice Administration.* New Delhi: APH Publishing; 2005, p. 320.

[27] Wikipedia. Indian Evidence Act. Available at: https://en.wikipedia.org/wiki/Indian_Evidence_Act (accessed on 16 December 2020).

[28] DNA. Women Groups Protest Anti-rape Ordinance. DNA, 2013. Available at: https://www.dnaindia.com/india/report-women-groups-protest-anti-rape-ordinance-1796191 (accessed on 16 December 2020).

[29] Reddy M. Despite Protest, Ordinance on Sexual Offences Promulgated. *The Hindu,* 2013. Available at: https://www.thehindu.com/news/national/despite-protest-ordinance-on-sexual-offences-promulgated/article4375214.ece (accessed on 16 December 2020).

[30] Anti-rape bill cleared by Lok Sabha. NDTV. 19 March 2013. Retrieved 4 February 2013.

[31] Lok Sabha Passes Anti-rape Bill. *Hindustan Times,* 19 March 2013. Retrieved 4th February 2019.

[32] *The Hindu.* Anti-rape Bill Passed. *The Hindu,* 2013. Available at: https://www.thehindu.com/news/national/antirape-bill-passed/article4534056.ece (accessed on 16 December 2020).

[33] Sexual Harassment of Transgenders. Available at: http://www.rediff.com visited on 7th July 2019.

[34] *Jiloha RC. Rape: Legal issues in mental health perspective.* Indian Journal of Psychiatry. 2013;*55(3):250–255.*

[35] Mehta S. Rape law in India: Problems in prosecution due to loopholes in the law. *SSRN Electronic Journal.* 2013 Apr. Available at: https://papers.ssrn.com/sol3/papers.cfm?abstract_id=2250448 (accessed on 16 December 2020).

[36] Indiankanoon.org. The Protection of Women from Domestic Violence Act, 2005. Available at: https://indiankanoon.org/doc/542601/ (accessed on 16 December 2020).

[37] Legislative.gov.in. The Protection of Children from Sexual Offences Act 2012. Act No. 32, 2012. Available at: http://legislative.gov.in/sites/default/files/A2012-32.pdf (accessed on 16 December 2020).

[38] Supreme Court decriminalises Section 377. Gay Sex Legalised. *The Times of India,* New Delhi, 7 September, 2018. Available at: timesofindia/com (accessed on 16 December 2020).

[39] Chief Labour Commissioner. Industrial Employment Act, 1946. Available at: https://clc.gov.in/clc/acts-rules/industrial-employment-standing-orders-act-1946 (accessed on 16 December 2020).

[40] India Code. Indecent Representation of Women (Prohibition) Act 1987. Ministry of Women and Child Welfare, Government of India. Available at: http://legislative.gov.in/sites/default/files/A1986-60_0.pdf (accessed on 16 December 2020).

[41] Mukherjee MK. Mrs. Rupan Deol Bajaj & Anr vs Kanwar Pal Singh Gill & Anr on 12 October, 1995. Available at: https://indiankanoon.org/doc/579822/ (accessed on 16 December 2020).

[42] Jungthapa V. Women's Group Shaken after Jaipur Court Dismisses Bhanwari Devi Rape Case and Clears Accused. *India Today*, 1995. Available at: https://www.indiatoday.in/magazine/special-report/story/19951215-womens-group-shaken-after-jaipur-court-dismisses-bhanwari-devi-rape-case-and-clears-accused-808044-1995-12-15 (accessed on 16 December 2020).

[43] Mathur K. Bhateri Rape Case: Backlash and Protest. *Economic and Political Weekly*, 1992. Available at: https://www.epw.in/journal/1992/41/commentary/bhateri-rape-case-backlash-and-protest.html (accessed on 16 December 2020).

[44] indiakanoon.org. Vishaka & Ors vs State of Rajasthan & Ors on 13 August, 1997. Available at: https://indiankanoon.org/doc/1031794/ (accessed on 16 December 2020).

[45] Lodha R. Medha Kotwal Lele & Ors vs U. O. I. & Ors on 19 October, 2012. Available at: https://indiankanoon.org/doc/48293767/ (accessed on 16 December 2020).

[46] Anand D. Apparel Export Promotion Council vs A. K. Chopra on 20 January, 1999. Available at: https://indiankanoon.org/doc/856194/ (accessed on 16 December 2020).

[47] Press Information Bureau. The Sexual Harassment of Women at Workplace (Prevention, Prohibition and Redressal) Act, 2013. The Gazette of India.

[48] Benson DJ, Thomson GE. Sexual harassment on a university campus: The confluence of authority relations, sexual interest and gender stratification. *Social Problems*. 1982 Feb 1;29(3):236–251. Available at: http://www.jstor.org/stable/800157 (accessed on 16 December 2020).

[49] Kalita P. Major General Fired for Sexual Harassment of Woman Officer. *The Times of India*, 2019. Available at: https://timesofindia.indiatimes.com/india/major-general-fired-for-sexual-harassment-of-woman-officer/articleshow/70708559.cms (accessed on 16 December 2020).

Sexual Harassment of Women at Workplace (Prevention, Prohibition and Redressal) Act, 2013

Sexual Harassment of Women at Workplace (Prevention, Prohibition and Redressal) Act, 2013, was passed by the Lok Sabha[1] on 3 September 2012 and the Rajya Sabha[2] on 26 February 2013,[1] and received President's assent on 23 April 2013.[2] The Act came into effect from 9 December 2013,[3] superseding the Vishaka Guidelines[3] for preventing sexual harassment that were introduced by the Supreme Court in 1997. The Vishaka Guidelines had helped establish the law that could serve to expand the scope of India's constitutional guarantees and bridge the gaps wherever found.[4] The Act is meant to ensure safe working spaces for women and build enabling work environments that respect women's right to equality of status and opportunity and are consistent with the Vishaka judgment.

[1] https://en.wikipedia.org/wiki/Lok_Sabha
[2] https://en.wikipedia.org/wiki/Rajya_Sabha
[3] https://en.wikipedia.org/wiki/Vishaka_Guidelines

The Act makes provisions for implementing the Convention on Elimination of all Forms of Discrimination against Women to protect them against sexual harassment at workplace.[5]

3.1. Provisions in the Act

Because of historical and sociocultural reasons, women require protection at their workplace to ensures that they feel secure at the place of their work to improve and enhance their participation in work for their economic empowerment and collective share in productivity.[6]

Although the accused harasser is primarily responsible for his offence, this Act holds the workplace responsible and accountable to ensure a safe and secure working environment for women.

The Act is spread over 8 chapters and 30 sections.[2] All the sections of the Act, through their chapters, have been discussed here in a sequence.

Chapter 1 comprises three sections. Section 1 gives preliminary descriptions, including short title, extent and commencement. Definitions of various terms used in the Act are embodied in Section 2. Some important definitions such as aggrieved women, workplace and sexual harassment, as incorporated in the Act, have been explained, here, in this chapter. These are as follows:

3.1.1. Aggrieved Woman

Aggrieved woman, around whom this Act revolves, is interchangeably used for the word 'victim' of sexual harassment in the book. According to the Act, an aggrieved woman could be an employee of an establishment or a household, of any age group, who alleges to have been sexually harassed by a person (Section 2(a)).

All age groups of women irrespective of their employment status and all women working or visiting any workplace in any capacity are protected under the Act. They all qualify the definition of an 'aggrieved woman' as per this Act.

The Act also includes co-workers or students subjected to sexual harassment. Women, who are working in dwelling places or houses as domestic help or otherwise, are also covered under this Act.[7]

3.1.2. Employee

A person employed at a workplace for any work, irrespective of his/her employment status, including a contractor, with or without the knowledge of the principal employer, is an employee. A person working voluntarily, a probationer, trainee, apprentice or called by any other such name, is an employee. A student pursuing his/her studies at an educational institution or a domestic help employed by someone to perform household chores also qualify the definition of an employee according to this Act (Section 2(f)).

3.1.3. Workplace

The place where a person is employed to work, where he/she spends a considerable amount of his/her time working with others or otherwise, whether in an office, educational institution, a residence of some person or any other such place, is the workplace. It includes both organized and unorganized sectors of employment. The workplace owned by Indian or foreign company located in India is also included in the definition (Section 2(o)).

The workplace also includes hospitals, nursing homes, sports institutions, stadium and dwelling place or a house.

The 'workplace' in the Vishaka Guidelines is assumed to be the traditional office set-up where there is a clear employer–employee relationship. However, the Act expands the definition to include organizations, department, office, branch unit, etc., in the public and private sector—organized and unorganized—hospitals, nursing homes, educational institutions, sports institutes, stadiums, sports complexes and any places visited by the employee during the course of employment, including transportation. Even non-traditional workplaces which involve telecommuting are covered under this law.[8], [9]

As per the Act, an unorganized sector is a place owned either by an individual or by self-employed workers engaged in the production or sale of goods or providing services of any kind. It also includes any place with less than 10 employees.

3.1.4. Sexual Harassment

Sexual harassment has been variously defined right from the time of its conceptualization, depending on the context and the reference. (A detailed description is given in Chapter 1). The 2013 Act[2] derives the definition of sexual harassment from Vishaka Guidelines.[4] According to Section 2(n) of the Act, any one or more of the following unwelcome acts constitute sexual harassment:

- 'Physical contact and advances
- A demand or request for sexual favours
- Making sexually coloured remarks
- Showing pornography
- Any other unwelcome physical, verbal or non-verbal conduct of sexual nature.'

Only the recipient decides whether a behaviour is innocuous or unwelcome. The subjective perception of the aggrieved party matters, which may vary from individual to individual. The harasser may not recognize his behaviour or conduct to be offensive and may blame the victim for being oversensitive. However, the Delhi High Court in 2010 affirmed it as a subjective experience of the victim within the framework of a prescribed description.[7]

Unwelcome behaviour or conduct needs to be understood from the aggrieved woman's perspective. There are many women who just ignore the offending remarks without making the harassers realize that they have hurt their sentiments. When their offensive comments are ignored by the victim, the harassers may be further encouraged to make such comments for other women. This behaviour needs to be stopped by making the perpetrators realize their unwelcome behaviour in order to stop the chain of such conduct.[10] A recent incident illustrates the fact in which a university professor in Kolkata equated a virgin woman with a 'sealed bottle' in his social media post which he asserted was for 'fun' in a closed group, but the state's women commission took it otherwise, and university authorities had to divest the don of his teaching assignments and an inquiry initiated by the Internal Complaints Committee (ICC) of the university.[11]

The Act prohibits sexual harassment at the workplace as specified in Section 3. Section 3(1) forbids 'women to be subjected to sexual harassment at any workplace', and Section 3(2) describes the following circumstances, which may amount to sexual harassment:

- Implied or explicit promise of preferential treatment in her employment
- Implied or explicit threat of detrimental treatment in her employment
- Implied or explicit threat about her present or future employment status
- Interference with her work or creating an intimidating or offensive or hostile work environment for her
- Humiliating treatment likely to affect her health or safety.

Many a time, it so happens that situations that start innocently end up in inappropriate and unprofessional behaviours. One should keep in mind that workplace sexual harassment is undesirable and often comprises subjective experience for the victim. It is the 'impact' and not the 'intent' that makes the difference, and it almost invariably occurs in a situation of power. It is quite possible that a woman experiences either an act of sexual harassment or a series of such events over a span of time. One should also remember that each case is unique and should be understood in its own context and accordance with the surrounding circumstances in totality.

3.1.4.1. Behaviours That Constitute Sexual Harassment

Following are some examples of behaviours amounting to sexual harassment:

- Sexually coloured comments by a male colleague at woman co-worker or in her presence who dislikes such comments.
- Telling vulgar jokes to a woman or in her presence which she doesn't like.

- Offensive remarks related to a woman co-worker's body or appearance, looks, gestures, movements, hair, eyes, lips, hips, breasts or other body parts which are spoken by a male and objected by the woman.
- Showing offensive pictures, posters, MMS, SMS, WhatsApp or emails she is not interested in.
- Asking sensitive questions about a woman's private and personal life, particularly about her sex life, which the woman perceives as an encroachment upon her privacy and feels uncomfortable. Exploration of sexual history by a clinician with her consent is not a case of sexual harassment.
- Intimidation, threats, blackmail around sexual favours.
- Social invitations by a male colleague, with sexual overtones—commonly understood as flirting.
- Unwelcome sexual advances which may or may not be accompanied by promises or threats, explicit or implicit.
- Retaliation against a woman employee who speaks up about unwelcome behaviour with sexual overtones.
- Touching inappropriately or pinching a female colleague on one pretext or the other which she may not like.
- Kissing or fondling a woman against her will.
- Getting very close for no apparent reason, brushing against or cornering a woman colleague.
- Asking for sexual favours repeatedly despite being turned down, rebuffed or reprimanded.
- Stalking a woman.
- Abuse of authority or power to threaten a woman's job or undermine her performance against sexual favours.
- Falsely accusing and undermining a woman behind closed doors for sexual favours.
- Controlling a woman's reputation by rumour-mongering about her private life in person or through electronic media.

3.1.4.2. Behaviours Depicting Underlying Sexual Harassment

Following are some examples of behaviours underlying sexual harassment:

- Without a valid reason, depriving a woman worker of group activities or assignments.

- Without a valid reason removing a woman employee from a position of importance.
- Isolating a woman employee by assigning her with demeaning and belittling jobs that are not part of her regular duties like asking to serve tea.
- Insulting, blaming, reprimanding, criticizing or condemning a woman employee in public or in the presence of co-workers.
- Making statements which may damage a woman's reputation or career, professional standing.
- Inappropriately giving too little or too much work.
- Constantly overruling authority without a just cause.
- Constantly blaming a woman for errors without a just cause.
- Monitoring everything that is done by a woman, taking undue interest in her or her work.
- Insulting or humiliating behaviours, repeated attempts to exclude or isolate a woman worker from the larger workgroup.
- Deliberately interfering with normal work conditions, sabotaging places or instruments of work related to a woman worker.
- Withholding a woman worker's access to resources such as time, budget, autonomy, and training opportunities often necessary to succeed.

3.1.4.3. Behaviours That May Not Constitute Sexual Harassment

Following are the behaviours which may not come under the ambit of sexual harassment behaviour:

- Monitoring work absences, pointing out faults in work
- Demanding work as per the job standards
- Routine exercise of management rights—inspecting the work performance
- Work related demands, for example, meeting deadlines or quality standards
- Conditions of works
- Constructive feedback about the work mistakes

Chapter 2 comprises Section 4, which pertains to the constitution of ICC. It relates to the redressal mechanism for a sexually harassed woman which she could approach. According to Section 4(1) of the Act, every employer of a workplace, in the organized sector, shall, by an order in writing, constitute a committee to be known as the ICC. The Act has made it mandatory for every employer to have ICC for his/her establishment.

3.1.5. Complaints Committees

3.1.5.1. Internal Complaints Committee (ICC)

It is a mandatory requirement for every office or the place of work to have a complaints committee to look into the complaints of the aggrieved women and to recommend interventions. According to Section 4(1) of the Act, 'every employer of a workplace shall, by an order in writing, constitute a Committee to be known as the "Internal Complaints Committee" (ICC), at each office or branch with 10 or more employees.'

Where the office or administrative unit of a workplace can be located in different places, divisions or sub-divisions, an ICC has to be set up at every administrative unit and office.

Section 4(2) of the Act pertains to the constitution of ICC, which has the following members nominated by the employer:

- Presiding officer, a woman employed at a senior level at workplace from amongst the employees. If a senior level woman employee is not available, the Presiding Officer is nominated from other offices or administrative units of the workplace. If no senior level woman employee is available there also, the Presiding Officer is nominated from any other workplace of the same employer or other department or organisation.
- At least two Members from amongst employees preferably committed to the cause of women with experience in social work or have legal knowledge.
- One member from amongst non-governmental organisations (NGO) or associations committed to the cause of women or a person familiar with the issues relating to sexual harassment.[4]

---

[4] Women constitute at least half of the nominated members.

Table 3.1. *Internal Complaints Committee (ICC)*

No.	Member	Eligibility Criteria for Nomination
1.	Chairperson/presiding officer	A senior woman employee of the organization or nominated from other offices of the same employer
2.	Two members (minimum)	From amongst employees committed to the cause of women/having legal knowledge/experience in social work
3.	External member	From amongst NGO/associations committed to the cause of women

Table 3.1 shows the constitution of ICC.

The external member is taken from an outside agency like an NGO. It could be a social worker with at least five years' experience in the field of social work, particularly in addressing workplace sexual harassment. It could be a person who is familiar with labour, service, civil or criminal law—a lawyer.

Since the services of an external member are borrowed from a person who is not the part of the organization where the ICC is constituted, he/she is entitled to fee and allowances of ₹200 per day for holding the proceedings of ICC and also the reimbursement of travel cost incurred.

Chapter 3 comprises Sections 5, 6, 7 and 8 pertaining to constitution of LCC.

3.1.5.2. *Local Complaints Committee (LCC)*

It is a mandatory requirement for every state government to have LCC in every district. The district officer is required to constitute LCC at his/her district, and if required at the block level depending upon the size and the population of the block so as to enable women in the unorganized sector or small establishments to work in an environment free of sexual harassment. LCC will receive complaints:

- From women working in an organization having less than 10 workers
- When the complaint is against the employer of an establishment
- From the domestic workers

Section 5 empowers the government to appoint a district magistrate or additional district magistrate or the collector or deputy collector as a district officer (DO) for every district to exercise powers or discharge functions under this Act. Section 6(1) of the Act empowers every DO to constitute 'LCC' in his/her district to receive complaints of sexual harassment.

As per Section 6(2), DO appoints one nodal officer in every block, taluka and tehsil in the rural or tribal area and ward or municipality in the urban area to receive complaints and forward the same to the concerned LCC within a period of seven days. Jurisdiction of LCC is the district where it is constituted and located as per Section 6(3).

Section 7(1) provides for the constitution of LCC with the following members[5] to be nominated by DO:

- Chairperson, an eminent woman social worker committed to the cause of women.
- One woman member working in block, taluka or tehsil or ward or municipality in the district
- Two Members, of whom at least one shall be a woman, from amongst non-governmental organisations (NGO) familiar with the issues relating to sexual harassment. One of them should, preferably, have a background and at least one woman belonging to the Scheduled Castes or the Scheduled Tribes or the Other Backward Classes or minority community notified by the Central Government.
- The concerned officer dealing with the social welfare or women and child development in the district, shall be an ex officio member.

Table 3.2 shows the constitution of LCC.

The chairperson is entitled to the prescribed allowances, and DO is responsible for their payment.

Because of the complex nature of workplace sexual harassment, there are several complexities involved in providing effective responses to workplace sexual harassment complaints. Due to this, external/third

---

[5] One of the nominees shall be a woman belonging to the SC/ST/OBC/ Minority community notified by the Central Government.

Table 3.2. Local Complaints Committee (LCC)

No.	Member	Eligibility Criteria for Nomination
1	Chairperson	An eminent woman from within the district in the field of social work and committed to the cause of women
2	Member[a]	Women working in the block, taluka or tehsil or ward or municipality in the district and having an interest in the welfare of women
3	2 Members	Nominated from amongst NGOs/associations/persons committed to the cause of women or familiar with the issues relating to sexual harassment, provided that: • At least one must be a woman • At least one must have a background of law or legal knowledge
4	Ex officio member	The concerned officer dealing with social welfare or women and child development in the district

Note: [a]One of the nominees shall be a woman belonging to the SC/ST/OBC/ minority community notified by the central government.

party representatives on the complaints committee(s) from civil society or legal backgrounds should possess the following qualities:

• Knowledge, skill and capacity to deal effectively with the workplace sexual harassment issues and complaints
• Strong grasp and practice in handling the legal aspects and their consequences

Such expertise hugely benefits complaints committees in terms of their capacity for fair and informed handling of complaints, leading to sound outcomes. These external third-party members are paid for their services on the complaints committees as prescribed.

Both the committees (ICC and LCC) prepare their annual report in a prescribed form and time every year and submit the same to the employer and DO under Section 21(1) of the Act. DO compiles these annual reports received from the committees in a brief report and forwards it to the state government for necessary action.

Chapter 4 pertains to complaint and comprises three sections, Sections 9, 10 and 11.

3.1.6. Complaint

Section 9 empowers an aggrieved woman to lodge a complaint to the complaints committee in writing within three months of the incident or within three months of the last episode of ongoing harassment. ICC, for the reasons to be recorded in writing, can extend the time, not exceeding three months, if it is satisfied that the circumstances were of such a nature that prevented the aggrieved woman from filing a complaint within the prescribed time period and the committee appreciated the genuineness of the delay. Six copies of the complaint need to be submitted by the aggrieved woman. The designated person or any member of the complaints committee may assist the victim to lodge a written complaint. If the aggrieved woman is unable to make the complaint due to physical or mental incapacity, death or otherwise, the legal heir can make a complaint on her behalf with her consent. The workplace having less than 10 employees cannot have ICC; therefore, an employee of such organization shall lodge her complaint with LCC of the district. Similarly, the complaint by a domestic help and the complaint against the employer of an establishment shall be lodged with LCC.

Under Section 10(1) of the Act, the complaints committees are required to provide for conciliation before initiating an inquiry if requested by the complainant (aggrieved woman). If a settlement is reached, then it is recorded, and its report is sent to the employer or DO as applicable. A copy each should also be given to the aggrieved women and the respondent, and no further inquiry is needed in such case.

Under Section 11(1), the concerned complaints committee shall proceed to make an inquiry in accordance with the service rules if no settlement is reached. The committee is empowered to summon respondent and witnesses and can ask for the production of documentary evidence. Complaints committees have the powers of civil courts for gathering evidence. To address the complaints and conduct an inquiry into the alleged harassment, the committee is required to complete the inquiry within 90 days. On completion of the inquiry, the report will be sent to the employer or DO, as applicable, and they are mandated to take action on the report within 60 days of receiving the report.[12]

Chapter 5 pertains to inquiry into complaint and comprises seven Sections. These are Sections 12, 13, 14, 15, 16, 17 and 18.

Under Section 12(1), on receiving the complaint, the committee may recommend to the employer the transfer of the aggrieved woman or the respondent to another working place to avoid further intimidation. It may also recommend granting leave to the aggrieved woman up to three months which will be in addition to her entitled leave. The committee may also recommend any other interim relief as may be prescribed.

3.1.7. Employer

The employer is a person under whose instructions and administrative control the employees work. According to Section 2(g) of the Act, an employer means:

- In relation to any department, organisation, undertaking, establishment, enterprise, institution, office, branch or unit of the appropriate Government or a local authority, the head of that department, organisation, undertaking, establishment. enterprise, institution, office, branch or unit or such other officer as the appropriate Government or the local authority, as the case may be, may by an order specify in this behalf
- In any workplace not covered under sub-clause (i), any person responsible for the management, supervision and control of the workplace. Management" includes the person or board or committee responsible for formulation and administration of polices for such organisation
- In relation to workplace covered under sub-clauses (1) and (ii), the person discharging contractual obligations with respect to his or her employees
- In relation to a dwelling place or house, a person or a household who employs or benefits from the employment of domestic worker, irrespective of the number, time period or type of such worker employed, or the nature of the employment or activities performed by the domestic worker;
- The head of the department, organisation, undertaking, establishment, enterprise, institution, office, branch or unit of the Appropriate Government or local authority or such officer specified in this behalf.

- Any person (whether contractual or not) responsible for the management, supervision and control of a designated workplace not covered under clause (i).
- A person or a household who employs or benefits from the employment of domestic worker or women employees.

Section 13 is about reporting the findings of the inquiry, and Section 14 pertains to punishment for false or malicious complaint and false evidence.

Section 18 is regarding appeal:

- Any person aggrieved from the recommendations made under subsection (2) of Section 13 or under clause (i) or clause (ii) of subsection (3) of Section 13 or subsection (1) or subsection (2) of Section
- 14 or Section 17 or non-implementation of such recommendations may prefer an appeal to the Court or Tribunal in accordance with the provisions of the service rules applicable to the said person or where no such service rules exist then, without prejudice to provisions contained in any other law for the time being in force, the person aggrieved may prefer an appeal in such manner as may be prescribed.
- The appeal under sub-section (1) shall be preferred within a period of ninety days of the recommendations.

Chapter 6 pertains to the duties of the employer and embodies Section 19.

Section 19 of the Act prescribes duties of the employer of a workplace in relation to the sexual harassment of the employees. The duties described are as follows:

3.1.7.1. Duties of the Employer

The following are the duties of the employer:

- It is the duty of the employer to provide a safe working environment to his/her employees, including safety from persons coming in contact at the workplace whether working there or otherwise.

- The employer should display the penal consequences of sexual harassments at conspicuous places of the workplace visible to all; he/she should also order constituting ICC for his/her workplace.
- The employer should organize workshops and awareness programmes at regular intervals to sensitize the employees. The employer is also responsible for the orientation programmes for members of ICC.
- The employer should make available necessary facilities required by ICC to deal with the complaints and conduct inquiries. The employer should also make the records available if the ICC requires them.
- The employer is required to assist in securing the attendance of the respondent and the witnesses before ICC when they are summoned.
- Any information required by ICC from the office of the establishment during the process of inquiry shall be made available by the employer.
- If the aggrieved woman chooses to file a complaint under IPC or other relevant laws, the employer is bound to assist her. He/she is not expected to dissuade her from doing so.
- The employer shall cause to initiate action under IPC or other relevant laws against the perpetrator or if the aggrieved woman so desires, where the perpetrator is not an employee, in the workplace at which the incident took place.
- The employer shall treat sexual harassment as misconduct and initiate action accordingly.
- The employer shall monitor and ensure timely submission of the report by ICC.

Chapter 7 deals with the duties and powers of DO and contains Section 20.

3.1.7.2. Duties and Powers of District Officer

According to Section 20 of the Act, DO has the following powers:

- DO is required to monitor the timely submission of reports furnished by LCC.

- He/she is to take necessary measures to engage NGOs for creation of awareness on sexual harassment and the rights of the women.

3.1.7.3. Miscellaneous Provisions of the Act

Chapter 8 contains miscellaneous provisions embodied in the remaining sections of the Act—Sections 21, 22, 23, 24, 25, 26, 27, 28, 29 and 30.

Section 21(1) directs ICC or LCC to prepare an annual report in a prescribed form within a prescribed time limit and submit to the employer or DO.

DO shall forward a brief report on the annual reports to the state government as per Section 21(2) of the Act for further necessary action on the part of the government.

Section 22 directs every employer to include the number of cases filed during the year and their disposal while preparing the report. At the places where no such report is required, the intimation of such number of cases is given to DO.

The government is responsible for monitoring the implementation of the Act. Section 23 provides that the appropriate government shall monitor the implementation of this Act and maintain data of the cases filed and disposed of in respect of all cases of sexual harassment at the workplace.

To ensure development and availability of educational material on the awareness about the Act, Section 24 provides that the government will generate finances and subject to the availability of financial resources. The appropriate government may:

- develop relevant information, education, communication training materials, and organise awareness programmes, to advance the understanding of the public of the provisions of this Act providing for protection against sexual harassment of woman at workplace.
- formulate orientation and training programmes for the members of the Local Complaints Committee.

In the public interest or in the interest of women employees at a workplace, the employer or DO shall furnish written information related to sexual harassment. The inspection report of the records and workplace is submitted within a prescribed period [Section 25(1)]34 that of the workplace.

According to Section 25(2), every employer and DO shall produce on demand before the officer making the inspection all information, records and other documents in his/her custody having a hearing on the subject matter of such inspection.

When the employer fails to perform his/her following duties:

- constitute an Internal Committee
- take action as prescribed under Sections 13, 14 and 22
- contravenes or attempts to contravene or abets contravention of other provisions of this Act or any rules made thereunder.

He/she shall be punishable with fine which may extend to ₹50,000 under Section 26(1).

According to Section 26(2), if the employer commits the offence again after having been convicted earlier of an offence punishable under this Act, shall be liable to 'twice the punishment, which might have been imposed on a first conviction, subject to the punishment being maximum provided for the same offence' provided that in case a higher punishment is prescribed under any other law for the time being in force or the offence for which the accused is being prosecuted, the court shall take due cognizance of the same while awarding the punishment 'of his licence or withdrawal or non-renewal or approval or cancellation of the registration, as the case may be, by the government or local authority required for carrying on his business or activity.'

According to Section 27(1) of the Act, no court shall take cognizance of any offence punishable under this Act or any rules made thereunder, save on a complaint made by the aggrieved woman or any person authorized by ICC or LCC in this behalf.

Section 27(2) does not permit any court inferior a court of metropolitan magistrate or a judicial magistrate of the first class to try any offence punishable under this Act.

All offences under this Act shall be non-cognizable as per Section 26(3). According to Section 28, the provisions of this Act shall be in addition to and not in derogation of other provisions.

Section 29(I) empowers the central government by notification to make rules to carry out the provisions of the Act. Section 29(2), in particular and without prejudice to the generality of the foregoing power, make rules for all or any of the following matters:

i. the fees or allowances to be paid to the Members under Section 4(1) for Internal Complaints Committee
ii. nomination of members under Section 7(1)[c]
iii. the fees or allowances to be paid to the Chairperson, and members under Section 7(1)
iv. the person who may make complaint under Section 9(2)
v. the manner of inquiry under Section 11(1)
vi. the powers for making an inquiry under Section 11(2)[c]
vii. the relief to be recommended under Section 12;(1)[c]
viii. the manner of action to be taken under Section 13(3)[i]
ix. the manner of action to be taken under Section 14(1) and (2).
x. the manner of action to be taken under Section 17;
xi. the manner of appeal under Section 18(1)
xii. the manner of organising workshops, awareness programmes for sensitising the employees and orientation programmes for the members of the Internal Committee under Section 19(c)
xiii. the form and time for preparation of annual report by Internal Committee and the Local Committee under Section 21(1)

According to Section 29(3), every rule made by the central government under this Act shall be laid at the earliest possible after it is made, before each House of Parliament, while it is in session, for a total period of 30 days which may be comprised in one session or in two or more successive sessions, and if, before the expiry of the session immediately following the session or the successive sessions aforesaid, both Houses agree in making any modification in the rule or both Houses agree that the rule should not be made, the rule shall, thereafter, have effect only in such modified form or be of no effect, as the case may be; so, however, that any such modification or annulment shall be without prejudice to the validity of anything previously done under that rule.

According to Section 29(4), any rule made under Section 8(4) by the state government be laid, as soon as may be after it is made, before each House of the State Legislature where it consists of two Houses or where such Legislature consists of one House, before that House.

Section 30(1) of the Act says that if any difficulty arises in giving effect to the provisions of this Act, the central government may, by order published in the official gazette, make such provisions, not inconsistent with the provisions of this Act, as may appear to it to be for removing the difficulty, provided that no such order shall be made under this section after the expiry of the period of two years from the commencement of this Act.

Every order made under Section 30(2) shall be laid, as soon as may be after it is made, before each House of Parliament.

3.2. Dissemination of Information and Awareness Generation

Under the Section 24 of the Act, the government has a legal responsibility to:

- Effectively communicate a policy that prohibits unwelcome behaviour that constitutes workplace sexual harassment, and provides a detailed framework for prevention, and redress processes.
- Carry out awareness and orientation for all employees.
- Create forums for dialogue i.e. Panchayati Raj Institutions, Gram Sabhas, Women's Groups, Urban Local Bodies or like bodies, as appropriate.
- Ensure capacity and skill building of Complaints Committees.
- Widely publicize names and contact details of Complaints Committee members.

The government is liable to frame a policy against sexual harassment and effectively and clearly communicate it to all by organizing awareness programmes at regular intervals, and wide publicity is given to their names and contact numbers of the members of the complaints committees.

The Act also covers students in schools and colleges as well as patients in hospitals.

The employers are expected to strictly adhere to the provisions of the Act. Penalties have been prescribed for employers for non-compliance or any lapses in compliance. Non-compliance with the provisions of the Act shall be punishable with a fine. Repeated violations may lead to higher penalties and cancellation of licence or registration to conduct business.[13]

The government can order an officer to inspect the workplace and the records related to sexual harassment in any organization.

In case of non-compliance with any provisions contained in the Act, the law prescribes a monetary penalty of up to ₹50,000, and a repetition of the same offence could result in the punishment being doubled and/or de-registration of the entity or revocation of any statutory business licenses.[7]

3.3. Difficulties in Implementation of the Act

Many organizations are not even aware of the existence of the Act[14] and many of those who are aware, are unwilling to streamline policies or set up appropriate mechanisms for effective implementation of the Act. Some employers just set up a complaints committee for their own safety than to help the victims because it is the mandatory requirement.[15], [16] Many private organizations discourage complaints to avoid any slur on the reputation of their organizations. Many corporate companies deny having cases and find it irrelevant to have ICC at their place. Mostly, there are no complaints because no one raises a complaint because of the fear of retaliation, stigma and the lack of confidence. In India, sexual harassment is a closeted form of gender discrimination and occurs at all levels of workplace settings.[15] The International Labour Organization[6] (ILO) notes that despite widespread prevalence, all the employers in India are not compliant to the Act.[16], [17] According to Federation of Indian Chamber of Commerce and Industry (FICCI),

---

[6] https://en.wikipedia.org/wiki/International_Labour_Organization

36 per cent of Indian companies and 25 per cent multinational corporation are not compliant with the Act.[18]

In case a woman reports the incident formally, the power dynamics against the aggrieved woman gets the complaint invalidated. If the harasser is a higher up in the ladder or more powerful administratively, the complaint is ignored, and victim's past sexual life or friendship with men in the past is brought into consideration to justify the perpetrator's conduct, and the game is turned against the victim.[19], [20]

In some cases, the nature of the job complicates the issue, and the victims prefer to ignore it. The hospitality industry, including hotels and restaurants, rarely report cases of sexual harassment as client satisfaction is their priority. Reporting against their clients is likely to adversely affect their business.[21] Hospitals also find it difficult, as there are different groups of people with different roles working and visiting the establishment every day, and a large number of people coming in and going out throughout the day—patients, their attendants, visitors, agents from pharmaceutical companies and so on. Women workers, particularly the nurses who come in direct contact of people, are more vulnerable. Similar is the case with the educational institutions where the redressal mechanism is non-existent in most of the places, and the students may be exploited by predatory male teachers.[22], [23]

A recent report illustrates the fact wherein 20 girls of a school in New Delhi incidentally opened up about their ordeal of sexual harassment when the members of the Women Commission were discussing the matter of street harassers with the women of a locality. They revealed the boys teased them, whistled at them, made catcalls and stalked them, and there was no one to complain about it. This shows ignorance of the victims about legal remedies and redressal mechanisms available in the country.[24]

Overall experiences with the implementation of the Act reveal many difficulties in many sectors for various reasons. Following measures are important to resolve these difficulties.

• **Awareness generation and capacity building by the employers:** Symbolic compliance of the Act only wards off the legal liability but does not reduce sexual harassment. Awareness programmes are required to ensure that employers are investing resources in creating awareness about the redressal mechanisms among the employees.

- **Selection of external member of the complaints committee:** The role of the external member is very crucial to deliver justice without bias. An independent and impartial person, having respect for the law and capacity to ensure the process in an unbiased manner, should be nominated by the employer.

- **Zero reporting of sexual harassment:** If there is no reporting of cases, it does not mean the problem does not occur. Victims do not report because of fear of retaliation, denial of promotion, stigma, lack of surety whether the action will be taken against the perpetrator or interruption in academic enhancement.

- **Employer's role:** The employer's role is to create awareness about the provisions of the Act in his/her organization. The employer is mandated to perform his/her duties as per the Act.

- **Responsibility of complaints committee:** When a complaint against a person at the top is made, there is often a failure of the management to help the aggrieved woman. At times, the complaints committee is reluctant to initiate the inquiry against a respondent occupying a high position in the organizational hierarchy. The Act empowers the complaints committee to investigate the complaints in an unbiased manner.

The Act insists for a written complaint by the victim to proceed further with the case, and the members of the ICC could render assistance to the individual victims in filing the complaint. Personal space and dignity of women who have to go through a bitter emotional experience are eroded; many of them are reluctant to make a complaint in writing but want to be helped. Some of them are willing to communicate verbally without giving a complaint in writing to avoid getting further meshed up with bureaucratic and legal hassles.[14] According to Chaudhuri's[21] report, women often feel that a legal battle could take a prolonged course. Several organizations take no action against the culprit in the absence of a written complaint, and the incident goes unreported, and the employer gets the credit of having no cases.

3.4. Criticism of the Act

No doubt the Act is beneficial to victimized individuals, it has spawned a defensive climate for the employers who focus more on protection against liability and less on the resolution of the issues. The mediation-driven outcome could enhance a women's self-esteem, but that is seldom possible to achieve in the current environment. Even when a woman receives a positive outcome to a formal complaint, she may encounter difficulties. Many male workers will avoid befriending her for fear of alleged sexism. Ratna Kapoor says that the law on sexual harassment actually causes greater repression instead of leading to respite.[12] In view of the magnitude of prevalence of sexual harassment, with increasing awareness, more and more cases are likely to come up on the surface and hence more and more inquiries. As a result, every workplace is likely to turn into a battlefield and ICC a full-time inquiry committee at the cost of the routine official work for which its members and the presiding officer are originally appointed.

Sexual harassment litigation may lead to polarization in the workplace. With ostracization of the victim, there may be retaliation from the perpetrator and his/her friends. There may be others who are sympathizers for the victim. There may be a prevalence of adversarial win–lose environment at the workplace. The Act also marginalizes different groups of women. The Gujarat National Law University, after conducting a critical analysis of this Act, highlighted the exclusion of certain workers,[25] and it took sustained campaigning by activists to have domestic workers included in the Act.

3.5. Clinical Aspects of the Act

There is no denying that the legal professionals have contributed immensely in providing victims with a powerful weapon; laws clarify the liability of employers for employees acting in discriminatory manners. Laws have led to the formulation of sexual harassment and discrimination policies within institutions, as well as the complaint channels that provide another means of redress. The legally mandated training of managers and administrators regarding the handling of sexual harassment complaints has heightened their awareness of and sensitivity to the importance of these issues, which has also been useful.

Litigation can seriously disturb psychiatric treatment, and a psychiatric diagnosis can favour establishing damages, as different from recovering psychologically. The litigation process can adversely affect the victims and disrupt their treatment.[26] Many clinicians, in fact, are reluctant to treat victims because they find the process of litigation intimidating. Many clinicians concentrate more on determining whether the victim's situation constituted harassment from a legal standpoint than on understanding the victim's symptomatology, appreciating the meaning of the event for the patient, and assisting her in recovering. The clinical treatment may be misused via:

- Forced psychiatric evaluations
- Forced psychiatric treatment
- Evaluation for fitness for duty, in which the clinician is in a conflict of interest with the victim

Confidentiality can be compromised in unethical ways. Gender bias within the courtroom, as described by Schafran[27] can also pose a problem for both clinicians and plaintiffs involved in the legal process.

Although many of the victims have the courage to withstand social pressure, some women are doubtful about their role. They blame themselves when treated inappropriately by their harassers or employers. This type of attitude develops from social learning, the cultural beliefs and the upbringing. The traditional upbringing enables women to develop skills and competence to be well-versed with household skills and fails to empower and emancipate them to fight for their own rights in the outside world. There is no denying that women are eminently capable and proficient at working outside their homes and pursuing practically all occupations that men are capable of pursuing. Yet many seem incapable of asserting themselves and standing up against the wrongs they are subjected to, particularly those of a sexual nature.

Many women are economically well off, highly educated and occupy a position of importance in their office, but still they are dependent on men. There is an inherent need for permission from male family members before asserting. Many of them carry low confidence and find it difficult to express and assert their rights without others' support. Majority of men are helpful and come forward to help women in distress; some men trivialize their problem and prevent them from asserting. Such women need to seek help from other women who have had a similar experience of sexual misconduct.

References

[1] Kapur N. The Sexual Harassment Bill Undermines the Innovative Spirit of Vishaka. Bar and Bench; 2018. Available at: Available at: https://www.barandbench.com/interviews/sexual-harassment-bill-undermines-innovative-spirit-vishaka-naina-kapur-lawyer-and-0 (accessed on 17 December 2020).

[2] Legislative Department. Sexual Harassment of Women at Workplace (Prevention, Prohibition and Redressal) Act, 2013 Ministry of Women and Child Development, Government of India; 2013. Available at: http://legislative.gov.in/sites/default/files/A2013-14.pdf (accessed on 17 December 2020).

[3] PTI. Law against Sexual Harassment at Workplace Comes into Effect. *The Times of India*; 2018. Available at: https://timesofindia.indiatimes.com/india/Law-against-sexual-harassment-at-workplace-comes-into-effect/articleshow/27308194.cms (accessed on 17 December 2020).

[4] Supreme Court of India. Vishaka & Ors vs State of Rajasthan & Ors. 1997. Available at: https://indiankanoon.org/doc/1031794/ (accessed on 17 December 2020).

[5] UN Women. Convention on the Elimination of all Forms of Discrimination against Women. Available at: https://www.un.org/womenwatch/daw/cedaw/ (accessed on 17 December 2020).

[6] Press Information Bureau. Protection of Women against Sexual Harassment at Workplace Bill, 2010. Government of India; 2010. Available at: https://pib.gov.in/newsite/erelease.aspx?relid=66781%7C (accessed on 17 December 2020).

[7] Ministry of Women and Child Welfare. Handbook of Sexual Harassment at Workplace. Government of India; 2015. Available at: https://www.iitk.ac.in/wc/data/Handbook%20on%20Sexual%20Harassment%20of%20Women%20at%20Workplace.pdf (accessed on 17 December 2020).

[8] Bag A. Is Your 'Workplace' Covered under the New Sexual Harassment Law? iPleaders; 2014. Available at: https://blog.ipleaders.in/is-your-workplace-covered-under-the-new-sexual-harassment-law/ (accessed on 17 December 2020).

[9]   Rouf Ahmad Bhat, Anita Deshpande. An overview of sexual harassment at workplace in India: an analytical study. International Journal of Innovative Research in Science, Engineering and Technology. 2017;6(7). Available at: www.ijirset.com (accessed on 17 December 2020).

[10] Osman SL. Victim resistance: Theory and data on understanding perceptions of sexual harassment. *Sex Roles*. 2004 Feb 1;50(3–4):267–275.

[11] TNN. 'Virgin girl is like sealed bottle,' Jadavpur University professor posts on Facebook, deletes it. *The Times of India*; 2019. Available at: https://timesofindia.indiatimes.com/city/kolkata/virgin-girl-is-like-sealed-bottle-jadavpur-university-professor-posts-on-facebook-deletes-it/articleshow/67519277.cms (accessed on 17 December 2020).

[12] Kapur R. *Erotic Justice: Law and the New Politics of Post-Colonialism*. Abingdon: Routledge–Cavendish; 2005.

[13] Ministry of Women and Child Development. The Protection of Women against Sexual Harassment at Work Place Bill, 2010. *PRS Legislative Research*. Available at: https://www.prsindia.org/billtrack/the-protection-of-women-against-sexual-harassment-at-work-place-bill-2010-1402/ (accessed on 17 December 2020).

[14] Petrocelli W, Repa B. *Sexual Harassment on the Job: What It Is and How to Stop It* (4th ed.). Pleasanton, CA: Nolo Press; 1998.

[15] Shukla S. Indecent Proposal. *Business Today*; 2002. Available at: http://archives.digitaltoday.in/businesstoday/20020901/cover1.html (accessed on 17 December 2020).

[16] Tejani Sheba. Sexual harassment at the workplace: Emerging problems and debates. *Economic and Political Weekly*. 2004; 39(41):4491–4494.

[17] Haspels N, Kasim ZM, Thomas C, McCann D. *Action against Sexual Harassment at Work in Asia and Pacific*. International Labour Organization; 2001. Available at: https://www.ilo.org/wcmsp5/groups/public/---asia/---ro-bangkok/documents/publication/wcms_bk_pb_159_en.pdf (accessed on 17 December 2020).

[18] FICCI. Fostering Safe Workplace. Available at: http://ficci.in/spdocument/20672/Fostering-safe.pdf (accessed on 17 December 2020).

[19] International Labour Organization. Rights and Protection of Domestic Workers in India. Available at: https://www.ilo.org/newdelhi/info/public/vid/WCMS_522314/lang--en/index.htm (accessed on 17 December 2020).

[20] Sarpotdar A. Sexual Harassment of Women: Reflections on the Private Sector. *Economic and Political Weekly*. 2013; 48(40):18–22.

[21] Chaudhuri P. Sexual Harassment at the Workplace: Experiences with Complaints Committees. *Economic and Political Weekly*. 2008; 43(17):99–106.

[22] Suroosh A. Sexual Harassment: News Story. Canadian Press, 23 December 2017.

[23] U.S. Department of Labor. Form LM-2 Labor Organization Annual Report. File No. 000-106; 2014. Available at: https://olmsapps.dol.gov/query/orgReport.do?rptId=562569&rptForm=LM2Form (accessed on 17 December 2020).

[24] TNN. Delhi: 20 Girls Open Up about Teasing by Boys in School. *The Times of India*; 2019. Available at: https://timesofindia.indiatimes.com/city/delhi/20-girls-open-up-about-teasing-by-boys-in-school/articleshow/69104888.cms (accessed on 17 December 2020).

[25] Sexual Harassment of Women at Workplace (Prevention, Prohibition and Redressal) Act, 2013: Critical Analysis [online]. Gujarat National Law University. http://sibresearch.org/uploads/2/7/9/9/2799227/riber_tk14-150_418 428.pdf, Retrieved 12 December 2014.

[26] Jensvold MF. The potential for misuse and abuse of psychiatry in workplace sexual harassment. In: Shrier DK, editor, *Sexual Harassment in the Workplace and Academia: Psychiatric Issues.* Washington DC, WA: American Psychiatric Press; 1996.

[27] Schafran LH. Sexual harassment cases in the courts, or therapy goes to war: Supporting a sexual harassment victim during litigation. In: Shrier DK, editor, *Sexual Harassment in the Workplace and academia.* Washington DC, WA: American Psychiatric Press; 1996, pp. 133–152.

CHAPTER 4

Procedure to Process the Complaint and Redressal Mechanism

A workplace is a common platform for the workers and other related persons of an establishment to perform their assigned task collectively or otherwise, where they spend considerable time together and interact. A safe and healthy environment at the place of work is an essential ingredient for the progress and development of both the employees and the organization. A healthy work environment in which persons of both sexes work and complement each other as equals encourages maximum productivity. Harassment of women employees certainly hampers the growth and productivity of the organization and makes the working environment hostile which negatively affects victims' physical and mental health. In order to prevent these unwanted adverse effects, sexual harassment should not go unreported, and the culprit should be brought to book in accordance with the law of the land to prevent hostility in the work environment.[1] It should be reflected in the institutional policy of every organization mandated by the law.[2]

It is not necessary that the incident takes place only at the place where the person is employed. Any event of work-related activity like official travels, working at customer's or client's premises or any work-related electronic communication constitutes a workplace for the purpose of the Act. Freelancer, consultant or a client to the workplace is also entitled to make a complaint under the Act.[3]

The experience of sexual harassment is not only a painful and agonizing event for the victim, but it also shatters her self-concept as a human being. Before deciding to raise a complaint, majority of the victims spend sleepless nights brooding over the trauma and the future prospects of continuing in the job. Their behaviour with people changes, their work productivity gets adversely affected and, in some cases, they avoid attending classes or work meetings out of fear of having to confront the harasser there, have fears of safety, avoid people, keep interactions minimal and avoid socializing.[4] The emotional impact becomes damaging for the victim and requires to be addressed in a sensitive manner by those who handle the complaints. If handled casually and callously, it can further expose the victim to emotional and mental health issues, which may be further damaging on account of stress and anxiety. The following is the procedure to process the complaint.

4.1. Complaint and Inquiry

4.1.1. How to Make a Complaint?

The first step to make a complaint is to approach the complaint committee of the organization where the complainant is employed. Every workplace with 10 or more employees has a complaints committee where the victim can lodge her complaint. Employers are legally bound to have ICC as a requirement mandated by the Act. Any victim or aggrieved woman may lodge her complaint in writing, to the ICC, within a period of three months from the date of the last incident of sexual harassment. However, ICC is empowered to extend the time period not exceeding another three months if it is satisfied that the circumstances prevented the complainant from filing a complaint within the prescribed period. The reasons for this extended period should be recorded in writing.[1] For the aggrieved women not able to submit a written complaint, the presiding office or any other member of the ICC shall render all reasonable assistance to make the complaint in writing. Six copies of the complaint are submitted to ICC.

Those complainants working in the organizations having less than 10 employees, domestic help and those who have a complaint against the employer of their organization can approach the nodal officer of the area of the LCC constituted by DO. DO designates a person, the nodal officer, in every block, taluka and tehsil in rural or tribal areas and wards or municipalities in the urban areas to receive workplace sexual harassment complaints from aggrieved women. Here also, the complaint has to be lodged within three months of the incident or within three months of the last episode of the ongoing harassment. The nodal officer forwards the complaint within seven days of receipt to the concerned LCC.[2]

4.1.2. Who Can Make a Complaint?

Routinely, it is the aggrieved woman or the victim who makes the complaint. When she is unable to do so, on account of her physical incapacity, her relative, friend, co-worker or an officer of the National Commission for Women or State Women's Commission or any person knowing the incident, can make the complaint. The complaint made by some other person on behalf of the victim is valid only when the aggrieved woman or the victim has given her consent for the same in writing under Section 9(2) of the Act.

If the victim is unable to lodge complaint due to her mental incapacity, some other individuals such as her relative or friend, a special educator, a qualified psychiatrist or psychologist, the guardian or authority under whose care she is receiving treatment or care and any person who knows about the incident, jointly with her relative or friend, can make a complaint. If some other unavoidable reasons prevent her to make a complaint, with her written consent or when the aggrieved woman is dead, a complaint may be filed by any person who has knowledge of the incident, with the written consent of her legal heir.

4.1.3. Content of the Complaint

Six copies of the complaint are submitted along with the details of the witnesses and the supporting documents to substantiate her complaint. Each incident of sexual harassment which the aggrieved woman suffered should be described in the complaint. The description should have the date and time of the incident along with the name of the place where the incident took place. The complaint should include respondent(s)' name(s) along with their working relationship with the victim.

If the aggrieved woman or the victim has not lodged the complaint in writing, the nodal officer or any other designated officer provides assistance in writing the complaint. Any document that can substantiate an allegation of sexual harassment such as text messages, emails and restaurant bills should be kept carefully for use as evidence to prove the case.

4.1.4. Receipt of Complaint

Once a complaint is received by ICC, it is forwarded immediately to the presiding officer, and other members of ICC are notified, and a meeting is called for discussion within three days of receipt of the complaint. The committee decides on its jurisdiction to deal or rejects the complaint prima facie and recommends to the employer that no action is required in the matter.

If ICC finds the case suitable to dealt with within it sends one copy of the complaint to the respondent within seven working days of the receipt of the complaint.

The accused or the respondent has to respond with his reply along with a list of supporting documents, including the names and addresses of witnesses within 10 working days from the date of receipt of the copy of the complaint.

This makes the inquiry committee begin with the investigations. A fair, prompt and impartial inquiry process is initiated in an environment of trust and confidence. The complaint is reviewed in the context of:

1. The Sexual Harassment of Women at Workplace (Prevention, Prohibition and Redressal) Act 2013
2. Service rules applicable
3. Policy of the organization against sexual harassment
4. Vishaka Guidelines and related laws
5. Clarity in the complaint
6. Additional information needed from the complainant

A written notice is sent to the complainant to acknowledge receipt of the complaint, and the accused is made aware of the allegations made against him, and the name of the complainant is informed to the accused.

4.1.5. Rights of the Aggrieved Woman

Every aggrieved woman enjoys certain rights accorded in the Act. The following are the rights of an aggrieved woman seeking redressal of her grievances:

1. An aggrieved woman has the right for a friendly environment and empathy for expressing herself fearlessly without inhibition or hesitation.
2. Throughout the process of inquiry, complainant's identity is kept confidential. It is the responsibility of ICC or LCC to maintain confidentiality.
3. Sexual history of the aggrieved woman is irrelevant for the current case. History is of no relevance in the current case of sexual harassment. Complainant's character or sexual life is independent of the complaint made.
4. If the complainant expects retaliation or fear of intimidation from the respondent, she is entitled to get her statement recorded in the absence of the respondent.
5. The complainant has the right to appeal if not satisfied with the recommendations or the findings of the complaints committee.

6. In case the complainant chooses to lodge criminal proceedings against the respondent, she is entitled to support in lodging FIR.

4.1.6. Rights of the Respondent

The accused in the complaint is entitled to the following rights:

1. Patient hearing by the complaints committee to present his case
2. Get a copy of evidence and the list of witnesses submitted by the complainant to the complaints committee
3. Confidentiality of his identity throughout the process of inquiry, and it is the responsibility of the complaints committee to maintain confidentiality
4. Appeal if not satisfied with the findings and recommendations of the complaints committee

4.1.7. Meeting and Informing the Aggrieved Woman

The aggrieved woman is informed and explained the options available for formal or informal resolution of the matter.

4.1.8. Informal Mechanism

The complaints committee is empowered to take initiative for conciliation if the complainant desires so. The complainant is provided with an opportunity for conciliation by making arrangement for communication with the respondent in the presence of the members of the committee. If she chooses to resolve the issue, possible ways are explored. To resolve the complaint through conciliation, procedures such as counselling, education, reorientation and warning the respondent to immediately cease undesirable behaviour, are used. A neutral conciliator is employed to settle the matter.

The severity of the situation should be assessed before recommending conciliation, and if necessary, the victim is advised and enabled to opt for the formal option. She should never be advised to directly resolve the matter. In case the informal process is successful, the conciliator records the resolution and forwards it to ICC or LCC, who, in turn, forward it to the concerned authorities for further action based on the resolution.

To prevent backlash or retaliation of any kind by the respondent or his friends against the victim, appropriate steps are taken to avoid any mishap. However, no monetary relief is allowed in conciliation cases. No monetary settlement is permissible at this stage. ICC or LCC will record the basis of the conciliation and copies of the settlement are given to both the parties for their record.

In case the respondent or the accused does not follow the conciliation settlement, the aggrieved woman or the victim will still have an option to approach ICC or LCC for proper inquiry of the incident.

The nodal officer or the member of ICC dealing with the case can neither suggest nor compel the complainant for conciliation. That is entirely her choice.

4.1.9. Formal Mechanism

If the matter is not settled by conciliation, or the conciliation is not followed, ICC or LCC shall make an inquiry or forward the case to the police. Assistance is provided to the aggrieved woman if she chooses to file a police complaint in relation to an offence under IPC.[5]

ICC or LCC will hold an inquiry into the matter, and both the accused and the complainant will be questioned. To proceed with the inquiry, notice is issued to both the parties keeping the safety of the complainant in mind. Specific documents and witnesses may be called upon, and the following points shall be considered while conducting the inquiry:

1. When the complainant wants formal redress, or the complaint is of serious nature.
2. The complaints committee must not have any conflict of interest.
3. The independent external member is required.

4.1.10. Respondent's Response

As mentioned earlier, the following is the procedure for the respondent:

1. A response is sought in accordance with the service rules.
2. The respondent is informed in writing within seven days of receiving a complaint by the complaints committee that a complaint has been received against him.
3. Within 10 days after receiving the information about the complaint against him, the respondent has to reply in writing to the complaints committee.

4.1.11. Relief Measures to Complainant

4.1.11.1. Interim Measures

A written request can be made by the complainant for her own transfer or the transfer of the respondent or leave (up to three months). The complaints committee can also be requested by her to restrain the respondent from reporting on her work performance or writing her confidential report or supervising her academic activities (in case she is in an educational institution). Even if she does not make such a request, the complaints committee is duty bound to take corrective action keeping the complainant's interest in mind. As an interim measure, the complaints committee may recommend the above reliefs summarized as follows:

- The transfer of the aggrieved woman or the respondent to another section or department as deemed fit by the committee.
- Grant a leave to the aggrieved woman up to a period of three months. This leave will be in addition to her usual claim on leave.
- Restrain the respondent from exercising any administrative authority, supervision or academic evaluation of the aggrieved woman.
- Grant such other relief to the aggrieved woman as the case may require.

It is essential to take these actions in order to prevent potential ongoing sexual harassment or any other harm to the complainant.

4.1.11.2. Support

While maintaining clear, timely communication with the parties throughout the process, The complaints committee shall provide the complainant with psychological or health-related needs if she requires.

4.1.12. Record Maintenance

Documentation of the proceedings is the essential feature of the inquiry process. For a sound inquiry, proper recording needs to be done, therefore, a separate file for every case is prepared and maintained by the complaints committee for future reference. The following points should be kept in mind while preparing the case file.

1. **Documentation:** For each complaint, there should be an independent and dedicated confidential file wherein all future developments are lucidly recorded and collected for further reference.
2. **Review law and policy:** The committee is required to have a clear knowledge and understanding of the Sexual Harassment of Women at Workplace (Prevention, Prohibition and Redressal) Act, 2013, rules of the Act and the relevant service rules. The workplace policy of the institute or the organization should be there in place to refer to. The committee should be aware of Vishaka Guidelines, existing practices and the related laws. All these documents should be available for ready reference.
3. **Make a list:** All the events and the dates mentioned in the complaint should be listed for further reference in chronological order for understanding the entire episode. A list of witnesses should be prepared if mentioned in the complaint.
4. **Supporting documents:** All the relevant documents related to the complaint should be procured and safely filed for review. The documents provided by the complainant and the respondent should also be carefully reviewed and examined.
5. **Timely action:** A plan should be chalked to ensure all critical elements are covered. No relevant point should be left out. It may include:
   a. Names of the parties and witnesses
   b. Documentary support that needs to be examined
   c. Timeline

4.1.13. Inquiry Process

The inquiry should be conducted in reference to the following facts:

4.1.13.1. Interview Plan for the Hearing

The presiding officer or chairperson shall convene the first hearing. The respondent, the aggrieved woman (complainant) and the witnesses are intimated at least seven working days in advance in writing, of the date, time and venue of the inquiry proceedings. The subsequent proceedings may be held on a day-to-day basis to be decided by the committee in consultation with both the parties:

- The complaints committee should decide the issues to pursue questioning, based on the results of the previous steps and before conducting interviews.
- Interviews may be conducted to secure relevant information related to the complaint.
- There should be separate and confidential interviews for all without bringing the complainant and the respondent face to face.

4.1.13.2. Responsibilities of Complaints Committee

For effectively addressing the workplace sexual harassment complaints, both ICC and LCC should be aware of their responsibilities while dealing with a complaint. Important responsibilities of the complaints committees are as follows:

- The committee should have a fair understanding of the Sexual Harassment Act, 2013, policy and the relevant service rules.
- The committee should collect all the relevant information and document it.
- The committee needs to identify the main issues in the complaint.
- The committee needs to prepare relevant questions rather than having an unstructured interview. The questions should be framed in accordance with the nature of the complaint.
- It should conduct necessary interviews providing a reasonable opportunity to the aggrieved woman and the respondent for presenting and defending their case without any kind of pressure.

- The committee should ensure parties are made aware of the process and their rights and responsibilities within its domain. The information should be conveyed lucidly in a language understood by the party.
- The committee should analyse information gathered in an unbiased manner.
- On the basis of evidence and findings, the committee should prepare the report and give its recommendations.

4.1.13.2. Duties of Complaints Committee

The following are the duties of the complaints committee:

- Every complaint should be treated in a dignified manner giving it full respect. It should not be treated as a 'troublemaking move' by the complainant.
- The committee should create a conducive environment to conduct the inquiry. No hostility should be expressed against either party.
- The committee members should not carry any preconceived biases against either the complainant or the respondent. Biases and prejudices have no place in a fair and just inquiry.
- The committee should be in a position to determine the extent of harm that has occurred due to sexual harassment.
- At no stage, the committee member(s) should get aggressive or hostile either with the complainant, the respondent or the witnesses during the inquiry process.
- The committee shouldn't insist on an illustrative or vivid description of an episode which may create an embarrassing situation for the aggrieved woman.
- When complainant, respondent or the witness is making a statement, he/she should be allowed to speak without interruption or suggestion. No leading questions should be asked.
- The committee should discuss the complaint without hiding anything from either party.
- During a redress process, the complaints committee should assure confidentiality, non-retaliation and recommend interim measures as needed to conduct a fair inquiry.

4.1.13.3. Rights of Complaints Committee

The following are the rights of the complaints committee:

- During the inquiry, the committee may do away with the face-to-face examination of the respondent, the aggrieved woman (complainant) and/or their witnesses, keeping in view the need to protect the aggrieved woman (complainant) or the witnesses from facing any serious health or safety problems.
- In the interest of justice, the committee may call any person to appear as a witness.
- The committee has the right to summon, as many times as required, the respondent, the aggrieved woman and any of the witnesses for the purpose of supplementary testimony and/or clarification.
- The committee has the power to summon any official papers or documents pertaining to the aggrieved woman as well as the respondent.
- The committee has the right to terminate the inquiry proceedings and to give an ex-parte decision on the complaint, should the respondent or complainant fail, without valid ground, to be present for three consecutive hearings convened by the presiding officer.

For such a termination or ex-parte order, the complaints committee should give a notice in writing, 15 days in advance, to the party concerned.

4.1.13.4. Competence of Complaints Committee

The committee making an inquiry against sexual harassment deals with a sensitive issue involving a woman's dignity and reputation and violation of her human rights. To deal with such complaints, the committee members have to be skilled, highly experienced and knowledgeable who could understand the complaint in a right perspective and deal effectively to resolve the problem in an unbiased manner. Complaints committees must effectively carry out their role in order to deliver justice to all concerned. Its members should have a sound knowledge of the Act, Vishaka Guidelines, applicable service rules, relevant laws and an understanding of workplace sexual harassment, policy and related issues. The committee must be able to synthesize information, that is, relevant documents, the law and interviews. Committees should be able to communicate effectively, write clearly, listen actively and conduct interviews in a calm and unbiased environment. They should be competent at showing empathy, being impartial and being thorough in their approach. They should be able to identify sexual harassment and its impact on the victim.

The committee needs to be trained in terms of skill and capacity to conduct a fair, informed inquiry into a sexual harassment complaint. If such training is absent, there will be inconsistent and unfair results, which can prove costly for all concerned.

4.1.14. Assessment of Collected Information

The information gathered by the complaints committee is reviewed in the light of its factual relevance to each aspect of the complaint. This will help determine whether there is enough information to make a finding on the complaint.

4.1.15. Reasoning

After receiving complete information and reviewing it satisfactorily, the committee will make its reasoned finding(s), which involves the following:

1. Identification of the substance of each aspect of the complaint
2. Determination, whether the unwelcome sexual harassment took place
3. Ensuring that the behaviour comes within the ambit of the definition of sexual harassment as per the Act or rules, policy, service rules or law
4. Comment on any underlying factor(s) that may have contributed to the incident such as minority status of the aggrieved woman,

hailing from the Dalit community, single woman employee in the establishment

5. Creation of a timeline to help establish the sequence of events related to the complaint
6. Comparison of similarities and differences within each of the statements made by the interviewees during the process of inquiry

4.1.16. Final Recommendation

4.1.16.1. Finding

The committee must arrive at a finding of whether the complaint is upheld, not upheld or inconclusive.

The committee shall share its finding with both the parties before finalizing the report and provide them with an opportunity to make representation against the findings if not satisfied. No party is allowed to bring in any legal practitioner to represent them in their case at any stage of the proceedings before the complaints committee.

4.1.16.2. Recommendations

Appropriate recommendations are made on the basis of the findings, which are as follows:

- When the complaints committee is unable to uphold the complaint, it shall recommend no action.
- When the complaints committee upholds the complaint, it may recommend such action as stated within the relevant policy or service rules, which may be from a warning to termination from the job. When there are no service rules, the recommended action may include:
  - Disciplinary action, including a written apology, reprimand, warning and censure
  - Withholding promotion/pay raise/increment
  - Termination
  - Counselling
  - Community service

- The complaints committee may also recommend financial compensation to the complainant while deciding the amount they shall take the following points into consideration:
    ○ Mental trauma, pain, suffering and emotional distress caused to the complainant by the incident of sexual harassment.
    ○ Medical expenses incurred on treatment of physical or mental illness due to sexual harassment, including medication, investigative procedures and psychotherapeutic interventions.
    ○ Loss of career opportunity resulted due to the incident.
    ○ Income and financial status of the respondent is also taken into consideration in view of his pay ability in a lump sum or instalments. If the amount is not paid it can be recovered as an arrear of land revenue.
- The complaints committee can also give additional recommendations to address the underlying factors contributing to sexual harassment at the workplace.
- If prima facie case exists, the complaint is forwarded to the police, within a period of seven days for registering the case under Section 509 of IPC and any other relevant provisions of the said code where applicable (Section 11).
- The inquiry by the complaints committee must be completed within a period of 90 days and a final report submitted to the employer or DO within 10 days thereafter. The report is also made available to the concerned parties—the complainant (aggrieved woman) and the accused will be provided with the report of investigation within 10 days of the completion of the investigation.
- The employer or DO is obliged to act on the recommendations within 60 days after receiving the report.

4.2. Action against Sexual Harasser

If the committee finally concludes that the accused had sexually harassed, as claimed by the complainant, the accused may be subject to the penal provisions already described. Except in cases where service rules exist, the complaints committee shall recommend to the employer or DO to take any action, including a written apology, warning, reprimand or censure, withholding of promotion, withholding of pay rise or increments, terminating the respondent from service or provide help

Table 4.1. Timelines Action

Lodging a complaint	Within three months of the last incident
Notice to the alleged harasser	Within seven days of receiving the complaint
Completion of the inquiry	Within a period of 90 days, the committee has to complete the inquiry and submit the report
Submission of the report by ICC/LCC	Within 10 days of completion of inquiry
Implementation of the recommendations of the committee by the employer or DO	Within 60 days of submission of the report
Appeal	Within 90 days of recommendation

in the form of counselling session or treatment, if needed, or order to carrying out community service. Any further legal recourse could be sought by the complainant.[6]

The complaint that one files with the committees is also monitored by the National Commission for Women to ensure proper redressal.

4.3. False Complaint or False Evidence

Except where service rules exist, in cases where the complaints committee concludes that the allegation levelled against the respondent is false, or the complainant has knowingly made a false complaint or produced any forged or misleading document, it may recommend action against the complainant, in accordance with the provisions of the Act or the service rules to the employer or DO. This action could amount to the same punishment that would have been levied on the accused had he been found guilty.[7]

However, the preconceived notions about the complaining woman should not be made the basis for dismissal of her complaint, it should be treated fairly. Because of the lesser numerical strength of women at most of the workplaces, the lack of evidence is understandable. The lack of evidence in favour of aggrieved woman (complainant) should not make the committee reject the case outrightly. Mere inability to substantiate a complaint or provide adequate proof will not attract legal action against the complainant. However, it is certainly an offence on the part of the complainant if she makes a false or malicious complaint or produces a forged or misleading document.

A recent case of a PhD scholar from Jawaharlal Nehru University in Delhi[8] who sought respite from Delhi High Court demonstrates the working of ICC of the University. The court asked the university authorities to immediately release the degree of the student and also place before the court the full report of the ICC that found the student's charges to be 'false and frivolous' and recommended her expulsion from the university.

The PhD scholar had challenged in the court the clean chit given by the ICC to the harasser, her professor and the guide, accused of sexually harassing and molesting her. The ICC found no substance in the student's complaint and debarred her entry into the university campus. Her PhD degree was also withheld for making a false complaint. The ICC also recommended that the complainant be given no job at the university. A copy of the committee's recommendations was not provided to the aggrieved woman. The ICC's action is against the spirit of the Act and defeats its very objective. The students' body of the university also criticized the inquiry committee, 'ICC has till date not done anything other than intimidation of the complainants, which was blatantly exposed when the current case came into light.' ICC, which is expected to deliver justice and restore harmony at the workplace, at times, works otherwise.

4.4. Annual Report

The complaints committee prepares its annual report containing the following details[9]:

1. Number of complaints received during the year and a description of the different aspects of the sexual harassment complaint
2. Number of complaints disposed of during the year, and the process followed should be mentioned in the report.

3. Number of cases pending for more than 90 days
4. Number of workshops or awareness programme against sexual harassment carried out during the year for the employees and the members of ICC
5. Nature of action taken by the employer or DO on the recommendation of the complaints committees
6. A description of the background information and documents that support or refute each aspect of the complaint
7. An analysis of the information obtained
8. Findings as stated above
9. Recommendations

4.5. Appeal

If the decision is not satisfactory or the findings or recommendations made by the complaints committee are not acceptable to the complainant or the respondent or the recommendations have not been implemented, the concerned party is free to approach an appropriate court or tribunal. Such action is taken under the service rules, and where no such service rules exist, the action is in such a manner as may be prescribed. Under Section 18, any person aggrieved from the recommendations made under various provisions of the Act may appeal to the appellate authority notified under clause (a) of Section 2 of the Industrial Employment (Standing Orders) Act, 1946.[10]

One can also post a complaint on the online portal created by the Ministry of Women and Child Development in 2013 via SHe-Box directly to the ministry. The complaint can be made at http://www.shebox.nic.in/, and the update on the complaint status can be checked.

4.6. SHe-Box (Sexual Harassment Electronic Box)

It is an online complaint platform launched by the Ministry of Women and Child Development. The subjects of sexual harassment at a workplace can reach this box to register their complaint. Employees of both private and public sector can avail this facility.

It is accessible at www.shebox.nic.in. Through this portal, there is an effective implementation of the Act, and speedy redressal of the grievances of the victim is possible. Once a complaint is received, it is immediately forwarded to the concerned ICC of the complainant's workplace or the concerned LCC. The Ministry of Women and Child Development closely monitors such complaints and ensures timely progress of inquiry conducted by the ICC or LCC and keep the complainant updated about the progress made. This facility also provides information related to dealing with workplace sexual harassment complaints.[2]

4.7. Complaint to National Commission for Women

A complaint can be filed online with the commission which provides a broad platform for filing a complaint as an alternative to other recourses. One can log on to the commission's website (http://ncw. nic.in/) and click on 'Register Online Complaint' or can directly go to their complaint page at http://ncw.nic.in/onlinecomplaintsv2/frmPubRegistration.aspx.

4.8. Complaint with Police

FIR can be filed to a police officer at the nearest police station under Section 154 of the Code of Criminal Procedure. FIR will be registered as a 'zero FIR', in case the police station is not the appropriate jurisdiction, and it would be transferred to the appropriate jurisdiction. No complaint can go unaddressed. FIR cannot be refused if the complaint does not relate to the area of the police station where the complainant has approached.

At the police stations, there is a separate 'Rapid Response Desk for Women', having a lady police officer. One can also directly approach a female police officer. If the lady police officer is not available, a lady constable can be approached. One can be accompanied by a family member or a friend or a lawyer for lodging the police complaint. The complaint can be lodged with a telephonic call or by email as well. One should always check the content of the complaint as noted by the police to make sure that there are no discrepancies.

No sexual harassment[1] complaint can be refused to be lodged by the police officer since it is a cognizable offence. However, in case if the police officer still refuses to do so, one can complain to an officer of a higher rank or the district judicial magistrate under Section 156(3) and Section-190 of the Code of Criminal Procedure with the help of a lawyer.

4.9. Confidentiality

Confidentiality of the entire inquiry process is essential according to the Act.[3] It prohibits the publication or divulging the contents of a complaint and the inquiry proceedings. Any breach of confidentiality will result in specific consequences. The Act prohibits the disclosure of[11]:

- Contents of the complaint
- Identity and address of complainant, respondent and witnesses
- Information related to conciliatory or inquiry proceedings or recommendations of the ICC/LCC
- Action taken by the employer or DO

Any person entrusted with the duty to handle or deal with the complaint, inquiry or any recommendations or action taken under the provisions of this Act shall be accountable.

The inquiry process under the Act should be confidential, and the breach of confidentiality invites a penalty of ₹5,000, except in the cases where dissemination of information regarding the justice secured without disclosure of name, address, identity and particulars of complainant or witnesses is reported. The manner in which a complaint is addressed will make all the difference to the equal rights of working women as well as the kind of workplace culture being promoted.

---

[1] https://lawrato.com/criminal-lawyers

4.10. Post-complaint Retaliation and Backlash

Retaliation and backlash are very common and the victim is often labelled as a troublemaker, on her own 'power trip' or the one looking for attention. Similar to rape[2] cases, she is blamed for her provocative appearance and dress. Her private life and her character come under intrusive scrutiny and attack.[3][4]

Ostracism from others, including her colleagues and friends, is generally observed after the complaint is made an aggrieved woman.

It is commonly observed that the women colleagues, at times, are not sympathetic to complainants. Their 'internalized sexism' (or jealousy over the apparent sexual attention towards the victim) may make them react towards the complainant in as much hostile manner as her male colleagues might. Also, their fear of themselves becoming harassment targets may motivate these women to respond with hostility. Women may also project hostility onto the victim to bond with male colleagues and build rapport with them.[5], [6]

Retaliatory negative action in response to the harassment complaint, by which the victim's career or educational advancement suffers significantly, is very common. When a complainant is given poor evaluations or her projects is not approved without a valid reason or she is denied a work opportunity she actually deserved or an academic advancement she was a right person for, her productivity at workplace is adversely affected. At some places, the complainant is fired from the job for creating trouble at the workplace ignoring her genuine distress. This may lead to unemployment if terminated from service, suspended or forced to resign and leaving the perpetrator to continue his criminal conduct for further addition to unemployment. Retaliation can result in further sexual harassment in various other forms is possible resulting from the act of retaliation.[7], [9]

When the victim is forced to leave the jot and search alternate workplaces to find a job, it is likely that the perpetrator or his friend

---

[2] https://en.wikipedia.org/wiki/Rape

[3] https://web.archive.org/web/20080516085341/http://www.uoregon.edu/~counsel/harass.htm

make it difficult for her to get one. They ensure that the victim is never hired again in the same office or never accepted in any other workplace. Retaliation can possibly result in:

4.10.1. Backlash Stress

At times, it is merely annoying, but it can a major impact on life, especially when it is prolonged and chronic or when there is retaliation against the victim who does not submit to the harassment or who complains about it openly. Even when the victim is able to maintain a healthy sense of anger, harassment can lead to self-stigmatization, isolation and a sense of being defective or a loser. Damage to her self-identity can occur around attempts at resolution of the situation when others blamer her. Backlash stress occurs when there is confusion about the changing norms while dealing with women in the workplace.[12]

Institutions are more concerned about their reputation, and the complaint channels are often constituted for their legal protection rather than actually helping the victims. Complaint procedures focus on the objective assessment of guilt and appropriate punishment, rather than focus on negotiating for the cessation of the behaviour and continuation of the work or academic relationship in an improved form. This mediation-driven outcome could, no doubt, enhance a women's self-esteem, but it is seldom possible to achieve in the current environment. Even when a woman receives a positive outcome to a formal complaint, she may encounter difficulties; many male workers will avoid befriending the victim or avoid providing any assistance, such as holding doors open or even wishing a 'good morning'. As a result, women are being handicapped by a lack of the necessary networking and mentorship at the place of their work.

The victim wants justice that can restore normalcy in her life and heal wounds to enable true rehabilitation back in her official work. Even after the conviction of the perpetrator, many victims of sexual harassment fail to find closure of the matter and face serious acceptance issues with the friends, colleagues and supervisors at the workplace.[13]

4.10.2. Restorative Justice

Currently, there is a growing demand for restorative justice. The process involves a conference where all the stakeholders—the victim, perpetrator, the families and if required representatives of the community—take part.

Counselling, which may not always be equipped to deliver justice as it appears in the mind of the victim, may be of great help beyond the legal framework as parallel support.

Restorative justice is based on the acknowledgement of harm and its impact as perceived by the victim. Next stage is to establish what she wants so that the impact of the harm can be mitigated. Then, the perpetrator is brought into the picture and encouraged to take responsibility to make him admit what he had done. In all such cases, psychological and legal counselling must be done.

Victims adopt several strategies to overcome the resultant psychological effects, including stress management[4] and therapy, cognitive behavioural therapy,[5][9] friends and family support and advocacy.[13] 'Some of them might require treatment in the form of pharmaco-therapy if they suffer from clinical depression or anxiety disorder.'

For various reasons, several women remain silent over the bitter experience of sexual harassment or retaliation and keep brooding within to suffer emotional distress. Lack of understanding or the fear drives them to accept the treatment meted out to them by the harasser and submit themselves passively to psychological trauma. The employers should come forward to help such aggrieved women instead of hushing these cases up, with the hope that they would get sorted out on their own.

References

[1] Ministry of Women and Child Development. Working Rules for Internal Complaints Committee. Government of India, 2013.

[2] Ministry of Women and Child Welfare. Handbook on Sexual Harassment of Women at Workplace (Prevention, Prohibition and Redressal) Act 2013.

---

[4] https://en.wikipedia.org/wiki/Stress_management
[5] https://en.wikipedia.org/wiki/Cognitive_behavioral_therapy

Government of India, 2015. Available at: https://www.iitk.ac.in/wc/data/Handbook%20on%20Sexual%20Harassment%20of%20Women%20at%20Workplace.pdf (accessed on 18 December 2020).

[3] Ministry of Women and Child Welfare. Sexual Harassment of Women at Workplace (Prevention, Prohibition and Redressal) Act 2013. Government of India. Available at: http://legislative.gov.in/sites/default/files/A2013-14.pdf (accessed on 18 December 2020).

[4] Dittman M. Sexual harassment too often leads to humiliation for victims. *American Psychological Association*. 2003 Oct;34(9):24. Available at: https://www.apa.org/monitor/oct03/harass (accessed on 18 December 2020).

[5] Schlesinger Library. Archieve-It partner colleges and universities. Available at: http://www.radcliffe.harvard.edu/schlesinger-library (accessed on 18 December 2020).

[6] Schneider KT. *Bystander Stress: The Effect of Organizational Tolerance of Sexual Harassment on Victim's Co-workers*. Champaign, IL: University of Illinois at Urbana-Champaign; 1996.

[7] Daubney M. Well Done, Feminism. Now Men Are Afraid to Help Women at Work. *The Telegraph*, 2015. Available at: https://www.telegraph.co.uk/men/relationships/11904203/Well-done-feminism.-Now-man-are-afraid-to-help-women-at-work.html (accessed on 18 December 2020).

[8] TNN. Delhi HC Breather for Jawaharlal Nehru University PhD Scholar. *The Times of India*, 2019. Available at: https://timesofindia.indiatimes.com/city/delhi/hc-breather-for-jnu-phd-scholar/articleshow/69364755.cms (accessed on 18 December 2020).

[9] Elsesser K. *Sex and the Office: Women, Men, and the Sex Partition That's Dividing the Workplace*. Lanham, MD: Rowman & Littlefield; 2015.

[10] Chief Labour Commissioner. Industrial Employment (Standing Orders) Act, 1946. Available at: https://clc.gov.in/clc/acts-rules/industrial-employ-ment-standing-orders-act-1946 (accessed on 18 December 2020).

[11] Foa EB, Street GP. Women and traumatic events. *The Journal of Clinical Psychiatry*. 2001;62(17):29–34.

[12] Schwartz D. How to Cope with the Current News Cycle as a Sexual Abuse Survivor. Lifehack. Available at: https://lifehacker.com/how-to-cope-with-the-current-news-cycle-as-a-sexual-abu-1820823444 (accessed on 18 December 2020).

[13] Olsen HB. How #MeToo Affects Sexual Assault Advocates. PacificStandard, 2017. Available at: https://psmag.com/social-justice/how-metoo-affects-sexual-assault-advocates (accessed on 18 December 2020).

CHAPTER 5

The Interpersonal Dynamics of Sexual Harassment

In recent years, academicians and researchers have identified an association between workplace sexual harassment and other serious sexual crimes like rape.[1]-[4] Some researchers point out a direct continuum and a significant overlap between the two.[4], [5] Types of violence and its impact on women have been amply studied in comparison to the study of the characteristics of the perpetrators who indulge in such type of violence.[6], [7] Moreover, there have been very few studies to compare the characteristics of sexual harassers with those of serious sexual offenders like rapists. In view of the fact that a continuum exists between sexual harassment and serious sexual crimes, if the characteristics of male sexual harassers are identified and properly understood, treatment for sexual offenders can be formulated and preventive strategies developed by the use of behaviour modification techniques.

Impact on the victim is the result of a complex series of interactions between the victim, the perpetrator, the victim's associates and the significant people in her personal life. If she happens to be a member of a socially marginalized group, such as the Dalit community of traditional

Indian society, the dynamics may take on special characteristics unique to Indian culture.[8], [9]

To understand dynamics and evolving treatment strategies, the study of perpetrator–victim interaction is of crucial importance. It is relatively a new area of research and clinicians have to identify a broader theoretical link between the dynamics of workplace sexual harassment and sexual harassment in the society in general.[10]

Social responses to childhood sexual abuse, domestic violence, sexual exploitation in a professional relationship, rape and sexual harassment are deeply rooted in the cultural fabric of gender discrimination.[11]-[13] All these sexual crimes reinforce the behaviour of:

- Traditional gender role socialization
- Female subordinate status
- Sexual objectification and devaluation of women
- Social complicity for exploitation for abuse of women

The ongoing research has culminated into focus on exploring the clinical and treatment implications of these similarities. Women subjected to rape, sexual assault and other forms of sexual crime share many clinical issues with the victims of sexual harassment, some of which are as follows:

- The victims in both situations have difficulty in extracting themselves from the abusive situations exacerbated by some form of physical, economic, emotional or social pressure.
- In both the situations, there is difficulty with sociocultural invalidation and non-supportive people around who are in hand in glove with the harasser.
- Both types of victims have similarities in psychological after-effects. They share specific similarities in resulting psychiatric illness like depression or post-traumatic stress disorder (PTSD).

The dynamic model of domestic violence also helps in understanding:

- The victim–perpetrator characteristics and interactions
- The impact of the external social environment on the interaction

Like battered women, the victims of sexual harassment often vary in terms of their:

- Individual histories
- Pre-abuse status
- The status of their relationship with the harasser
- Status within the work hierarchy or household
- Type and severity of discriminatory treatment
- Response to their situation
- Resources and the support available to them

5.1. Why Sexual Harassment at the Workplace?

Sexual harassment is a common occurrence all over the world, in almost all cultural settings and manifests in power relations. Victims are often dependent on men not only for financial reasons, but they also need men around for their social well-being and security—an unmarried girl needs her father and a married woman her husband. In male-dominated societies, women are generally less powerful, often lack the confidence to take the initiative independently and are socialized to suffer in silence. They are generally not encouraged to protest. With such a mindset, women enter the workforce where they meet the men with patriarchal orientation and continue with the same attitude of male dominance.

Why women endure sexual intimidation silently is due to a complex dynamic interaction of various factors, some of which are described as follows:

5.1.1. Violence and Male Self-perception

In most societies across the globe, the relationship between men and women includes a considerable amount of violence against women. Studies show that in the USA, violence against women is very common; 1 out of every 10 women suffers sexual violence during her lifetime, while more than 50 per cent of all women living with men have experienced a battering or similar incident of domestic violence.

In certain communities of traditional Indian society, wife beating has been accepted as a norm to control the behaviour and sexuality of women which they tolerated and accepted as their gender role and suffered silently without protest.[12]

Violence exists in the workplace as it does in society in general. Some scholars are of the opinion that the dominant role of men in society is very closely connected to male hostility towards women at the workplace.[13] Surveys indicate that the leading definition of masculinity in men's perception is 'being a breadwinner for his family', thus making women dependent on men for their survival and other needs. In traditional Indian society, particularly in the rural areas, the dependence of women on men goes to the extent that men are equated to God; they are considered the incarnation of Almighty (pati parmeshwar), and any sort of intimidation by them is acceptable without resentment.[14] Women, entering the workforce outside the confines of the household, makes many men perceive the feminist drive for economic equality as a threat to their traditional role and an attempt to disorganize the social order and challenge their unquestioned superior position.[12]

5.1.2. Economics of Women's Work

The 1995 World Conference on Women by United Nations to develop a plan to ensure a more equitable future for women remains elusive as two-thirds of the world's work is performed by women, especially in the unorganized sectors.

Women earn significantly less than men worldwide. Middle East countries have the widest gender gap in economic opportunities. Women in India earn 65 per cent of their male colleagues' earnings for performing the same amount of work.

Women make 80 per cent of consumer goods in the USA and 70 per cent in Canada, but this does not change the ground reality of economic disparity they suffer.

Till recently, it was not easy for a woman to get a job in male-dominated workplaces. However, with the changing socio-economic scenario, in recent times, women have made their presence felt everywhere, in every sphere of the workplace. This massive global influx of women into the labour market during the last 50 years has been prompted by necessity, women's movement for equality, access to educational facilities at par with men, as some of the many reasons. To avoid financial discomfort and to make their both ends meet, both the partners work to earn money and get the household going.

The changing trend in the workforce has a far-reaching impact on global demography. Surveys carried out between 1980 and 1990 reveal that two out of every five working women were the sole bread earners for their families, and within that group, more than 25 per cent had dependent children to look after.[15] Female-headed households are quite common in many Asian societies showing the need for women to work to run their household.

In India, according to the National Sample Survey Office, the worker population ratio for females[1] aged 15 years and above was 25.8 per cent in 2015–2016. Despite rapid economic growth, just a quarter of women aged 15 and above participated in the labour force.

Despite their scanty representation in the workforce, working women are perceived by men as competitors when they start earning and contribute to running the household. In the initial years, they were discouraged to join the labour force, reminding them of their primary role to bring up children and look after the household. Discrimination is limited not only when they join the labour market, but they also have a tough competition in the workplace after they join the job.

'Women earn lesser (65% of what men earn) than their male colleagues' for performing the same work,[2][16] and for that too, some of them are exploited sexually to continue in the work. They are subjected to demand for sexual favours in exchange for employment, to keep from being fired, demoted or otherwise adversely affected at work.

---

[1] https://www.livemint.com/Companies/Jf6nR0giRAWIeO94zexvdM/Why-so-few-women-work-in-India.html

[2] https://www.catalyst.org/research/women-in-the-workforce-india/#footnote26_098zxy5

Creation of a hostile environment at the workplace, in the first place, and better service conditions for sexual favours, in the second, make sexual harassment rampant at most of the establishments, whether educational institutions or offices, for the women.

Low labour force participation rate for women in India is also due to an increase in women continuing their education and then getting married and looking after domestic chores or joining white-collar jobs, the availability of flexible scheduling and the proximity of work locations. Another noticeable change is that the rural women who were traditionally engaged in the unorganized sector are leaving India's labour workforce at a faster rate than urban women. Young women are moving into non-traditional professional jobs.

5.1.3. Discrimination as a Form of Workplace Control

Catherine MacKinnon[17] studied the connection between sex discrimination and sexual harassment. According to her, when women began to enter the workforce, they were employed in low-ranking positions. They had to be dependent upon the approval and goodwill of male superiors for getting into the job, retention of the job and advancement in the career. Their being at the mercy of male superiors adds direct economic clout to male sexual demands.

This has remained an important reason for women to be sexually harassed, and most of them occupied junior job positions and depended heavily on their male seniors to carry out their routine office work. Sexual favours helped them stay in the work and continue there, particularly in those places where the work culture was lax and unprofessional. Women in such places continued to stay in the work to meet their daily life needs accepting sexual harassment as an integral component of their job requirement.

There are certain jobs traditionally performed by women only. Jobs of receptionists, secretaries, nurses and maids in the households, often performed by women, have vulnerability for exploitation. They are, generally, given menial, degrading tasks which their male counterparts would never like to perform. They are often called demeaning names, and they are led to believe that a certain amount of male domination and sexism is normal for the positions they are holding. If the woman worker hailed from a minority social background particularly from a Dalit community, she is addressed with vulgar casteist and sexist remarks and profane names. Such behaviour of male colleagues undermines women's position and reinforces the idea that women workers are of little value in the workplace. Women who try to break into traditionally all-male work, such as construction jobs, medicine, investment banking, police and armed forces, often suffer even more intense harassment clearly aimed at forcing them to leave or submit to the sexual advances of their male counterparts.[18]

5.2. Forms of Sexual Harassment

Depending on how the victim suffers sexual harassment, it has been described in two forms by the US courts.

5.2.1. Quid Pro Quo

Quid pro quo refers to promise of preferential or detrimental treatment by the employer or others in power in employment depending upon acceptance of or refusal of sexual advances. It is a subtle or express threat to a woman's present or future employment status. In return for sexual favours, the woman gets benefits in the job or advancement in academic pursuits and blockage of these benefits for refusing to sexually submit. Submission to or rejection of the demand for sexual favours determine the job stability, promotions and other job or academic benefits for a working woman or a student.

5.2.3. Hostile Work Environment

Hostile work environment created by perpetrators for women workers is another form of sexual harassment. It leads to humiliating treatment for a woman which affects not only her dignity, but her health and safety is also adversely affected. It is more common at the workplace where a woman is unable to enjoy equal status in terms of various job-related benefits.

5.3. Types of Sexual Harassment

Depending on the type of 'perpetrator's mode of action' or motivational actions, sexual harassment can be categorized into various perpetrator-harassment types. These categories, as described below, often overlap with each other.

5.3.1. In Academic Institutions

Dziech and Weiner[19] describe two types of harassment perpetrated by the harassers in educational institutions. These types are as follows.

1. **Public harasser:** One who is a casual, sociable and apparently a friendly person engaged in public relationships with his students in which he frequently tells sexual jokes. It is a less severe form of sexual harassment which the students take casually and often ignore.
2. **Private harasser:** One who appears to be professional and conservative in public and maintains a serious public profile, but privately he is involved in a severe form of 'quid pro quo' sexual harassment—making sexual advances for academic favours.

These two types are in a continuum, and within these two types, a teacher or academician may adopt five different roles to initiate sexual intimacy:

a. 'Counsellor–helper type' is one who takes undue personal interest in the student, and the information, thus, obtained from the student is used in initiating unwelcome sexual advances.
b. 'Confident type' of the harasser is a teacher who treats all the students equally, helps them with personal favours and encourages intimate personal meetings by inviting them at home or other places to talk freely. During these meetings, he shares his personal information, such as difficulties in his marital life. In the process, he either traps the student or leaves her feeling obliged to concede to his wishes.
c. 'Intellectual seducer' is a teacher who first impresses the student with his academic prowess and then uses academic pretence to obtain personal information of the student and her vulnerability which he subsequently exploits for sexual favours.

d. 'Opportunist harasser' uses opportunities such as field trips, laboratory work or meeting at his home as excuses to minimize inhibitions towards touching her, sitting closer to her to pursue further or making sexual jokes under the cover of frankness.

e. 'Power broker type of harasser' is a teacher who uses his authority directly over the grades, assessment, evaluation of answer-books, publications, recommendations, etc., to bargain for sexual favours.

Zalk[20] re-affirms public–private types as two extremes of a continuum; there are many who fall in between and have mixed characteristics. He suggests following three types of such perpetrators:

1. 'The untouchable' who feels superior and entitled to sexual activity with his students versus the 'risk taker' who knows his behaviour is wrong.
2. 'The secure-demander' who actively solicits sexual favours versus 'receptive non-initiator'.
3. 'The infatuator' who believes he is in love with his student versus one who has no personal interest in the student but 'takes pleasure in sexual encounter'.

Most professors or teachers who sexually harass their students interact along the continuum of each of these three types. These types emphasize problematic behaviours in a superior–subordinate relationship of a fiduciary nature and are not readily applicable to co-worker hostile environment harassment that occurs in the workplace.

5.3.2. On the Basis of the Victim's Perspective

Women often do not share their experiences of sexual harassment and open up only with an assurance of confidentiality. They choose to remain silent despite the fact that the law is in their favour.[21] Dilemmas and internal struggles often dominate many victims' mind before deciding to lodge a complaint or open up before someone.[22] Some victims tend to minimize their painful experience by ignoring the harasser for violating their dignity and rights; they ignore them either because of the hierarchical status of the harassers who are in a position of power or discount them otherwise. They trivialize the incident by saying, 'the person is well behaved and gentle and respects women in general. It could be just a stand-alone case; the person is otherwise known for his impeccable image.' Victims tend to safeguard themselves by denying or discounting the importance of such experiences, which may send signals that they do not have misgivings about being treated disrespectfully. Sexual harassment is compared with a slow poisoning process, which starts slowly with indecent body language and if not resisted, culminates into demand for sexual favours and physical contact. It continues because many women find it difficult to take action due to job insecurity and for fear of their own reputation.[23] Some women remain silent and refuse to report due to the stigma attached to it.[24]

Harassment can also be classified on the basis of harasser's behaviour towards the victim. Depending upon the victims reporting on their harassers' behaviour and on the basis of their perceptions of the motivation of the perpetrator, sexual harassment is classified into three types. These are as follows.

1. **Male gender role:** In this, a male harasser objectifies women as a sex object.
2. **Power-dominant harasser:** This type of harasser is hostile and sexually aggressive towards women.
3. **Psychological characteristics of the harasser:** The harasser enjoys power over the victim, exploits emotional weakness, immaturity and personal problems of the victim.

The most common motivation is power over the victimized individual or of a related fear that the harasser might be losing power at work if he is not assertive. Aspects of the male gender role include objectification of women into sexual objects, hostility toward women and seeing men as the dominant sexual aggressors. Psychological characteristics reported in the victims are emotional weakness, feeling of insecurity, behavioural immaturity and personal problems in abundance.

5.3.3. On the Basis of Psychological Functions

Pryor et al.[25] have described four types of perpetrators on the basis of their psychological profile, which are as follows.

1. **Sexual exploitation:** This type of sexual harassment is based either on sexual or hostile intent, and within each of these, there is sexual exploitation, which describes a situation in which perpetrator imposes sexual intimacy due to power differential which makes the victim vulnerable. This is a professor–student form of exploitation.

2. **Sexual miscommunication:** This is the type where the perpetrator is interested in establishing a non-exploitative sexual relationship at work and misperceives victim's friendliness as sexual interest and insensitive to lack of her interest in him. Such a misperception can contribute to courtship rape.

3. **Misogyny:** This type is based on hostile motivation. The perpetrator carries a hostile and degrading attitude towards women at the workplace. He may use this attitude to exclude women from the workgroup and impede their advancement in the organization. This is quite common in male-dominated places where women are perceived as growing threatening minority. A non-sexual hostile environment may become contributory in gender discrimination.

4. **Homo-anathema:** This is based on the hostile motivation of the perpetrator who harasses the victims because they are homosexual. Men target women they perceive gay.

5.3.4. When Key Decision-maker Is the Perpetrator

If the key decision-makers in a workplace carry biased opinion against women employees, they often make unwelcome sexual statements which hurt the dignity of women. According to Mary Rowe,[26] the biases against women employees occurring at the level of individuals who are decision-makers are highly significant because of the power invested in the decision-makers in the hierarchy. These decisions may carry a negative impact on self-esteem, working, promotional avenues and scope of new learning for the women. Impact of these decisions is cumulative, like drops of water collecting in a bucket which the author calls 'micro-inequities'. Depending on the motivation of the perpetrator, Rowe divided micro-inequities into four categories, which are as follows.

1. **Unconscious slights and invisibility problems:** The harasser rates the office work of a woman differently from that of a male employee. He may ignore or devalue a female employee or attribute the success of the work to a male colleague. He often leaves women out of both formal and informal work networks, and the victims may not perceive conscious malice of perpetrator, which creates confusion regarding how to respond.

2. **Conscious slights and harassment:** The harasser is overtly hostile towards women, depicting them as incompetent or inappropriate for their work role, or he barrages women with unwanted devaluing attention based on gender by over-scrutinizing their work.

3. **Poor service:** The harasser does not equitably promote women or provide them with training and educational opportunities. The perpetrator overtly discourages them from opportunities because they are women.

4. **Exploitation:** The perpetrator pays women less without giving due credit for work done or places them in positions where they cannot deliver work that would lead to promotion. The harasser utilizes women's training and abilities in the intentional services of promoting male subordinates.

Micro-inequities have an adverse effect on the victims' health and overall well-being. Lenhart[27] describes the negative impact of these micro-inequities as follows:

- The aggrieved woman perceives herself negatively on receiving negative feedback from significant authorities, which is a potent negative reinforcement to her work performance and confidence.
- Even a capable female worker finds it impossible to perform quality work because of micro-inequities or being overloaded with routine or personal work by the perpetrator that stifles creativity and stability of the victim.

- Micro-inequities induce negative reinforcement to create high levels of anxiety and a sense of helplessness in victims which is often highly demoralizing. Continued micro-inequities, which are irrational, intermittent, and do not occur in the context of merit or striving for excellence, may lead to severe depression in the victim.
- If women respond to micro-inequities, they are branded as over-reactive and troublemakers, which may further lead to discrimination. If they ignore, they permit situations to continue that may damage their careers, but micro-inequities take up time and energy and thus reduce efficiency, leading to lesser productivity.
- Micro-inequities exaggerate the polarity between men and women, making it harder for them to work together in a team.
- Women have few role models to help them deal with methods for redress. Women supervisors often react with a sense of denial, helplessness or identification with the aggressor. For their own safety, they often do not support the victim and justify the stand of the perpetrator. This defensive attitude of woman supervisors serves to address their own insecurities.
- Power politics operate in micro-inequities. In this, the perpetrators are often in authoritative positions, and the women are often in subordinate positions.
- Micro-inequities are especially detrimental if they occur at the vulnerable point when a woman is attempting to consolidate her career and her maternal role in her household at the same time. Many women have been socialized to be sensitive to anger and disapproval directed at them, as well as inhibited in asserting their own anger. This makes the impact of micro-inequities especially significant and difficult to address.
- Micro-inequities are extremely difficult to stop in skewed groups (groups where women are in a significant minority) due to the intergroup dynamics already described.

Continued experience of these disturbing situations can lead the victim to unhappy cycles of avoidance behaviour, declining self-esteem, withdrawal, resignation, poor work performance, and fantasies of violence. These difficulties are not easily legislated out of existence and are difficult to address within existing complaint channels.

5.4. Characteristics of Sexual Harassers

Sexual harassers are not a homogenous group of people; they include heterogeneous individuals with no clearly defined clinical psychopathology. Individual traits often seen in these people can be grouped as follows[5]:

- Harassers who exhibit heightened hostility, particularly against women
- Harassers have high anger in conflicting situations
- Harassers have a high need for power and control
- Presence of enabling factors in the environment

An individual's harassing behaviour is embedded in his relationship with the victim, which, in turn, is embedded in the policies and practices of the workplace environment. Victim's work approach, which is embedded in the norms and the values of the larger sociocultural environment, is exploited by the harasser under these circumstances.

It is difficult to clearly delineate the specific characteristics of the harassers as the majority of the cases go unreported, and frequently the harassers deny any culpability.

5.4.1. Socio-demographic Characteristics of Perpetrators

The typical demographic and social characteristics of sexual harassers are that they are often married co-workers or superiors who are older than their victims and generally hail from the same social and ethnic background. The women of lower social strata in traditional Indian society are more vulnerable and very often harassed by men of higher and dominant caste members. Therefore, the harassers in India, in general, are from upper social strata of society particularly in the rural areas of the workplace where they are socially and materially powerful in addition to a superior hierarchical position at work. More serious forms of sexual harassment are committed by supervisors or superiors of the victims; severity of the harassment is directly linked to the harasser's victimization and its effect on other women as well.

People who harass women are mostly males, generally married, better educated and more powerful than their victims.[28] But it is not always necessary that harasser is powerful and hierarchically better placed than the victim. According to some studies, there are instances where subordinates and peers have harassed women more frequent.[29] These studies reveal the victims of similar status (or even superior status) becoming a target. Since people with varying hierarchical statuses work together, covering both white- and blue-collar workers, sexual harassment occurs at all levels, indicating that sexual harassment is all pervasive across all socio-economic strata of the society. However, in rural areas of India, the women from the lower strata of society working in the fields of their landlords, an unorganized sector, are often sexually harassed and assaulted by the kin of the landlords who are superior to the victims both socially and materially.[14] Here, the power dynamics play an important role.

In their study of women managers, Poonam Sahgal and Aastha Dang[22] found that sexual harassers were often married men with a senior position at the workplace and mostly high performers enjoying a good reputation among the employees. In this study, when perpetrators were confronted by the victims, their response was, 'what can you do? Or no one will believe you!' and 'remember I am the one who will be doing your appraisal.' These are the usual explanations harassers give to their victims.

In view of these research findings, it may be misleading to generate a typical profile of the sexual harasser based upon sociodemographic factors. Sexual harassers appear to permeate all social strata, occupational levels and age categories. Typical sexual harassers can be categorized as follows:

1. Married co-workers, older than their victims and often belong to the same racial or ethnic groups.
2. Hostile environment harassers are more common than 'quid pro quo' harassers.
3. A severe form of sexual harassment is committed by supervisors or superiors.

5.5. Character Traits of Sexual Harassers

Several scales are in use to identify the personal characteristics of the men with proclivities towards harassment. Commonly used scales to identify the characteristics of sexual harassers include the Likelihood to Sexually Harass (LSH) and the Modern Sexism Scale. The traits identified by these scales are as follows[30]:

1. A belief in rape myths, such as a woman's underlying desire and wish to be raped.
2. Proclivity for sexual violence.
3. A belief that the relationship between a man and a woman is always antagonistic and adversarial.
4. A belief that men are always powerful, hypermasculine and dominant and women are submissive and compliant.
5. Sexual harassers have diminished capacity for empathy and the ability to appreciate others situation.
6. Low acceptance of feministic beliefs.
7. They have a tendency to connect sexuality to dominance, putting women at an inferior position.
8. Male harassers carry a desire for status.
9. They have a desire for continuing discrimination and antagonism towards women's demands at the workplace.

Many forms of gender discrimination such as job segregation, discrimination in institutional policies, keeping girl students in *purdah* in educational institutions and not allowing them to use mobile phones or wear particular type of dresses do not constitute individual interaction with the specific perpetrators. When the individual interactions do exist:

1. Acceptance of traditional sex role stereotype
2. Lack of capacity to appreciate another person's situation
3. Denial of continuing workplace discrimination

5.6. Personality Profile of Sexual Harassers

Sexual harassment includes a wide range of behaviours from mild but unwelcome sexually coloured remarks and transgressions to sexual abuse or sexual assault.[19], [31] In most societies, sexual harassment is illegal, but simple teasing or minor isolated incidents which do not impose a general civil code are not taken seriously. It is taken seriously only when it is frequent or severe enough to create a hostile and offensive work environment. When committed by an employer, it is illegal employment discrimination. One of the difficulties underlying sexual harassment is the involvement of a wide range of behaviours, and at times, it may not be possible for a victim to describe what she experienced. Moreover, behaviours and motives of the harassers vary from individual to individual.[28] The common features shared by the perpetrators of sexual harassment included lack of social conscience and empathy, social immaturity, irresponsibility, childish outlook, manipulativeness, attention seeking and exploitative behaviours.[31], [32]

In their study, Rapaport and Burkhart[33] also had similar findings in their study that sexual harassers are often irresponsible in their commitment; they lack a social conscience and exaggerated the situation to justify their misdeeds and legitimize their violence, particularly against women when it is related to the endorsement of sexually coercive behaviours. According to a study, there is a close link between LSH and the acceptance of interpersonal violence towards women[34] measured by use of the instruments such as Socialization Scale and Narcissistic Personality Inventory.[35] Results show that the psychopathic traits of exploitation of others and lack of empathy are both commonly associated with rapists and offenders of other serious sexual crimes like abusing children for sex.[36] When sexual harassment escalates, it poses a potential risk for more serious sexual crimes like rape. This link highlights the importance of future research to explore the psychopathology of sexual harassers in more details to fully understand the gap between sexual harassment and rape. At present, this area of research is largely neglected.

5.7. Sexual Harassment Proclivity

The most commonly used instrument to measure men's inclination to sexually harass a woman is the LHS Scale[5] developed by Pryor and Meyers.[37] This is the most effective and commonly used instrument to measure a person's inclination to sexually harass someone. The instrument comprises 10 hypothetical situations with a series of self-reporting measures for respondents to indicate their choice of sexually harassing behaviour. The choice is expressed without the fear of any retaliatory action from any quarter. In the recent years, this instrument has been modified to develop Sexual Harassment Proclivity Scale by Bingham and Burleson,[38] but the original LSH Scale is still in use to assess male proclivity to sexually harass women in a given situation. This scale's validity has been tested for rape and rape-related attitudes and other adverse sex-related behaviours. Subjects scoring high on this scale have the tendency to engage in behaviours which are harassment-type acts; in fact, they prefer this type of acts as compared to those men who are low on the measurement with the scale. Subjects high on LSH Scale, when provided with a real reason to touch a woman confederate, will engage in more attempts of sexual touching as compared to those subjects who are low on LSH measurement.[39]

5.8. Types of Sexual Harassers

Martha Langelan[40] describes four types of harassers based on their characteristics.

1. **Predatory harasser:** This type is the one who gets a sexual thrill from humiliating a female. Just to see how the victims react, he frequently harasses women by involving in sexual extortion. The victims who do not retaliate may even become a target of severe sexual assault like rape.
2. **Dominance harasser:** This type of perpetrator engages in harassing behaviour to boost his ego and feel proud of his conduct.
3. **Strategic or territorial harasser:** This is the type of harasser who seeks to maintain group privilege in a job or physical location, that is, a man harassing a female employee in a predominantly male occupation or on an outdoor assignment where the victim is the only female.
4. **Street harasser:** This one is the harasser who is active in a public place where harassment is performed by a stranger which may be verbal or non-verbal behaviour, sexual remarks on victim's looks or her presence in the public place.[41]

There is another classification of sexual harassers, again based on personality characteristics. This classification divides sexual harassers into four groups, which are as follows[42]:

1. The dark triad
2. Moral disengagement
3. Working in a male-dominated field
4. Hostile attitudes towards women

These four groups are described as follows.

5.8.1. The Dark Triad

The dark triad constitutes three personality traits—narcissism,[3] psychopathy[4] and Machiavellianism.[5] The combination of these three characteristics is called 'dark' because of the resultant malevolent qualities which emerge in a person with these traits. Research on the dark triad has been carried out by psychologists and business management personnel to know that the subjects who score high on these traits are more likely to commit criminal acts, cause social distress and create severe problems for an organization, particularly when they hold leadership positions. These persons have a strong association with a 'callous-manipulative' interpersonal style. A sexual harasser belonging to the dark triad group carries all three characteristics, namely narcissism, psychopathy and Machiavellianism, which are described as follows:

'Narcissism' has the characteristic features of grandiosity, pride, egotism and lack of empathy.[6] A narcissistic person has a grandiose view of one's abilities, along with lack of empathy and an intense need for admiration from others. Regardless of the fact whether or not others like them, narcissists do need others to think of them as powerful, impressive and important persons. They may justify sexual harassment on the grounds that they were deprived of a sexual experience they deserved.

---

[3] https://en.wikipedia.org/wiki/Narcissism
[4] https://en.wikipedia.org/wiki/Psychopathy
[5] https://en.wikipedia.org/wiki/Machiavellianism
[6] https://en.wikipedia.org/wiki/Empathy

'Psychopathy' has two characteristics—fearless dominance and aggressive impulsivity. Psychopathic individuals are bold, daring, manipulative and exploitative. They have no empathy but are practised mimickers of empathetic expressions since this is useful for exploiting their victims. Psychopaths harass others sexually just to fulfil their need. If the situation permits (or they may create the situation), they will exploit it to the full and won't let it go just like that.

'Machiavellianism' is named after Niccolò Machiavelli, the Italian Renaissance politician. It represents an unscrupulous, deceptive philosophy of politics used for attaining long-term goals at any cost.

The triad characteristics put together to make a person essentially gleeful, enthusiastic in exploiting others, deceptive and manipulative. With added characteristics of callousness to others' and grandiosity makes a perfect combination for sexual harassment. In a study of 2,000 community members,[42] researchers found that—unsurprisingly—each of the three dark triad characteristics augmented the tendency to sexually harass others.

5.8.2. Moral Disengagement

'Moral disengagement' is a cognitive process by which individuals construct their own version of reality without applicability of moral principles, and they justify their corruption by their own explanations. Such people choose their behaviour to correspond with their values, and sometimes, through moral disengagement, they may even alter their values to justify their behaviour.

'Moral disengagement' as a concept was first proposed by a noted psychologist, Albert Bandura,[43] whose theory, when applied to sexual harassment,[7] has several parts.

1. **Moral justification or portrayal of harassment as acceptable:** As Harvey Weinstein explained,[44] 'I came of age in the '60s and '70s when all the rules about behaviour and workplaces were different.'

---

[7] https://www.uky.edu/~eushe2/Bandura/Bandura1990JSI.pdf

2. **Euphemistic labelling:** Use of sanitized substitutions for describing their offensive actions, like Bill Cosby's[45] characterization of his sexual assaults as 'rendezvous'.
3. **Displacement of responsibility:** Attribution of the harassment to external factors, like Weinstein's[44] 'that was the culture then.'
4. **Advantageous comparison:** The assertion that the behaviour could have been worse if others were involved and distortion of consequences through which the person plays down the harm done through his actions.
5. **Dehumanization and attribution of blame:** These respectively do away with concern for the victim and blame her for causing the incident. Bill O'Reilly[46] did this when commenting that a woman who was raped and killed was 'moronic' as she wore a miniskirt and a halter top, and that, 'every predator in the world shall pick that up.'

Harassers are invariably at ease since, due to moral disengagement, they take it for granted that whatever they did was normal and could not cause any harm.

Sexual harassers, again due to moral disengagement, alter their prevalent values to justify their actions. In this way, they maintain their positive self-image of being decent, even morally upstanding individuals.

5.8.3. Working in a Male-dominated Field

In cohesive male workgroup settings at the workplace, social norms are often condoned, and hostile environment prevails for the women who are in minority. The hostility may emanate from an authority figure or peers within the workgroup. Once a man with proclivities to harass witnesses another man sexually harassing a woman, he too is likely to begin harassing women or join the harasser.[48] This role model effect is persistent in the environments where men are in majority and women are very few. Sometimes, several co-worker men sexually harass one single woman working in the group. The males identify with the group norm and experience less personal responsibility for their behaviour. This is especially prevalent when a woman is a sole member of a workgroup or she represents a threatening minority in a situation where workers are competing for limited resources. This situation is often characterized by a hostile environment and other disparate treatment along with hostile environment discrimination of a non-sexual nature. For example, a Dalit woman, a potential competitor for the next promotion along with others is often harassed with casteist comments. The Dalit women in India, who are, by and large, quite a few in numerical strength in the offices and have reached there with the benefit of reservation in jobs, are often targets of not only sexual harassment, they are discriminated against and hated for alleged encroaching upon the limited job opportunities available at the workplace.[14] These behaviours serve as a means for driving women from jobs where they were not wanted in the first place[45], [47] and explain the high turnover rate for women in male-dominated blue-collar jobs.[13]

5.8.4. Hostile Attitudes towards Women

Traditional and deeply embedded sexual scripts define women as sexual objects, subordinates and nurturers and men as sexual aggressors and superiors who are expected to push the limit. Gutek[48] found evidence of such gender role stereotyping in the victim–harasser interactions preceding actual events of sexual harassment. This propensity for gender roles to take precedence over work roles also explains the phenomena of counter-power sexual harassment, in which women who occupy positions of power in the workplace are still harassed by their subordinates such as a female college professor is harassed by male students.[13]

5.9. Who Commit Sexual Harassment and Why?

Information on the characteristic features of the sexual harassers is scanty because it is not easy to gather reliable information about those who commit sexual harassment. Whereas 25 per cent of women reported sexual harassment in a US study, only 10 per cent of men admitted their behaviour could have amounted to sexual harassment.[49] Very few people would be ready to accept that they have committed sexual harassment, thereby generating data to explain the patterns of their sexual harassment behaviours becomes difficult. Since a majority of the harassers don't perceive their behaviour to be harassment and do not cooperate for an interview, this makes it hard to identify their characteristics. This way, the majority of the harassers simply get away without scientific scrutiny.

Sexual harassment revolves around power dynamics, and it is fundamentally about exerting power.[8] But that is not always true, the harasser may not occupy prominent or powerful positions in the organization's hierarchy. Even people in supervisory roles are targets[9] for sexual harassment by their subordinates. The problem of sexual harassment is not limited to male-dominated organizations; the manufacturing, healthcare and retail[10] industries all account for similar percentages of the sex-based discrimination complaints filed with the Equal Employment Opportunity Commission.[50]

The environment is equally responsible for contributing to the incidents of sexual harassment at a particular workplace. Some individuals may be, by nature, more aggressive, dominating and sexist, but it depends upon the workplace culture to make it acceptable or unacceptable, and in a culture where harassment is tolerated, such characteristics are not frowned upon rather they are accepted and even encouraged.[19], [52]

The workplace cultures normalizing unacceptable behaviours towards women encourage workplaces to become a fertile ground for sexual harassment. If a woman is unable to voice her grievance to stop offensive behaviour before it turns to a severe form, this behaviour can possibly escalate as the workplace environment does not discourage him in doing so.

Some perpetrators and victims who make an out-of-court settlement and maintain confidentiality do not figure in the official records and thus contribute to the insufficiency of data on sexual harassers. As a result, the case details remain secret, and the harasser may even be

---

[8] https://onlinelibrary.wiley.com/doi/full/10.1111/gwao.12117

[9] https://www.ncbi.nlm.nih.gov/pmc/articles/PMC3544188/

[10] https://fivethirtyeight.com/features/sexual-harassment-isnt-just-a-silicon-valley-problem/

allowed to continue working in the same job. Private settlements also make it tough to find out whether a workplace has a positive or negative climate and can convey to others at the organization that sexual harassment can be quietly tolerated. Pina et al.[51] emphasized the importance of workplace environment in determining whether sexual harassment takes place or not; characteristics of the harassers are not that important according to him. What is really controllable is culture.

Victims' information about the harasser is not enough; her account does not provide much information on perpetrators' motives or patterns. More data on the perpetrators' perspective is needed, which will be particularly important in helping identify their personality characteristics to design preventive strategies. According to Lengelan Martha,[40] the organizations need to be more transparent about problematic behaviours of their employees. Settlements made confidentially could erode women's confidence. They should report harassment to know if a particular individual has a history so that they can be sure whether or not they are overreacting or imagining things. If the women at the workplace know who perpetrates harassment, they can be certain about the behaviour they are experiencing being part of a larger pattern.[34]

Researchers in recent years have demonstrated how power distorts people's perception of other people and changes people's behaviour. Powerful people are more self-focused, more likely to see others as objects or tools and overestimate the extent to which he/she is liked by them.

5.10. Contextual Factors

Sexual harassment occurs in some specific context, and the environmental factors play a crucial role in influencing harassers' behaviour in the society, in general, and the workplace, in particular. The conditions that encourage the harasser to repeat his unwanted behaviour act as a facilitator in the environment.[47] Similar to the perpetrators of domestic violence, sexual harassers at the workplace usually have some form of power (organizational status, situational such as being an examiner, physical such as being with the victim in isolation) over their victims, who are often isolated. The isolation could be possibly because of the less number of females in the workplace, nature of the job (male psychotherapist with a female patient) or because of the harassers' ability to place the victim in an isolated situation such as a secretary or research assistant asked to work for late hours when other employees of the establishment have left.[51] The more significant the power is differential, the more severe is the harassment.[52] Like a perpetrator in case of rape and sexual assault, the sexual harasser works alone and uses physical force combined with psychological, economic or political threats to silence the victim. He induces fear, shame and embarrassment and separates her from validation and support from the environment.[53] Places where the numerical strength of working women is lesser and the work situation demands them to work in isolation, it is difficult for the women to validate their discriminatory experience and seek redress. The numerical isolation leaves a woman vulnerable to gender discrimination, including sexual harassment.

Characteristics of the work or academic environment that increase the risk of sexual harassment are many; in an academic setting,[18], [54] the following contextual factors have been identified for sexual harassment:

1. Professors and guides in educational institutions often enjoy high autonomy and low scrutiny. Research scholars and students are generally at the mercy of their guides or professors for their academic pursuits.
2. Often, there is diffusion of authority for faculty members' behaviour. There is no clear demarcation between personal and academic behaviours between a teacher and the student. The teacher is likely to use his behaviour to exploit student's vulnerability, and the student may have no reasons to protest.
3. In the majority of the universities, there are no well-defined guidelines regarding faculty–student relationships, and the teacher can go to any extent without restrictions in the absence of any laid down demarcation.
4. In-group loyalties of students and resistance of peers to report abusive faculty members is an inevitable feature of a university campus.

5. Low numbers of women faculty members and administrators and the lack of acceptance of women's concerns by the university authorities are other contextual factors which add to the problem.

6. Often, there is no action taken against a complaint made by a female student. This belief leads the female students to tolerate sexual advances silently without opening their mouths in protest.

7. Generally, there is a lack of cohesiveness among students regarding sexual harassment, and there are many who may not agree with the victim regarding her difficulties. This approach makes the environment hostile.

In non-academic workplaces, the predictors of sexual harassment are often identified as related to management, sex ratios and organizational factors. These factors are as follows:

1. Management is, at times, insensitive to the difficulties faced by the women employees, particularly about sexual harassment.

2. The victimized woman reporting her difficulties to a male boss may not be helpful, rather it disinhibits other men to harass her, and the boss my exploit her difficult situation.

3. Women in minority at the workplace could be a contributory factor for sexual harassment. They might be discriminated against and their cases of sexual harassment may not be taken seriously.

4. Unequal opportunity for males and females within the organization may also become a contributory factor for sexual harassment.

5. A woman who holds a job requiring her to have frequent contact with men is exposed to the possibility of sexual harassment. A woman working as an office secretary, a nurse in the hospital with male patients and attendants around or an air hostess in a plane is at risk of sexual harassment.

6. A woman holding a job that is considered non-traditional for women like working in police or armed forces.

7. A woman having a job that is perceived as difficult to get and high in status can possibly become the target of sexual harassment.

8. A woman holding a job that is predominantly female employment and is associated with a woman being perceived as a sex object, such as a secretary, receptionist, waitress, bargirl or maid in the domestic setting.

9. A woman having a job that is low in the hierarchy like a female attendant in an office or a sanitation worker.

10. The workplace where a majority of workers are males consists of cohesive male workgroups that perceive women colleagues as outsiders.

Many of these factors are also applicable to other forms of sex discrimination in the workplace.

The unprofessional environment at the workplace, often created by the strong cohesive male workgroups dominating the office workplace and perceiving women as outsiders, serves as a strong breeding ground for sexual harassment. In the unprofessional workplaces, particularly in the unorganized sectors, the boundaries between work and personal life may be blurred. At such places, co-workers may regularly engage in consensual sexual relationships; there may not be a dress code, and provocative dress-wearing is not objected, office flirtations are common, and sexual jokes are the part of the usual conversation. Such workplaces are often characterized by obscene language usage, swearing, practical jokes, petty office politics, disrespectful behaviours toward employees and women, in particular, and expectations that women will perform non-job-related tasks, such as babysitting, making coffee, running errands, shopping and cleaning the workplace. Many women may not like such an environment, but they are unable to open their mouths in protest. Gutek[48] documents increased harassment in unprofessional settings which have also been associated with higher levels of other forms of discrimination, in accordance with Nieva's sex-role model of discrimination.[55]

5.11. Characteristics of Victims

In their study, Barnett and LaViolette[10] have found the victims of sexual harassment and those of domestic violence sharing similar characteristics. Authors have described the common characteristics as follows:

1. They carry a sense of humiliation and tendency to conceal the event with the hope that the situation will improve in future.

2. They harbour a sense of betrayal of trust and abuse of power and perceive themselves as the victims of circumstances.
3. They carry a fear of retaliation and economic hardship if an incident is reported or revealed. This fear often keeps them silent.
4. There are physical, economic and social power differences between the victim and the harasser in both the situations.
5. They feel isolated from support as the harasser and others tend to minimize the event. The victim feels helpless in both situations.

Unmarried young girls, particularly the new entrants in the job, are at the great risk of sexual harassment. They are more vulnerable to be harassed compared to the married and senior women because the new entrants in the job are often unaware of the work culture of the organization; they are not aware whether any policy against sexual harassment is in place or not.[11] Women hailing from low socio-economic status and deprived communities of traditional Indian society, particularly from the rural areas and Dalit communities, are at a greater risk because of sociocultural and historical reasons.[14] The women with high-visibility positions in a work hierarchy are also vulnerable to sexual harassment and become an easy target of the harassers.

Sahgal and Dang[22] found in their study on women managers that certain kinds of behaviour or demeanour make women more susceptible to harassment. Those women who are friendly and outgoing or smoke or drink and wear unconventional (not necessarily provocative) attire are likely to be perceived as 'willing' and 'open' for a man to make advances and thus become the victims of sexual harassment. Women who are divorced or separated from their husbands are more likely to experience sexual harassment at workplaces, as they are deemed to be 'available' by the reason of their being unguarded by a male. In their study of five divorced women in their sample, the researchers found, three had encountered sexual harassment at their respective workplaces.

5.12. Response Pattern of Victims

There is often a mixture of responses in the form of fear and shame, sympathy for the harasser's family, stemming from the thought as to why his family should suffer because of harasser's actions if he is punished on account of her report. Social conditioning of women that they are to 'compromise', 'adjust' and 'ignore' whatever they go through normalizes most of the harassment incidents that they face. According to Kapoor and Dhingra,[56] women subjected to harassment go through a series of psychological difficulties which may ultimately culminate into severe depression and suicidal behaviour. There is a great impact on their lives in many negative ways, both physically and emotionally.

The response pattern of victims of sexual harassment and cases of domestic violence is more or less similar and presents in the following way:

1. Fear of retaliation or exacerbation of the situation
2. Fear of not being believed by others
3. Fear of revenge from the harasser or the perpetrator
4. Fear of economic and other penalties
5. Hope for improvement that often suppresses what is really going on

Events of sexual harassment often raise the question of culpability in the victim. This could be because of cultural reasons that women remain in an abusive relationship or work situations which are discriminatory in nature. Under such circumstances, women are at the receiving end, and their disadvantageous position is a part of cultural norms. Sexual harassment is part of their social position.

Knapp et al.[12] describe a comprehensive typology of victim responses into four groups, occurring along two intersecting axes:

1. **Self-focus:** The victim focuses her effort on managing internal cognitions and emotions.
2. **Initiator focus:** The victim focuses on problem-solving and altering the external situation.
3. **Self-response:** The victim's attempt to cope with the situation alone.
4. **Supported response:** The victim's attempt to cope with the utilization of another party, such as superiors, a mentor, physician, psychiatrist, spouse, co-worker and some law agency.

Gutek and Koss[13] substitute the terms 'indirect' and 'direct' for the terms 'self-focus' and 'initiator focus', respectively, and 'individual involved' versus 'other involved' for 'self-response' and 'supported response'. They further described a similar typology according to what the victim has self-response initiator focus and the victims of sexual harassment can and should handle it herself, speaking directly with the harasser.

Other studies indicate that most victims utilize some version of self-response, self-focus style.[57] This style is seldom effective in stopping sexual harassment which usually persists and at times escalates in the absence of a direct response.[8], [57] Even so, it is used constantly even for sexual harassment that includes rape.

In a study, 81 per cent of the rape victims stayed in job and continued working in the same workplace environment, 67 per cent remained in active contact with their harassers, and 21 per cent utilized workplace complaints channel for redressal of their grievances. Only 10 per cent of the rape victims had left their job to find some other place to work. Leaving a job leads the harasser free to target others and leaves the victim to search for another job and suffer career burden.[58], [59]

Bjorn[60] suggests the following three reasons why the 'indirect individual response' involved responses are popular, despite their being ineffective in stopping sexual harassment:

1. They allow the victim to manage the situation without disturbing the work or interfering the relationship with mentors, co-workers.
2. They are perceived by the victim as less risky.
3. Some kinds of sexual harassments are ambiguous and, therefore, are not likely to induce a direct response.

Individual involvement responses focused directly on the initiator are less frequent than individual involved response focused on self; however, the response involving the third party is even less common, perhaps because they require that the victims identify behaviour as sexual harassment and make the incident public.

Use of formal complaint and the legal channel is in less than 10 per cent cases and seldom more than 20 per cent, even for sexual harassment involving rape, though these channels are instituted by the society and institutions and considered more effective in stopping sexual harassment. Individual reasons for low utilization rates provide an explanation. They include[61]:

1. Failure to recognize the behaviour as harassment
2. Lack of knowledge of avenues of redressal
3. Fear of retaliation by the harasser, supervisors, management and co-workers
4. Fear of economic or career development repercussion
5. Shame and humiliation
6. Wishes to protect and not harm the harasser, with whom the victim has a relationship
7. Fear that the complaint will not be taken seriously or accomplish anything
8. Fear of negative impact on the family
9. Fear of emotional stress and time connected with reporting
10. A belief that the victim should handle the situation herself
11. Hope that the situation will improve with time
12. A belief that the situation is not serious enough to merit complaint
13. A belief in traditional gender role
14. A belief that the victim should be blamed for sexual harassment as she only provides an opportunity to the harasser to harass

The general perception among people is that the victim should act assertively to report harassment. However, research findings don't support this perception as being effective and beneficial for the victim. In fact, the research supports the concerns of many victims that the reporting has no positive impact on them rather worsens the overall situation for them.

Assertive, direct and initiator focused responses to sexual harassment often result in continued harassment, a high incident of retaliatory and punitive response from the harasser. It also results in a hostile work environment and increased psychological and somatic sequel for the victims who may suffer mental health problems.

Sexual harassment and other gender discriminations often occur together. Other forms of discriminations inhibit the victim's efficiency in dealing with sexual harassment and vice versa. It is also possible:

1. That the victim would suffer negative consequences of either harassment or discrimination
2. That other forms of discrimination could enhance the negative effects of sexual harassment
3. That sexual harassment and other forms of discrimination is not one-time experience, but it unfolds that waxes and wanes over time.

The factors which influence the reaction of the victims of sexual harassment may vary from individual to individual. The response pattern may be influenced by the following factors:

5.12.1. Environmental and Contextual Factors

Those experiencing the severest form of sexual harassment are most likely to respond in direct and assertive manner; less severely harassed are more likely to respond indirectly, avoid the harassment, joke about the harassing situation and laugh it away or minimize it. Women with higher organizational powers, high job skills, power superior to the harasser respond directly and assertively.

Women with fewer personal resources, low self-esteem, low skills and with a sense of being trapped in the job tend to choose individual responses.

Women with traditional sex-role attitude are also less likely to respond directly. If the supervisor or the mentor is supportive and powerful and the person handling the complaints credible, and the co-workers, friends and the family members are supportive, it has a positive impact on victim's decision.

5.12.2. Characteristics of Job Salient for Indirect Response

Following are the characteristics of indirect response, which are related to the workplace:

1. Lack of mobility due to a high degree of specialization or long-term nature of the project

2. Lack of transfer opportunities
3. Vulnerability to informal blackmailing
4. Loyalty to an institution due to a highly valued, high status or visible position

5.13. Polarizing Dynamics

The victim and those close to her often report on the intense and polarizing impact of sexual harassment. As the definition of sexual harassment varies, the reaction to sexual harassment also varies from victim to victim. It is often accompanied by an intense effect. It is not only because of individual perception differences but also because of the dynamics of dominant–subordinate interactions. In comparison to men, women are more likely to define an event as sexual harassment and also to perceive the event as threatening, negative or both in the outcome. On the other hand, men are more likely to perceive women's friendly and frank behaviour as indicative of sexual interest and to see the workplace as an equitable and conducive environment. Researchers observe that the dominant people in society and at the workplace, who are often males, label, organize and define the social and work realities without integrating the perceptions and experiences of subordinates, considering them insignificant. They not only resist but also punish those who raise issues. The current grievances redressal mechanism which assigns blame of wrongdoing on the accused further enhances the polarization processes. The victim may face hardship with valida-tion and support not only within her workplace but also within her personal life. Because of deeply ingrained and unconscious gender-based and dominant–subordinate based differences in perception and the strong association of male with dominant and female with subor-dinate, there will be an intense polarization process surrounding these issues. This impact will be felt by victimized individuals, perpetrators, their superiors and their co-workers, as well as by significant people in their personal lives. Because of this polarization process, significant disruptions in the victim's work and personal relations are common in discrimination or harassment situations, especially if the sufferer files a complaint or a lawsuit. These experiences are as traumatic for the victim as the sexual harassment itself was.

An aggrieved woman may lose a valued mentor or a supervisor if they are the perpetrators of sexual harassment or if they fail to support and validate her experience and efforts for redress. Colleagues at the workplace may ostracize her as a troublemaker or a slut and even may capitalize on any managerial retaliatory actions by taking over her work, her position or both if she is demoted or removed from a particular assignment. They may side with the perpetrator and the work organization and either retaliate against her directly or fail to validate or support her efforts for redress, even if they have witnessed the event of sexual harassment. Co-workers who have been sympathizers in private may not come forward openly as they may be frightened to join the complainant. The institution may publicly deny harassment and praise the organization, or it may even promote other women to discredit the victim's claims of sexual harassment. The female supervisor may become too demoralized to help, and the spouse and the significant others in victim's life may identify with the perpetrator or become worried that the woman is having an affair or in some way invited sexual overtures because of which harassment took place. They may become intrusive into the workplace to protect her or insist upon her taking impulsive legal action. The father of the victim may overidentify with management and discourage assertive action or overidentify with his daughter and insist that the woman take actions that may not be in her best interest. He may also intrude into his daughter's workplace to handle the situation himself. The mother may feel embarrassed by the public exposure of her daughter in a sexual situation or feel guilty that she did not sufficiently prepare her daughter for the inequities in the workplace. The daughter may identify with the mother who is victimized and feels frightened or discouraged. The complexities of the polarization process are unlimited. The mental health implications of this process are of great significance and discussed at another place in the book.[62]

5.14. Transference: What Counts as Harassment from a Patient?

Sexual harassment is quite common in the medical profession. Women are more commonly subjected to harassment than men.[63] Junior professionals are particularly more common victims of sexual harassment than senior colleagues. There have also been accounts of physicians who experience harassment at the hands of patients and their attendants more than often. Medical professionals are generally ill-equipped to handle this type of encounter.[64]

Mental health professionals, particularly psychiatrists are more vulnerable to unwanted sexual conduct. Around 86 per cent of psychiatry residents in a study reported deliberate physical contact, excessive proximity (e.g., leaning over or cornering), letters, unrelated telephone calls and being exposed to sexual material, with most offences having been perpetrated by patients and male colleagues at the workplace.[65] According to reports from all hospital settings, that is, in the emergency department, female physicians have reported it from patients in their offices as well.[64]

Some patients, by reason of their mental disorder, may show sexually inappropriate behaviour and the treating psychiatrists are unclear how to respond to patients' advances which they do not always regard as 'sexual harassment' and believe it to be the part of their psychopathology. While dealing with the cases of mania or schizophrenia or confused state, unwanted sexual advances by the patient may not necessarily be sexual harassment in true sense. It could be the product of psychosis. However, the psychological impact on victims should be acknowledged even when the behaviour of the perpetrator is explained by the diagnosis of a psychiatric condition.[65]

Health professionals from other specialities may take such remarks as sexual, which may, in fact, be part of the patient's psychopathology. A psychiatrist has to carefully examine the patient to differentiate whether it was the part of the illness or otherwise. Carefully hearing these statements, evaluating their genesis, conducting a detailed mental status examination and reaching a specific conclusion is the part of psychiatrist's duty.

A patient undergoing psychotherapy is allowed to speak anything irrespective of its relevance, and the therapist analyses the content of the patient's thought from a psychological perspective. At times, it may make the therapist uneasy, particularly when a female therapist is treating the patient. The therapist should be able to differentiate the nature of thought making her uncomfortable whether they are patient's genuine concerns or simply harassing tactics. Certain behaviours may not fall in the ambit of sexual harassment, but they are inappropriate and offending for the therapist. It could just be a professional hazard of being a psychotherapist.

Sexual fantasies during the psychotherapeutic process are common, which may lead to erotic transference towards the therapist or vice versa. Transference is the central component of psychotherapy that is applicable to female psychiatrists treating male patients as well as male psychiatrists treating female patients.

Transference in psychotherapy sessions is very common. It is an unconscious feeling that is transposed onto another significant individual—here, a therapist. In sexualized transference, the patient's fantasies about the therapist contain elements of reverence, romance, intimacy, sensuality or sexuality, whereas, in erotic transference, there is an irrational preoccupation with the therapist with demands for love and sexual fulfilment. The patient fails to develop appropriate insight and uses psychotherapy sessions for the opportunity to be close to the therapist with the hope of reciprocation.[66]

It is important for the therapist to avoid indulging in an unethical relationship with the patient and deviating from the standard practice of psychotherapy. The therapist needs to be alert to patients who dress seductively, attempt to give gifts, contact on social media or outside the appointment time, ask frequent questions about therapist's sex life or refuse to talk about subjects other than sex.[67]

5.15. Protection against Allegation of Sexual Harassment

Psychotherapy allows discussion on several sensitive issues including the client's sexual history which may be discussed not only during psychotherapeutic sessions but also during pharmacotherapy to establish a diagnosis.

When the patient is uncomfortable with sex-related questions asked by the therapist, the clinician should explain the relevance of the questions and should proceed slowly. The clinician should also seek to explore and understand the discomfort of the client regarding the questions related to sex. Therapists should not avoid necessary questions about sex out of concern that the client might misinterpret them as sexual harassment.

5.16. Secondary Victims of Sexual Harassment

The primary victims of sexual harassment behaviour are those who are directly involved in the experience, but there are others at the workplace who witness this behaviour, often on a continuous basis, may also get affected. They are the secondary victims of sexual harassment. Occasionally, these secondary victims file complaints of hostile environment and discrimination, and the negative consequences to these individuals can equal or even surpass those affecting the primary victim. This type of victims are likely to remain silent, keep working in the hostile environment for a long time, and they are placed at risk for negative psychological consequences, even though they are not directly involved in the discriminatory interaction. This may harm the overall productivity of the workplace.

Case Illustration

A recently reported case of sexual harassment[68] can be taken up for understanding the interpersonal dynamics:

The case comes from Air India where the complainant woman works as a captain. She alleged sexual harassment by a commander of the same organization. The incident of sexual harassment took place at Hyderabad on 5 May 2019 where the aggrieved woman was being trained by the said commander. The commander suggested the aggrieved woman accompany him for dinner after the class in a city restaurant to which she agreed as she had worked with him in few flights where he was a pilot and considered him to be a decent person.

In the restaurant, the commander began to talk about the unhappy married life he was leading and the severity of depression he was suffering from. He was also critical of other women colleagues of the airline and made lewd comments about their looks, character and work profile. Then he asked uncomfortable questions for which the complainant was not prepared. To her utter shock, the perpetrator asked her questions about her sex life. He asked, 'How do you manage without sex in absence of your husband who is living far away? Don't you need to have sex every day? Do you masturbate?' The aggrieved woman had never expected such questions and asked him to stop and called a taxi to leave and go back to the room where she was staying for the training. While waiting for the taxi, the commander continued with embarrassing questions, and his behaviour worsened. All this happened without any prompting or encouragement from the woman's side. She was left shocked at her instructor's behaviour and felt extremely uncomfortable, scared and humiliated. Even after she reached her room, the man continued messaging her to meet him which she ignored and didn't respond to. After a while, when he got no response from her, he wrote a threatening message that he would come to her room.

She responded then to explain how disturbed she was with his behaviour ... to which he replied that he was only providing her with options. He was not like other men who forced themselves on women. The case has been reported to the authorities.

In this case, the incident took place during the course of a training programme at a place where both the perpetrator and the victim were present in their respective official capacities. The perpetrator is a married man, older than the victim, at a senior position than the complainant in the organizational hierarchy, enjoying more power to influence the victim. The perpetrator has a tendency to undermine women's position, which is evident from the lewd comments he makes against the women working in the organization. Such a harasser is often labelled as 'sexual exploitation' type, in which sexual harassment is based either on sexual or hostile intent, and within each of these, there is sexual exploitation which describes the situation in which perpetrator imposes sexual intimacy due to power differential, which makes the victim vulnerable. The perpetrator tries to gain sexual favours by sharing his difficulties in his own marital life. He has diminished capacity for empathy and lacks the ability to appreciate others situation. He is least concerned about the victim's feelings and continues to text messages despite her protest and non-acceptance of his advances. The perpetrator is a 'private harasser' type who appears to be professional and conservative in public as he had portrayed himself as a decent person at the workplace, but privately, he behaved otherwise. This man gives 'moral justification' for his behaviour as he says that he had only provided options to the victim, unlike other men who just pounce upon when finding a woman.

The victim, in this case, is in a junior position and carries a sense of humiliation and harbours a sense of betrayal of trust by a man who she considered a decent person and agreed to have dinner with. She also felt the abuse of power by the perpetrator.

References

[1] Brunswig KA, O'Donohue W. Relapse Prevention, Harm Reduction, and Sexual Harassment: Confronting Sexual Misbehavior in the Workplace. Workshop Presented at the 17th Annual Meeting of the Association for the Treatment of Sexual Abusers, 1998. Vancouver, British Columbia, Canada.

[2] Griffin S. *Rape: The Power of Consciousness*. New York, NY: Harper and Row; 1979 and Groth AN. *Men Who Rape: The Psychology of the Offender*. New York, NY: Plenum Press, 1979.

[3] Koss M. The under detection of rape: Methodological choices, influence incidences estimates. *Journal of Social Issues*. 1992 Apr;48(1):61–76.

[4] Watts C, Zimmerman C. Violence against women: Global scope and magnitude. *The Lancet*. 2002;359 (9313):1232–1237.

[5] Crowell NA, Burgess AW. *Understanding Violence against Women*. Washington DC, WA: National Academy Press; 1996.

[6] Pryor JB. Sexual harassment proclivities in men. *Sex Roles*. 1987 Sep;17(5–6):269–290.

[7] Lapierre LM, Spector PE, Leck JD. Sexual versus nonsexual workplace aggression and victims' overall job satisfaction: A meta-analysis. *Journal of Occupational Health Psychology*. 1990 Apr;10(2):155–169.

[8] Willness C, Steel P, Lee K. A meta-analysis of the antecedents and consequences of workplace sexual harassment. *Personnel Psychology*. 2007 Mar;60(1):127–162.

[9] O'Donohue W, Downs K, Yeater EA. Sexual harassment: A review of the literature. *Aggression and Violent Behavior*. 1987;3(2):111–128.

[10] Barnett OW, LaViolette AD. *It Could Happen to Anyone. Why Battered Women Stay*. Newbury Park, CA: SAGE Publications; 1993.

[11] Fain TC, Anderson DL. Sexual harassment: Organizational cintext and diffuse status. *Sex Roles*. 1987 Sep 1;17(5–6):291–311.

[12] Knapp DE, Faley RH, Ekeberg SE, Dubois CLZ. Determinants of target responses to sexual harassment: A conceptual framework. *Academy of Management Review*. 1997 Jul 1;22(3):687–729.

[13] Gutek BA, Koss MP. Changed women and changed organizations: Consequences of and coping with sexual harassment. *Journal of Vocational Behavior.* 1993 Feb 1;42(1):28–48.

[14] Jiloha RC. *Native Indian: In Search of Identity.* New Delhi: Blumoon Books; 1995.

[15] Alam S. Women and poverty in Bangladesh. *Women Studies International Forum.* 1985: 8(4):17–18.

[16] World Economic Forum. The Global Gender Gap Report 2017. Available at: https://www.weforum.org/reports/the-global-gender-gap-report-2017 (accessed on 21 December 2020).

[17] Catharine MacKinnon. *Sexual Harassment of Working Women: A Case of Sex Discrimination.* New Haven, CT: Yale University Press; 1979.

[18] Loy PH, Stewart LP. The extent and effects of the sexual harassment of working women. *Journal of Sociological Focus.* 1984 Jan 1;17(1):65–66.

[19] Dziech BW, Weiner L. *The Lecherous Professor: Sexual Harassment on Campus.* Boston, MA: Beacon Press; 1984.

[20] Zalk SR. Men in the Academy: A Psychological Profile of Harassment. In: Paludi MA, editor. *Ivory Power: Sexual Harassment on Campus.* Albany, NY: State University of New York Press; 1990, pp. 141–175.

[21] Stanko E. I Second That Emotion: Reflections on Feminism, Emotionality and Research on Sexual Violence. In: Schwartz M, editor. *Researching Sexual Violence against Women: Methodological and Personal Perspective.* London: SAGE Publications; 1997.

[22] Sahgal P, Dang A. Experiences of Women Managers and Organisations. *Economic & Political Weekly,* 2017. Available at: https://www.epw.in/system/files/pdf/2017_52/22/SA_LII_22_030617_Punam_Sahgal.pdf (accessed on 21 December 2020).

[23] *Saheli.* Another Occupational Hazard: Sexual Harassment and the Working Woman. Delhi, 1998.

[24] Sakshi. Study on Sexual Harassment at Workplace. Delhi, 2001.

[25] Pryor JB; LaVite CM and Stoller LM. A social psychological analysis of sexual harassment: The person/situation interaction. *Journal of Vocational Behaviour.* 1993 Feb 1;42(1):68–83.

[26] Rowe M. Saturn's Rings Phenomenon. American Association of University Women. 1974, pp. 1–9. Available at: https://mitsloan.mit.edu/shared/ods/documents/?DocumentID=3986 (accessed on 21 December 2020).

[27] Lenhart S. Physical and mental health aspects of sexual harassment. In: Shrier DK, editor. *Clinical Practice Series, No. 38. Sexual Harassment in the Workplace and Academia: Psychiatric Issues* (pp. 21–38). Arlington, TX: American Psychiatric Association; 1996.

[28] Kosson DS, Kelly JC, White JW. Psychopathy-related traits predict self-reported sexual aggression among college men. *Journal of Interpersonal Violence.* 1997 Apr;12(2): 241–254.

138 Sexual Harassment of Women at Workplaces

[29] De Souza E, Fansler AG. Contra-power sexual harassment: A survey of students and faculty members. *Sex Roles*. 2003 Jun 1;48(11-12): 529-542.

[30] Pludi MA, Barickman RB. *Academic and Workplace Sexual Harassment: A Resource Manual*. Albany, NY: SUNY Press; 1991, pp. 2-5.

[31] Fitzgerald L. Why didn't she first report him? The psychological and legal implications of women's response to sexual harassment. *Journal of Social Issues*. 1995 Apr;51(1):117-138.

[32] Begany JJ, Milburn MA. Psychological predictors of sexual harassment: Authoritarianism, hostile sexism and rape myths. *Psychology of Men and Masculinity*. 2002 Jul;3(2):119-126.

[33] Rapaport K, Burkhart BR. Personality and attitudinal characteristics of sexually coercive college males. *Journal of Abnormal Psychology*. 1984 May;93(2):216-222.

[34] Gough HG. Theory and measurement of socialization. *Journal of Consulting Psychology*. 1960 Feb;24(1):23-30.

[35] Raskin RN, Hall, CS. A narcissistic personality inventory. *Psychological Reports*. 1979; 45:590.

[36] Bowman Cynthia Grant. Street Harassment and informal Ghettoization of women. *Harvard Law Review*. 1993;106(3):717-780.

[37] Pryor JB, Meyers AB. Men who sexually harass women. In: Schlesinger LB, editor. *Serial Offenders: Current Thought, Recent Findings, Unusual Syndromes*. Boca Raton, FL: CRC Press; 2000, pp. 207-228.

[38] Bingham SG, Burleson BR. The development of a Sexual Harassment Proclivity Scale: Construct validation and relationship to communication competence. *Communication Quarterly*.1996 Jun 1;44(3):308-332

[39] Siebler F, Sabelus S, Bohner G. A refined computer harassment paradigm: Validation and test of hypotheses about target characteristics. *Psychology of Women Quarterly*.2008 Mar;32(1):22-35.

[40] Lengelan M. *Back off: How to Confront and Stop Sexual Harassment*. New York, NY: Touchstone; 1993.

[41] Bowman CG. Street harassment and informal Ghettoization of women. *Harvard Law Review*. 1993; 106(3):717-780.

[42] Zeigler-Hill V, Besser A, Campbell WK. The dark triad and sexual harassment proclivity. *Personality and Individual Differences*. 2016;89:47-54.

[43] Bandura A. Moral disengagement in the perpetration of inhumanities. *Personality and Social Psychology Review*. 1999 Aug;3(3):193-209.

[44] *The New York Times*. Statement from Harvey Weinstein. 2017. Available at: https://www.nytimes.com/interactive/2017/10/05/us/statement-from-harvey-weinstein.html?src=twr (accessed on 21 December 2020).

[45] Stern Marlow. Bill Cosby's Long List of Accusers (So Far): 18 Alleged Sexual Assault Victims Between 1965-2004. *The Daily Beast*. Available at: https://www.thedailybeast.com/bill-cosbys-long-list-of-accusers-so-far-18-alleged-sexual-assault-victims-between-1965-2004 (accessed on 21 December 2020).

[46] Media Matters. O'Reilly: Rape, Murder Victim Was 'Wearing a Miniskirt and a Halter Top.... [E]very Predator in the World is Gonna Pick That up at 2 in the Morning.' Available at: https://www.mediamatters.org/bill-oreilly/oreilly-rape-murder-victim-was-wearing-miniskirt-and-halter-top-every-predator-world (accessed on 21 December 2020).

[47] Pryor J, Whelan N. A typology of sexual harassment: Characteristics of harassers and the social circumstances under which sexual harassment occurs. In: O'Donohue W, editor. *Sexual Harassment: Theory, Research, and Treatment.* Boston, MA: Allyn & Bacon; 1997.

[48] Gutek BA. *Sex and the Workplace.* San Francisco, CA: Jossey-Bass; 1985.

[49] US Merit Systems Protection Board. *Sexual Harassment in the Federal Government: An Update.* Washington DC, WA: US Government Printing Office; 1987.

[50] Equal Employment Opportunity Commission. https://www.google.com/url Retrived on Retrieved 25 December 2019.

[51] Pina A, Gannon TA, Saunders B. An overview of the literature on sexual harassment: Perpetrator, theory, and treatment issues. *Aggression and Violent Behavior.* 2009;14(2):126–138.

[52] McLaughlin H. http://www.eeoc.gov/laws/statutes/cra-1991.cfm Retrived 25 December 2018.

[53] Cleveland J, McNamara K. In: Stockdale M, editor. *Sexual Harassment in the Workplace.* Thousand Oaks, CA: SAGE Publications; 1996, pp. 217–240.

[54] Bondurant B, White J. Men who sexually harass: An embedded perspective. In Schrier D, editor. *Sexual Harassment in the Workplace and Academia.* Washington DC, WA: American Psychiatric Press; 1996, pp. 59–79.

[55] Benson KA. Comments on Crocker's: An analysis of university definitions of sexual harassment. *Signs.* 1984;9:516–519.

[56] Kapoor V, Dhingra K. Sexual harassment against women in India. *International Journal of Sustainable Development.* 2013;6(10):85–92.

[57] Furr S. Men and women in cross-gender careers. In: Daimant L, Lee JA, editors. *The Psychology of Sex, Gender, and Jobs: Issues and Solutions.* Westport, CT: Praeger; 2002.

[58] O'Leary-Kelly AM, Bowes-Sperry L, Bates CA, Lean ER. Sexual harassment at work: A decade (plus) of progress. *Journal of Management.* 1996;35(3):503–536.

[59] Dansky BS, Kilpatrick DS. The effects of sexual harassment. In: O'Donohue W, editor. *Sexual Harassment: Theory, Research, and Treatment.* Boston, MA: Allyn and Bacon; 1997, pp. 152–174.

[60] Björkqvist K, Österman K, Hjelt-Bäck M. Aggression among university employees. *Aggressive Behavior.* 1994;20(3):173–184.

[61] Bernstein AE, Lenhart SA. *The Psychodynamic Treatment.* Washington DC, WA: American Psychiatric Press; 1993.

[62] Jagsi R. Sexual harassment in medicine #metoo. *New England Journal of Medicine.* 2018;378(3):209–211.

[63] DeFilippis EM. Putting the 'she' in doctor. *JAMA Internal Medicine.* 2018;178(3):323–324.

[64] Morgan JF, Porter S. Sexual harassment of psychiatric trainees: Experiences and attitudes. *Postgraduate Medical Journal.* 1999;75:410–413.

[65] Phillips SP, Schneider MS. Sexual harassment of female doctors by patients. *New England Journal of Medicine.* 1993;329(26):1936–1939.

[66] Ladson D, Welton R. Recognizing and managing erotic and eroticized transferences. *Psychiatry (Edgmont).* 2007 Apr;4(4):47–50.

[67] Freud S. Observations on transference-love: Further recommendations on the technique of psycho-analysis III. *The Journal Psychotherapy Practice and Research.* 1993;2(2):171–180.

[68] Sinha S. Pilot Accuses AI Commander of Harassment. *The Times of India,* 2019. Available at: https://timesofindia.indiatimes.com/business/india-business/pilot-accuses-ai-commander-of-harassment/articleshow/69334260.cms (accessed on 21 December 2020).

CHAPTER 6

Workplace Environment and Theories of Sexual Harassment

In both the occurrence and prevention of sexual harassment, workplace environment plays a significant role. There are many establishments, educational institutions and other workplaces where both men and women can work in an environment that is stress-free, harmonious and conducive. There are many others that remain under the grip of stressors and hostility regularly. It is necessary to know the environment of the place where the people work. This understanding also helps to know how the victims of sexual harassment could recover from their adverse experiences and re-establish themselves in the same workplace environment. The structural and environmental conditions of workplace or educational institutions may contribute to discriminatory events and serve as a breeding ground for sexual harassment. For several reasons, these conditions have clinical significance for several, such as follows:

- In evaluating victims with work-related complaints, they allow the clinician to focus on external as well as intra-psychic factors.
- These conditions help the victim to avoid immobilization and internalization of guilt and shame.
- They help the therapist and the victim in collaborating to formulate an effective and adaptive coping plan.

Before theories of harassment are constructed, it is essential to know various aspects of the environment. Some aspects of environment are discussed further.

6.1. Environment and the Workplace

6.1.1. Environment at the Workplace and Educational Institutions

Over the last 50 years, the demography of the workplace has rapidly changed and significant change has been witnessed in offices and academic settings with the impact of gender. Gender impact has increased manifolds with significant gains and equally significant stagnation in gender equity. In the early 1970s, women began to enter the employment market in significantly large numbers, and their numbers have continued to increase since then. In 1970, in the USA, 43 per cent of women were either employed or seeking employment and their number increased to 60 per cent within the next two decades. Similar gender equity occurred in India in the distribution of men and women entering previously male-dominated professional schools, such as law and medicine, and the proportion of female managers increased from 16 per cent in 1970 to 44 per cent in 1998.[1]

At the time of Independence of the country in 1947, literacy rate among women in India was almost negligible; traditionally, women observed purdah when in public places, which restricted their work jurisdiction to domestic chores and raising their children. During the last seven decades, India's population has grown rapidly and so has its economy. The traditional social role of women in the country has been disrupted by rapid urbanization and other demographic changes. With the advent of education in free India, a considerable change has occurred in the pattern of women's education and their childbearing practices. The enrolment of girls in primary school came at par with boys, and universal enrolment was achieved in 2015.

Between 1994 and 2010, the number of women in the age group of 15 to 24 years attending an educational institution in the country rose to more than double (from 16.1% to 36%). The number of women enrolled in tertiary educational institutions also came at par with men

(27% of women compared to the same percentage of men) during the same period.[2]

However, the number of women entering the labour force in India has been scanty and female labour force participation (FLFP) rates remain low compared to the Western world and compared to men in the country. Despite women's educational gains in the country, only 28.5 per cent of them were in the labour force in 2017, compared to 82 per cent of men. Gender discrimination in employment is most obvious. In 2011–2012, only 43 per cent of the 11.7 million working women in urban areas were in regular wage and salaried positions (up from 28.5% in 1993–1994). Recent trends show that more young women are opting for newer professional jobs like communications; however, their participation remains much lower compared to men's participation.[3]

There is no doubt that women's labour force participation rate in India is lower than other countries in the world; employed women in general show an increase in the number of mothers of young children and single mothers. Changes in women's attitudes and expectations regarding work outside the home have occurred alongside changes in numbers.[4] In women's sense of themselves, career and salaried employments play a more salient role and are thus impacted by the work environment. This impact is of great psychological significance when viewed from the point of women's traditional role. Traditional roles of men and women are in great flux and perceptions of their roles are influenced by several variations between traditional and egalitarian attitudes that exist among individuals, their families and their workplace contacts. Thus, two women with similar credentials, career attitudes and goals may have very different experiences, depending on the attitudes of their colleagues, co-workers, mentors, bosses, teachers and significant individuals in their personal lives.[2] Therefore, in determining interpersonal relations, the workplace environment plays a major role.

At most of the places, the persons at top positions making policy decisions are generally males. If they carry traditional gender stereotypical beliefs about men and women, they can either resist promoting women altogether or only help women who are significantly junior or subordinate to them.[1] Discrimination is not only in appointments and promotions; on average, a full-time female worker receives less pay than a full-time male worker, just 62 per cent of what their male counterparts receive for doing the same amount of work. Female-dominated occupations still receive lower pay than male-dominated occupations. Furthermore, the disparity in earnings of two genders appears to be escalating after a period of decline.[5] Sex segregation remains a defining element of occupational structure in many organizations that affects the choices for both men and women, and still confines women to lower paying and female-dominated occupations and positions.[6] Women with high positions in work and educational institutions are few, and the continued gender stereotyping operates against women seeking top positions, despite changes in opportunities and attitudes for women at other levels. Women find it difficult to influence the policies and structures of their work and educational environments. For many women, their traditionally held responsibilities such as childcare, eldercare and other duties as a homemaker take a back seat and they come out in growing numbers for employment in offices or as students in educational institutions outside the confines of home. Women continue to carry out most domestic responsibilities, and many of them are expected to continue doing so in addition to outdoor work.[7]

6.1.2. Emerging Trends in Work Environment

Since the 1990s, globalization, recession and advancements in information technology have resulted in the following[1]:

- Radical and continuous restructuring of work organization
- Information overload and accelerated work pace

During the past few decades, there has been considerable erosion in the fundamental employer–employee contract, which used to promise long-term stable employment and advancement in the work hierarchy, in return for hard work, high performance and loyalty. The erosion has affected the morale, motivation and employee loyalty and provided an opportunity for change. Most of the organizations, ranging from manufacturing companies to educational institutions, now rely more on a small core of permanent full-time employees working in-house, supplemented by a much larger pool of part-time and contract employees working on specific projects or tasks for a defined period. Employees ranging from factory line workers to administrators, college professors and physicians in the hospitals have the experience of fewer people doing more work with less job security.[8] Employee value proposition (EVP) is redundant in today's workforce. It is the employee experience (EX) which is relevant in the era of technologies causing intense competition for unimaginable skills and compatibilities. Flourishing companies reposition their employees' EVP to move to individual value proposition (IVP) creating effective persons and designing customized programmes and communication road maps. They strengthen their employees' emotional connection to the organization expanding EVP's scope to encompass the following:

• Contractual experience that gives high returns on investment
• Attracting the right talent with a good start
• Emotional connect experience—the desire of employees to be proud of the work they do and the organization they work for

The purpose-driven employees transcend contractual experiences to be motivated by the work. Such employees not only create their own engagement experiences but spread it virally to their colleagues at work.

Many changes have come up due to this transaction in the workplace environment which has gender implications, such as flexible workplace, job insecurity and longer working time. These changes make it difficult for many to adjust in the new environment. Traditionally, women have been workers with flexible attitudes towards work with easy adaptability. In the changed work environment, they should be preferred more[9] because their career aspirations and management styles are focused on performing the duty, achieving expertise and job satisfaction, rather than on personal gains like promotions. The management profile of changing times demands good communication skills, flexibility in approach, a capacity to mentor others and good leadership skills. In a culture of rapid change, whether women will find a conducive workplace environment remains to be seen. One possibility is that the career paths regress back to the traditional styles within these new organizations and men still remain at the topmost positions, or they relinquish power in this time of change.[10]

As a consequence of prevailing job insecurity, both men and women may adapt to more egalitarian roles in the home where women are the sole providers for their families. With the changed environment, men may become active at home and share some of the emotional burden of family life. Will the employees continue the trend towards working longer hours to guard against job loss, or will they rebel and become more assertive in moving from organization to organization according to their needs? There is a possibility of a new trend of horizontal, rather than vertical, movement. Longer working hours in the office will create more stress at home, with children being deprived of parental care and families' stress spill into the workplace. Home-based work in virtual organizations can provide caretakers with more employment opportunities and egalitarian integration that can possibly reinforce gender inequities, with employers paying less to predominantly female home-based workers and more money to men maintaining the traditional boundaries between home and work. It is clear that many of the fundamental tenets of gendered organizations are affected by the recent radical changes in the work and educational environments, such as follows:

- The male model of work
- Continuous full-time careers based on advancement
- The physical and psychological separation of work and family

There is possibility of shifts in gender roles, but not certain by any means. Women have shown their presence at the workplace in significantly large numbers for the last 30 years, and they have made considerable gains. Many of them have reached significantly higher positions in their work organizations, giving a favourable tilt to the work environment. Many men have shown their increasing involvement in family life, but still this involvement is not at par with women. However, work and educational organizations, to a considerable extent, continue to be led by men and structured according to male values. The evolving global economy will affect jobs and introduce gender roles from other cultures. The impact of the activities of the terrorists and other world conflicts and the potential repercussions on the economic and working climate remains to be seen. It is possible that these emerging structural changes in the workplace alone may alter the embedded gender elements that currently exist, unless the need to challenge gender role inequities is articulated and specifically pursued in the larger sociocultural arena.[11]

6.1.3. Environments Creating Discriminatory Experience for Women

During the last two decades, researchers from various disciplines have constructed theories to explain the current inequity between the sexes in the work and educational environments. Some theories explain sex discrimination in general, and others apply specifically to sexual harassment. Many of these aetiologic theories overlap, and some lend themselves to psychological interpretation more than others. In general, these models point to an interaction between the following:

- Socio-environmental factors impacting on the workplace, such as sex role prescriptions or labour market conditions
- Structural factors of the workplace such as hierarchical and power differentials, interactions between working groups and employees, and biases at the level of key decision-makers
- Individual factors, such as motivation, attitudes, personality and coping strategies

Understanding of the aetiologic factors of sexual harassment can help both clinicians and victims to assess the external factors contributing to the victim's situation. This not only provides an opportunity to analyse the problem and develop effective coping strategies but also prevents the likelihood of internalizing guilt, shame and responsibility for the situation of the victimized person.

6.2. Behavioural and Conceptual Models: Theories of Sexual Harassment

The aforementioned observations conclude that the occurrence of sexual harassment cannot be explained by any single cause or single theoretical framework.[9] The perception about sexual harassment is influenced by characteristic features of both the people who observe the sexual harassment situation and the contextual factors. Age, sex, job position, prior harassment history, etc., are examples of observer's characteristics, whereas the contextual factors are coercion, how physically attractive the initiator is and any differences in status between individuals. Important theories hypothesize the joint or sole contribution of power, reward, society, biology, individual perception, external factors and climate.

To explain the phenomenon of sexual harassment from different perspectives, several widely accepted models have been documented in the literature, which explain various aspects of sexual harassment of women at the place of their work. Terpstra and Baker[12] explain the aetiology of sexual harassment on three levels, namely:

- The *environmental* level, such as socio-economic inequities, sex role prescriptions, legal sanctions, and economic and labour market conditions
- The *organizational* level, such as hierarchical and power differentials, organizational climates, sex ratios, employee composition and disparate compensation and benefit structures
- The *individual* levels, such as motivation, attitudes, personality, communication, leadership styles and strategies of workplace victims and offenders

Four explanatory models remain the main focus of research on sexual harassment, three of which were developed by Tangri et. al.[13],[14] and the fourth by Gutek and associates.[15] The theories are conveniently classified as follows:

1. Single-factor theories
   a. Sociocultural
   b. Organizational
2. Sex role spillover theory
   a. Natural–biological
3. Social–cognitive theories
4. Multi-factor theory
   a. Four-factor theory

In order to understand it from a correct perspective, various levels of theory, whether a single-factor theory or multi-factorial, need to be differentiated. The general focus of single-factor theories is on one single factor hypothesized to contribute to the phenomena of sexual harassment, such as biology, social or cultural factors, while multi-factorial descriptions are overarching theories that include a number of single factors in the aetiological explanation of the phenomena of sexual harassment.

6.2.1. Single-factor Theories

6.2.1.1. Sociocultural Theory

Sociocultural theory is largely feminist in orientation pertaining to the social and political aspects in which sexual harassment occurs at a workplace.[16] Unequal distribution of resources such as power and status between men and women leads to sexual harassment as a consequence of a larger male-dominated social system, in which men have the final say in decision-making. Sexual harassment is the assertion of personal authority by men on the basis of their gender. Women are the victims in male-dominated populations in the workplace. Research by Tangri and Hayes[14] provides a stronger empirical evidence for organizational and sociocultural models of sexual harassment that view predatory male behaviour as arising from power and status disparities between two sexes. They explain sexually harassing behaviour by men as a result of the gender inequality and sexism that exists in a particular society or the work setting, stemming from power and status.[15] Feminist perspective of sexual harassment is linked to the phenomenon to the sexist ideology of male dominance and male superiority. Sexual harassment occurs because of the perceived inferior social status that serves to maintain the already established gender stratification by emphasizing sex role expectations. Women's subservient role is not only a consequence but also a cause of sexual harassment.[14] It helps to maintain the current male–female social status in accordance with the accepted sex status norms and, therefore, helps to maintain male dominance by intimidating and discouraging women from working beyond the domestic chores and bringing up of children. In organizations where sexual harassment thrives and their members carry over the already existing gender roles, women are the worst sufferers.

Also important is the way people are brought up during their childhood. Men and women are brought up and socialized in the manner of stereotyped interactions expected of males and females in a given culture; men are expected to be aggressive and dominating, and women to be passive, meek, submissive and accepting.[15] It makes men believe that their behaviours as aggressive and dominant are justified, whereas women blame themselves for being victimized and accept their role prescribed by the society.[13], [15] This concept is applicable to different settings of a society, including the workplace and educational institutions, thus promoting gender inequality and sexual harassment everywhere.

The feminist sociocultural theory is constructed on the basis of gender issues, patriarchy and dominance. Traditional Indian society, which is patriarch in form, has often been credited with bringing to light the issue of sexual harassment[17] and opening up newer avenues of enquiry for researchers. In these settings, in most of the cases, perpetrators are males, and harassment is more predominant in male-dominated workplaces. This observation goes in favour of the feminist sociocultural explanation[18]; however, this explanation appears to be over-inclusive and simplistic in nature. Later, the gender role socialization is expanded to include other behaviours. They permit more infusions of different behaviours to be accepted as normal for each gender.[19] No doubt, sexual harassment is all-pervasive, most people do not indulge in this antisocial conduct, and the overarching nature of the feminist sociocultural theory does not explain as to why this is the case.

6.2.1.2. Organizational Theory

Since all aspects of sexual harassment are not explainable by the sociocultural model, it should also be examined from institutional perspective which is the breeding place for harassment. Chances of sexual harassment increase when there is a power difference, prominent hierarchical structure, lesser number of women than men at the workplace and differences in status within the organization. Organizational theory explains the possibility of sexual harassment occurring when these factors are present.[14], [15] The structures and situations of the workplace present the opportunity to influence behaviour towards sexual harassment due to power and authority relationships and hierarchy. It is an abuse of power because of the following reasons:

- Ratios of males to females within those positions often lead to power abuse
- Norms and the social climate of organizational life permits abuse of power
- Non-availability of an effective formal and informal grievance redressal mechanism

Asymmetrical relations between supervisors, who are often males, and female subordinates show consistent negative reactions of victimized women. Victimized women have the tendency to suffer further harassment at higher levels of personal vulnerability and dependence on their jobs.

The explanation of sexual harassment revolves around the concept of power.[20] Because of this power play, in traditional Indian society where men typically enjoy more social and economic power than women, stereotypes prevail that men are goal-oriented, powerful, aggressive, decision-makers and breadwinners for the family and women are passive–receptive and family-oriented members whose primary duty is to raise the children and manage the household.[21], [22] The caste, an embodiment of the hierarchical social structure, a prominent feature of the Indian social fabric, permits men of higher castes to take liberty of sexual favours with a woman of lower caste. In the unorganized sector of workplace in rural areas, low-caste women summoned to work in the agricultural fields of landlords often suffer sexual harassment. Landlords' men (powerful) are at liberty to inflict harassment of all sorts on women, including sexual harassment.[23]

It is not only the males in power, organizational theory also predicts that harassment may also be perpetrated by females who occupy positions of power in the organization. Moreover, it is not always the powerful who is perpetrator, women in power also get sexually harassed by their subordinates at times. Sexual harassment inflicted by a colleague or a subordinate is, in fact, an attempt to gain power or at least equalize the power differences between the harasser and the victim within the organization. According to McLaughlin et al.,[24] the motivation for sexual harassment is not directed by sexual desire, but by exercising dominance and controlling women who are considered non-conformist having captured positions traditionally held by men. Sexual harassment is often deeply entrenched within organizational practices and policies, and therefore needs to be evaluated as per the specific situation. Chamberlain et al.[25] argue that the role of work culture either augments or minimizes such instances. Employees on contract and economically weaker employees are more vulnerable to sexual harassment. Therefore, this theory also explains the prospect of harassing individuals to reassert or equalize power differences.

In addition to the organizational power differentials, the immediate context of the harassment and factors such as permissiveness, gendered occupational lines and organizational ethics, norms and policies also affect the occurrence of sexual harassment.[26] It is often more prevalent where there is no clear anti-sexual harassment policy or complaint procedure mechanism, because at such places there is no fear of punishment. It also depends on how permissive the organizational climate is, the extent of perceived risk of the potential victims complaining, the possibility and availability of punishment for harassers and the consideration of complaints by the organization and colleagues. In the absence of adequate measures, the victim is scared of retaliation in case she complains and, therefore, chooses to silently suffers the unwanted behaviour of the harasser. This attitude strengthens the conviction of the organization of having no case of sexual harassment; since there are no complaints, no redressal mechanism provisions are required.

Regardless of making complaint, the victims go through the distress of harassment. Their distress does not minimize whether they respond actively or passively. Ideally, they should lodge a complaint to get justice; however, the gap between ideal and actual responses can be predicted on the perceived strength of the offending behaviour, the coping strategy chosen and the difference in organizational status between the harasser and the harassed. In case they complain, co-workers can become hostile and if they do not complain, they undergo emotional trauma and suffer silently. The subordinates fear taking action due to the threat of retaliation, while seniors avoid taking action due to the absence of institutional supportive policies.[27]

Organizational theory identifies and tests certain factors related to the occurrence of sexual harassment. Meta-analysis of various studies reveals that tolerance and the gendered nature of a workplace (proportion of women in a working group) play an important part in the occurrence of sexual harassment. It is the strongest empirical predictor of sexual harassment at a particular workplace. Where there is co-worker solidarity and better grievance redressal mechanisms, such organizations have lesser incidents of sexual harassment, whereas large organizations providing anonymity to their employees have more cases of women being sexually harassed.

Women colleagues at the workplace often stay away, dissuade from taking a justifiable stand in support of their own woman colleague without pausing to think that the same harassment could have happened with them as well. Support from the family members and society is crucial; in a majority of cases, family and colleagues strengthen a woman's feeling of helplessness by discouraging her to assert her right and advise her to stay quiet. Harassment is therefore not only limited to the behaviour confronted by women at the workplace; it also relates to the desperation that society and family can impose upon a woman by discouraging her to talk openly about it. These self-appointed agents of society and religion render a woman's attempt undesirable. This attitude is by and large very common in Indian society where women are often silenced for the fear of damage to the reputation likely to spoil marriage prospects of the victim if she happens to be unmarried.[28] This approach prevents aggrieved women from speaking and most of the cases go unreported.

This theory fails to focus on individual differences of people that can influence the occurrence of sexual harassment. Nevertheless, this theory focuses on the need for strong measures to combat sexual harassment within the organization.[29]

6.2.2. Sex Role Spillover Theory

Sex role spillover theory by Gutek and Morasch[15] describes sexual harassment behaviour as a behaviour carried over by the harasser to the workplace in accordance with gender-based role expectations. In this theory, the researchers explain that the contextual or situational factors and the gender-based beliefs and expectations of the harasser are combined to explain the phenomenon of sexual harassment. For example, the harasser believes that women should stay at home and look after their children, which is his gender-based belief about women, and there are chances that he will sexually harass a woman when he sees her at the workplace, which is a contextual or situational factor. According to this theory, to work together at a common platform, men and women who come from different sociocultural, educational, economic, religious and caste backgrounds bring with them their preconceived and pre-existing gender-based beliefs and convictions inherited from their respective sociocultural milieu for their application at the workplace; for example, women should not be employed in powerful positions, should wear burqa at workplace, should avoid eye-to-eye contact with men and should not mix up freely with males in public places. This theory explains that the perpetrator's beliefs about gender override the belief about workers' equality at the workplace. In such a conflicting situation, where the sex role stereotypes held by the perpetrator are different from the work roles of the particular genders at the place of work, harassment is likely to occur. Any contextual or situational factor may trigger such behaviour. Therefore, women may undergo sexual harassment in non-traditional work situations while being a taxi driver, a police officer or even a high-ranking CEO. This theory provides a more comprehensive explanation than any other theory and makes a more fitting tool for a close understanding of sexual harassment. Its only limitations are that it minimizes the impact of perpetrator characteristics or any other organizational or situational variables that may surface and thus fails to explain the phenomenon in depth and totality.[30], [31] However, some of the predictions of this theory have been tested and validated, particularly those applied to women. At the workplace where men are in majority, women actually feel they are treated differently from male colleagues, whereas women working in integrated settings are least likely to report sexual harassment, even of the most severe kind (i.e., sexual coercion or rape). However, this theory is unable to put forth parallel arguments for men and women as fundamental differences exist between female and male sex roles. More research is needed to understand the ways in which sex role spillover affects men, since there are lesser numbers of men in non-traditional work environments.

Sex role spillover is exacerbated by skewed sex ratios and influences women in two ways:

- Women employees at workplace or students in educational institutions of non-traditional settings under a token status will be treated as role deviants because their sex does not correspond to the sex roles normally associated with their occupation. They are perceived and treated differently from their male colleagues. Chances of discrimination are more in such situations.
- Women in traditionally female areas will experience a different type of sex role spillover, in which their sex role and work role merge together. They may not be aware that some of their treatment in the work setting is based on their sex.

These types of occupations tend to be devalued and under-rewarded because of the sex type associated with them. This model is compatible with the sociocultural model of harassment and gains support from research that demonstrates a greater incidence of sexual and gender-based harassment of women working in non-traditional areas.[32]

6.2.2.1. Natural–biological Theory

According to natural–biological theory, sexual harassment is an expression of sexual attraction, a natural element in mate-seeking. Males have a naturally stronger inner drive for sexual aggression to find a mate, as compared to women.[33] The higher sex drive in men creates a mismatch between the sexual desire of men and women, and the male sex drive manifests when they remain close at the workplace and leads to sexually aggressive expression, which culminates into sexual harassment. Men use power instrumentally in these situations, according to the evolutionary perspective, in order to obtain sexual access. Such attempts to gain sexual access are also likely to result in more coercive sexual behaviours, such as rape.

Natural–biological theory explains the sexually aggressive behaviour on the basis of innate human instincts potentially driving men to behave in such a manner. It also unifies evolutionary perspectives to explain sexual harassment as a natural expression of men. This theory has several limitations and does not appreciate the gravity of the serious adverse effects it causes on society and individual victims, because it trivializes the phenomenon as a normal reproductive ritual of males. It is unable to effectively explain sexual harassment because it appears to be treated in a very simplistic way, disregarding all societal and personal factors involved in its manifestation and the adverse impact it has. Moreover, hypothesis of this theory cannot be tested as replicability is not possible.

6.2.3. Social–cognitive Theories

Clinicians and researchers have acknowledged the importance of social–cognitive factors in the manifestation of sexual harassment at the workplace. These factors have been utilized to understand and explain the phenomenon in its relevant perspective. It is a matter of common observation that when a person commits deviant sexual acts, he often tries to diminish his feelings of guilt and shame by making excuses or justifications for his behaviour rationalizing his conduct. These excuses, justifications and rationalizations are, in fact, cognitive distortions or errors in the thinking process of the perpetrator that allow him to absolve himself of the responsibility he has to bear for his antisocial act.

Distorted thinking in sex offenders is a common occurrence; it is identified and explained frequently in research to explain the behaviour of the perpetrator. Distorted thinking commonly observed in perpetrators includes thinking errors such as denial, minimization of harm done, claiming the right or entitlement to behaviour and blaming the victim for his conduct.

There is sufficient empirical evidence and statistical support to infer that many sex offenders hold feelings of resentment and use these feelings as justification for their behaviours. They are more concerned about self-protective and self-serving aims due to low self-esteem, poor relationships with others and emotional discomfort or anxiety. If their behaviours are challenged, they reframe the situation to maintain feelings of self-worth.

Sexual offenders carry a strong sense of entitlement, with the belief that the need to offend was more important than the negative consequences experienced by the victim. The sense of entitlement in those offenders who commit the crime of incest leads them to decrease their self-control; thinking errors lead them to pay attention to information that is consistent with their distorted beliefs and to reject information that is inconsistent with their beliefs. Egocentricity or self-interest allows them to justify their deviant sexual behaviour on the basis that it satisfies the needs. The offender sees the victim as deserving of victimization. He has distorted views of what the victim wants from him. Sexual offenders display a consistent tendency to blame others or negate personal responsibility through their distorted thinking.

Cognitive distortion of sex offenders depends on how they process their internal and external cues. Research reveals that they misinterpret social cues and have difficulty recognizing and interpreting the emotional state of others, they are unable to make good choices on the basis of the information they perceive and they do not take perceptions of others into account in making decisions about their own behaviour.

These observations have been made in the studies on offenders of serious sexual crimes like rape and not the sexual harassers per say. Considering rape and sexual harassment in one continuum, social–cognitive theories that play a fundamental role in explaining rape,[34] it can be proposed that the same social–cognitive explanations may be used to understand sexual harassment. To date, however, empirical and theoretical attention to the social–cognitive processes that regulate workplace harassment is not enough and more research with a particular focus on sexual harassers is needed.

The following are the underlying fundamental components of a social–cognitive explanation of any phenomenon:

- Long-term memory content and structure
- Social–cognitive processing
- Cognitive products

Men who score high on the scale of likelihood to sexually harass (LSH) tend to link their sexuality with their power. In their experiment, Pryor, LaVite and Stoller[35] asked participants to view and memorize certain pairings of words that were neutral, sexually charged and power-related. Men who scored high on the scale of LSH remembered more sex–power pairings than had actually been presented compared to men who scored low on the scale of LSH. It shows that men who scored high on the scale of LSH perceived a frequent but otherwise illusory correlation between sex and power-related words.

The majority of men tease women for fun or entertainment without realizing that they are hurting the sentiments of women or creating a hostile environment around them. They may not be consciously aware that their behaviour could be harmful for others or the victims. Protest or resentment expressed by their victim is perceived by the harasser as an overreaction and exaggeration by them and they try to justify their remarks as light jokes to cheer them up or make them happy.[36]

In their study, Bargh et al.[37] demonstrated an automatic link between power and sex and its consequences in men high in likelihood to sexual harassment. The control condition was to complete words unrelated to the power concept to know how the priming procedure affects men's appraisal of a female confederate. Although low-scoring LSH men showed no difference in their sexual attraction towards the female confederate, men who scored high on the scale of LSH, who had been primed by the power words, found the female confederate more attractive; they would have liked to become more familiar with her provided there was any scope to do so.

Men who scored high on the scale of LSH did not appear to be aware of the underlying reason for finding the female confederate attractive, instead stating that the female's attractiveness was the underlying cause or that the female confederate was more of their type. These results suggest that placing men who hold certain structural schemas between power and sex into contextual positions of power is highly likely to affect their sexual behaviour towards women without them even being conscious of such harassment.[38] These findings may explain why some men who sexually harass appear to have difficulty in perspective taking, since, from their frame of reference, no sexual harassment has ever taken place. Men who engage in sexual coercion as measured by the LSH do not demonstrate the same effect of power on sexual attraction as men who engage in sexual aggression as measured by the scale of attraction to sexual aggression (ASA).[39]

Participants who scored high on the LSH scale had a bidirectional power–sex connection, whereas those who scored high on the ASA scale demonstrated a unidirectional power-then-sex association. The latter indicates that it is the power-then-sex association that is the critical factor for men who sexually harass women.[19]

6.2.4. Multi-factor Theory

This theory comprises four factors that explain sexual harassment at the workplace.

6.2.4.1. Four-factor Theory

Four-factor theory comprises some key components of many of the single-factor theories discussed already, which are consolidated into one theory. The researchers borrowed the concept of Finkelhor's four-factor theory of child sexual abuse[40] to develop the only multi-factor theory of sexual harassment which is widely used at present. According to the hypothesis proposed by O'Hare and O'Donohue,[41] the presence of four basic conditions for a case of sexual harassment could be there. These four conditions are as follows:

- The individual must be *induced* to harass (e.g., driven by any combination of power, control or sexual attraction)
- The individual must be able to work around *internal inhibitions* not to harass (e.g., moral restraints)

- The individual must be able to *overcome formal barriers* to harassment (e.g., specific organizational workplace barriers such as professionalism, ethics and institutional policy)
- The individual must be able to *overcome victim's resistance* (e.g., assertiveness or the victim's relative status within the workplace).

To test the predictive validity of their theory, the authors used a self-reporting data collection mechanism from female faculty, staff and students. They hypothesized that women who reported themselves to be more physically attractive would report higher frequencies of sexual harassment. Women with more workspace privacy, greater knowledge of complaint procedures and institutional policy and who worked in an environment characterized by gender equality, professionalism and more equal sex ratios would report less harassment. Finally, women who rated themselves more feminine as measured via Bem's Sex-Role Inventory[42] and who held lower positions within their organization were more likely to suffer harassment. The four-factor theory provides a better explanation than any single-factor theory (organizational, sex role spillover or sociocultural) of sexual harassment. The key factors behind sexual harassment were found to be poor knowledge about complaint procedures, unprofessional work culture and sexist attitudes of harassers.[43]

The conclusion drawn from these results points to the fact that harassment intervention should proceed at the organizational level, since this is where the predominant risk of sexual harassment occurs. A well-defined redressal mechanism and an effective anti-sexual harassment policy of the organization will go a long way to prevent sexual harassment at the workplace.

The primary strength of the four-factor theory of sexual harassment is that it combines previously isolated individual theories, such as sociocultural and organizational, into one multi-factorial theory (evidence of unifying power and apparent explanatory depth and external consistency). This theory also explains relatively stronger empirical adequacy compared with previously discussed single-factor theories. It is a great step forward for a field that has been primarily dominated by relatively impoverished single-factor explanations of sexual harassment, unable to explain various aspects of sexual harassment.

Multi-factorial theory also has some limitations for its usefulness as a resource for professionals working on sexual harassment. Only the organizational and victim-relevant factors of the theory have been adequately tested. There is a very large explanatory and empirical gap in our understanding of sexual harassment behaviour. Further exploration is needed to address certain unanswered issues.[42]

The work culture of the workplace plays a significant role in either increasing or decreasing instances of sexual harassment. Organizations with co-worker solidarity and better grievance redressal mechanisms face less of these problems, whereas larger organizations that provide anonymity to their workers report more cases of women being sexually harassed.[25], [43], [44]

According to these theories, typically, sexual harassers lack guilt and are more likely to endorse myths related to sexual assault, blame the victimized women for their own sexual harassment conduct instead of accepting or even acknowledging their fault, rather, they often blame women's behaviour for what they perceive as seductive and provocative, compelling them to sexually assault such victims. They justify their behaviour by exonerating themselves with their own explanations in such situations. They have problems identifying the unfairness of their act because of their distorted cognition. Harassers hold harassment-supportive cognitive content that biases their cognitive processing, leading to automatic and unconscious, harassment-type behaviours.

Although the research does not provide a clear social–cognitive explanation for sexual harassment, it indicates some substantial empirical evidence for adapting such a theory for the explanation of sexual harassment. The essence of social–cognitive theory is that men who engage in antisocial behaviours hold behaviour-supporting belief content in long-term memory that bias their social information processing in an antisocial manner. That is the reason why many of the rapists justify their act as genuine and as a result of victim's sexually inviting gestures and behaviour.

Those who are involved in the treatment of sexual harassment have yet to find a clear cause for sexual harassment behaviour. No doubt, researchers have given several plausible explanations with their important findings about the genesis of sexual harassment behaviour, there are still many unanswered questions about sexual harassment. The essence of the research findings can be concluded as follows:

- There is no single factor or cause for occurrence of sexual harassment, a combination of factors possibly contributes to the manifestation of sexual harassment behaviour.
- Adverse childhood experiences, poor attachment to others, particularly caregivers, contribute to the development of sexual offending behaviours.
- Sexual harassment could possibly be a learned behaviour and the learning of harassment behaviour is influenced by reinforcement and punishment available in a particular society (social aspects of sexual harassment are covered in detail in the next chapter).
- Cognitive distortions or faulty thinking errors and the related patterns maintain deviant sexual behaviour.
- Exposure to sexually violent material contributes to hostility towards women. Acceptance of myths about unwanted sexual conduct, decreased empathy and compassion for victims and increased acceptance of physical violence towards women contribute immensely to the occurrence of sexual harassment behaviour.
- Sexual harassers have a problem with self-regulation of emotions and impulse control. Both of these problems are related to sexual harassment behaviour, but a causal link has not been clearly established so far.

Those who indulge in sexual coercion, but maintain negative attitudes towards women, go for short-term relationships. Self-interested motivation contributes to aggressive thoughts than compassion or empathy. Those who indulge in sexual harassment behaviour have strong self-interested motivation.

References

[1] Lenhart S. *Clinical Aspects of Sexual Harassment and Gender Discrimination: Psychological Consequences and Treatment Interventions.* New York, NY; Hove: Brunner-Routledge; 2004.
[2] World Bank. *India Development Update, March 2018: India's Growth Story.* Washington, DC: World Bank; 2018. Available at https://openknowledge. worldbank.org/handle/10986/29515 (accessed on 7 December 2019).

[3] Fletcher EK, Pande R, Moore CT. *Women and Work in India: Descriptive Evidence and a Review of Potential Policies* (Faculty Working Paper No. 339). Cambridge, MA: Harvard College; 2017.

[4] World Economic Forum. *The Global Gender Gap Report 2018*. Geneva: World Economic Forum; 2018.

[5] International Labour Organization. *India Labour Market Update*. New Delhi: ILO Country Office for India; 2017. Available at https://www.ilo.org/wcmsp5/groups/public/---asia/---ro-bangkok/---sro-new_delhi/documents/publication/wcms_568701.pdf (accessed on 17 December 2020).

[6] Pryor JB, Giedd JL, Williams KB. Social psychological model for predicting sexual harassment. *Journal of Social Issues*. 1995;51(1–2):69–78.

[7] Roos PA, Gatta ML. The Gender Gap in Earnings: Trends, Explanations and Prospects. In: G. Powell, ed. *Handbook of Gender and Work*. Thousand Oaks, CA: SAGE; 1999. pp. 95–124.

[8] Dupuis P. Improve Workplace Experience to Un-lease Employee Potential. *The Times of India*, 2019. Available at https://timesofindia.indiatimes.com/business/india-business/improve-workplace-experience-to-unleash-employee-potential/articleshow/69432701.cms (accessed on 17 December 2020).

[9] Jacobs JA. The Sex Segregation of Occupations: Prospects for the 21st Century. In: G. Powell, ed. *Handbook of Gender and Work*. Thousand Oaks, CA: SAGE; 1999. pp. 125–144.

[10] Cooper CL, Lewis S. Gender and the Changing Nature of Work. In: G. Powell, ed. *Handbook of Gender and Work*. Thousand Oaks, CA: SAGE; 1999. pp. 37–47.

[11] Skaine R. *Power and Gender: Issues in Sexual Dominance and Harassment*. Jefferson, NC: McFarland; 1996.

[12] Terpstra DE, Baker DD. Psychological and demographic correlates of perceptions of sexual harassment. *Genetic, Social and General Psychology Monographs*. 1986;112(4): 459–478.

[13] Tangri SS, Burt MR, Johnson LB. Sexual harassment at work: Three explanatory models. *Journal of Social Issues*. 1982;38(4):33–54.

[14] Tangri S, Hayes S. Theories of Sexual Harassment. In: W. O'Donohue, ed. *Sexual Harassment: Theory, Research, and Treatment*. Boston, MA: Allyn & Bacon; 1997. pp. 112–128.

[15] Gutek BA, Morasch B. Sex ratios, sex-role spill-over and sexual harassment of women at work. *Journal of Social Issues*. 1982;38(4):55–57.

[16] Farley L. *Sexual Shakedown: The Sexual Harassment of Women on the Job*. New York, NY: McGraw-Hill; 1987.

[17] Farrell M. Sexual Harassment in the Indian Workplace: An Exploratory Study in Civil Society Organisations. *Madhya Pradesh Journal of Social Sciences*. 2013;18(1). Available at https://www.questia.com/library/journal/1G1–412800303/sexual-harassment-in-the-indian-workplace-an-exploratory (accessed on 17 December 2020).

[18] Gruber JE. How women handle sexual harassment: A literature review. *Sociology and Social Science.* 1989;74(1):3–9.

[19] Ward T, Polaschek DLL, Beech AR. *Theories of Sexual Offending. Wiley Series in Forensic Clinical Psychology.* Hoboken, NJ: Wiley; 2006.

[20] Newton-Smith W. *A Companion to the Philosophy of Science.* Oxford: Blackwell; 2002.

[21] Cleveland J, McNamara K. In: Understanding Sexual Harassment: Contributions from Research on Domestic Violence and Organizational Change. M. Stockdale, ed. *Sexual Harassment in the Workplace.* Thousand Oaks, CA: SAGE; 1996. pp. 217–240.

[22] Allgeier ER, McCormick NB. *Changing Boundaries: Gender Roles and Sexual Behaviour.* Palo Alto, CA: Mayfield; 1983.

[23] Jiloha RC. *The Native Indian: In Search of Identity.* New Delhi: Blumoon Books; 1995.

[24] McLaughlin H, Uggen C, Blackstone A. Sexual harassment, workplace authority and the paradox of power. *American Sociological Review.* 2012;77(4):625–648.

[25] Lindsay C, Crowley M, Tope D, Hodson R. Sexual harassment in organisational context. *Work and Occupations.* 2008;35(3):262–295.

[26] Eagly AH, Mladinic A. Gender stereotypes and attitudes toward women and men. *Personality and Social Psychology Bulletin.* 1989;111:543–558.

[27] Salin D, Tenhiala A, Roberge ME, Berdahl J. 'I wish I had…' target reflections on responses to workplace mistreatment. *Human Relations.* 2014;3(7):18–27.

[28] Sahgal P, Dang A. Experiences of women managers and organisations. *Economic & Political Weekly.* 2017;52(22):13–15.

[29] Gannon TA, Pina A. Firesetting: Psychopathology, theory and treatment. *Aggression and Violent Behaviour.* 2009;15(3):126–138. Available at https://psycnet.apa.org/record/2010-05791-002 (accessed on 17 December 2020).

[30] Willness C, Steel P, Lee K. A meta-analysis of the antecedents and consequences of workplace sexual harassment. *Personnel Psychology.* 2007;60(1):127–162.

[31] Fain TC, Anderton DL. Sexual harassment: Organizational context and diffuse status. *Sex Roles.* 1987;17(5–6):291–311.

[32] Shullman S, Fitzgerald L. *The Development and Validation of an Objectively Scored Measure of Sexual Harassment* (Paper presented at the American Psychological Association, Los Angeles, CA; 1985).

[33] Barak A, Pitterman Y, Yitzhaki R. An empirical test of the role of power differential in originating sexual harassment. *Basic and Applied Social Psychology.* 1995;17(4):479–517.

[34] Drieschner K, Lange A. A review of cognitive factors in the aetiology of rape: Theories, empirical studies and implications. *Clinical Psychology Review.* 1999;19(1):57–77.

[35] Pryor JB, LaVite CM, Stoller LM. A social psychological analysis of sexual harassment: The person/situation interaction. *Journal of Vocational Behavior.* 1993;42(1)68–83.

[36] Fitzgerald LF. Sexual Harassment: The Definition and Measurement of a Construct. In: M. Paludi, ed. Sexual Harassment on College Campuses: Abusing the Ivory Power. Albany, NY: SUNY Press; 1996. pp. 25–47.

[37] Bargh JA, Raymond P, Pryor JB, Strack F. The attractiveness of the underlying: An automatic power–sex association and its consequences for sexual harassment. *Journal of Personality and Social Psychology.* 1995;68(5):768–781.

[38] Polaschek DLL, Ward T. The implicit theories of potential rapists: What our questionnaires tell us. *Aggression and Violent Behavior.* 2002;7(4):385–406.

[39] Malamuth N, Dean KE. Attraction to Sexual Aggression. In: A. Parrot & L. Bechhofer, eds. *Acquaintance Rape: The Hidden Crime.* New York, NY: Wiley; 1991. pp. 57–69.

[40] Ward T, Hudson SM. Finkelhor's pre-condition model of child sexual abuse: A critique. *Journal of Psychology, Crime and Law.* 2001;7(4).291–307.

[41] O'Hare E, O'Donohue W. Sexual harassment: Identifying risk factors. *Archives of Sexual Behavior.*1998;27(6):561–579.

[42] Bem SL. Gender schema theory and its implications for child development: Raising gender-aschematic children in a gender-schematic society. *Journal of International Relations.* 1983;8(4):598–616.

[43] De Coster S, Estes SB, Mueller C. Routine activities and sexual harassment in the workplace. *Work and Occupations.* 1999;26(1):21–49.

[44] Quinn B. Sexual harassment and masculinity: The power and meaning of 'girl watching'. *Gender & Society.* 2002;16(3):386–402.

Social Aspects of Sexual Harassment

With genetic and biochemical factors that make up the biological substratum of behaviour, sociocultural factors contribute immensely to the expression of human behaviour in general and sexual behaviour in particular.[1] Social *norms, mores* and *sanctions* guide the regulation of a person's behaviour in a given sociocultural milieu.[2] Socialization imparts the skills and habits required for expression of a particular behaviour, including sexual behaviour, and makes the person appreciate what society expects as appropriate rather than inappropriate.

Most societies adhere to hetero-normativity or heterosexual unions as a normal expression of sex with the consensual approval of the involved parties. Since heterosexuality involves males and females, mutual agreement of both parties makes it acceptable to society in general and the law of the land in particular. The acceptance or rejection of non-consensual or forced sexual expression varies from society to society depending on how sexuality is viewed in a particular social context. Marital rape by a husband with his lawful wife is a normal union in some societies, while others take it otherwise.[3]

There are no universally agreed sexual norms applicable to all societies. Sexual norms in a particular society depend upon the extent to which it allows its expression. Currently, hetero-normativity in societies is evaluated along a continuum of consensual approach or mutual agreement on forced sex or rape, with mutual love as the privileged mode of sexual expression.

Sexual aggression against women, a historical phenomenon in all cultures, varies from society to society depending on the status of women that societies accord during a particular period. Disrobing Draupadi of her clothes in full court view in Mahabharata, though frowned upon by some, was accepted and held appropriate by the powerful, though it could be an offence under the Indian Penal Code in current times. The historical and cultural context of a workplace may carry a different meaning for different people working at one place.

Sexual harassment of women involves intrapersonal and interpersonal factors as well as social and cultural variables. The role of social processes is quite important as explained by various hypotheses based on the relationship between social interaction and sexual aggression.

Sociocultural constructions of gender and power play a crucial role in unfolding of sexual behaviour and may manifest themselves in different forms. Although such behaviour manifests at the individual level, theory holds that *cultural* forces support and perpetuate it. Although sexual harassment is culturally driven, very few studies address cultural influences on sexual harassment processes. The social aspects of sexual harassment are discussed further.

7.1. Factors Influencing Sexual Behaviour Socialization

How socializing agents impress sexual norms on the members of a society depend on three primary agents: religion, law and media.

7.1.1. Religion

By and large, all religions dictate their adherents to follow the proper and holy ways as per the tenets of religious teachings that they should accept to live their lives. Religions regulate the sexual behaviour of their followers according to the commandments embodied in the scriptures of these religions. Christianity values abstinence from sexual expression and believes that to engage in sexual activity, men and women should wait until marriage. Followers of the Jewish faith promote sexual activity between married couples to reinforce the marital bond and produce children. Like most of the other denominations of monotheistic religions, Islam encourages sexual activity, as long as it is practised by married partners. In the Indian subcontinent, where several religions and people constitute a multiple society, with their diverse faiths and social mannerism, sexuality is expressed as per the dictates of their religious teachings. The traditional Hindu religious group, a majority society in India, an embodiment of caste system, assigning inferior and superior status to its members, allows its followers to express their sexuality according to their place in the hierarchical system. The high-caste Hindus share a cultural bias; they observe self-restraint, bordering upon asceticism. They observe several taboos, succumbing to many pleasures including sex.[4] Complete abstinence from flesh and observance of celibacy is considered meritorious for a pious Hindu, not only because religion demands so but also because it is believed to be beneficial for health and spiritual well-being. Sexual dealings in the traditional low castes of the Hindu social order were quite lax and sexual irregularities were commonly observed in the members of the lower castes. Premarital immorality was common, and a visitor had the liberty with the host's wife or daughter. Sexual harassment was acceptable to some extent in these social groups.[5]

People may not strictly or stringently adhere to the guidelines of their faith; an individual learns from childhood through the instructions from elders regarding appropriate and inappropriate sexual behaviour in the context of his or her religion. Almost all religions consider sexual harassment of a woman inappropriate and discourage such behaviour. *Religion not only frowns upon the occurrence of sexual harassment but also provides guidelines.*

7.1.2. Legal System

The law directs a society to adhere to the rules and regulations of the land warranting a punitive action in the case of a violation. For socially acceptable sexual behaviour, individuals are instructed on proper sexual conduct through abiding by the law, which simultaneously reflects and creates social norms regarding sexual behaviour. Law in India teaches citizens to believe that prostitution, rape, adultery and sodomy are improper forms of sexual expression and are hence illegal and liable to punitive action.

Legal status of gay provides an understanding of how the law mirrors and moulds Indian understanding of sexual norms in historical perspective. Until recently, laws prohibiting anal sex between two consenting males had been on the books in the Indian Penal Code. However, the attitude of society towards sexual orientation has significantly changed during the last few years, and Lesbian, Gay, Bisexual and Transgender (LGBT) people are better tolerated and accepted in Indian society, especially in large cities. However, for the fear of discrimination and disgrace, most LGBT people in India remain closeted, because, at large, society still sees homosexuality as shameful and disgraceful. Discrimination is still present, particularly in rural areas, where LGBT people often face rejection from their families; they are forced to have heterosexual marriage to stay in mainstream society. However, recently, a Gurgaon court recognized lesbian marriage[6] and the Supreme Court of the country decriminalized homosexuality by declaring Section 377[1] unconstitutional.[7] It called 2013 ruling 'arbitrary and retrograde'. Historically, homosexuality was never a crime in ancient India but was criminalized by the British during their rule and since then it carried a social taboo, and society often looked down on homosexuals.[8]

In another development, recently, the Delhi High Court affirmed the application of Section 354A to transgender (women) victims of sexual harassment. Now, transgenders can also pursue a criminal case of sexual harassment against their perpetrators.[9] The Court, in an inclusive move, has ruled that now transgender persons can use Section 354A to register complaints of sexual harassment. The judgement brings the transgenders at par with males and females for their fundamental rights.

---

[1] Available at https://en.wikipedia.org/wiki/Section_377_of_the_Indian_Penal_Code (accessed on 18 December 2020).

The Adultery Law[10] was often criticized as gender discriminatory in the sense that women could not be prosecuted for adultery. However, it was also argued that the adultery laws maintained social norms in societies justifying violence and oppression of women in certain societies of India, or in the form of individual acts of violence committed by husbands or relatives against women, such as honour killings and beatings. The law treated a married woman as the 'property' of her husband on the ground that her relationship with other married persons depended on the 'consent or connivance of her husband', which also meant that a woman could sleep outside her marriage with the 'consent' of her husband. The law gave power to a man to control the sexuality of his lawfully wedded wife in order to assert the sole claim to her body and use it the way he wanted. In law and in practice, the United Nations Working Group on Discrimination Against Women and Girls was deeply concerned about the criminalization and penalization of women through adultery law in India and stated that such a law and its enforcement caused discrimination and violence against women.[11] The National Commission for Women also criticized the law of being anti-feminist and consequently recommended that the law be deleted or reduced to a civil offence.[12]

The Court stated that the law is based on discrimination as it punishes only the man and spares the woman. There is no rationale in treating one party involved in adultery as a victim and the other as a criminal. The premise that the woman is always the 'victim' not only undermines the notion of women's agency but is also completely unfair to men in current times when women hold positions of authority in almost all fields.

In a historic judgement, the Supreme Court struck down this 158-year-old colonial-era law. Section 497 of Indian Penal Code, 1860, and Section 198 of Criminal Procedure Code, 1973, which prohibits wives from filing adultery complaints, were declared unconstitutional by the five judges' bench, thereby decriminalizing the offence of adultery.[10]

The impact of this judgement on marriages in India will be far-reaching, and it is impossible to ignore the adverse fallout. In a country with steeply rising divorce rates and cases of marital infidelity, the decriminalization of adultery is likely to endanger the institution of marriage. Not only does it create the risk of fostering extramarital affairs, it leaves little children in the lurch, catalysing the break-up of marriages. It is likely that cases of sexual harassment of women will increase.

Law plays a crucial role in moulding of social norms in a given society. The law in India disapproves sexual harassment in one way or another, but it is still highly common at the places of work and educational institutions. In view of its gravity, the Supreme Court in its historical judgement laid down *Vishaka* Guidelines[13] to be followed by establishments and educational institutions in dealing with complaints of sexual harassment until legislation to deal with the problem was enacted. The Sexual Harassment of Women at Workplace (Prevention, Prohibition and Redressal) Act, 2013,[14] came to ensure safe working spaces for women and to build enabling work environments that respect women's right to equality of status and opportunity. Consistent with the *Vishaka* judgement, the Act aims to ensure women's right to workplace equality and freedom from sexual harassment.

7.1.3. Media

During recent times, people have been encountering normative discourses of sexuality through the media which has created a tremendous impact on their minds. People tend to replicate the behaviours that they see on television serials, in movies or in the print media. Sexual representations of this type are typically hetero-normative and contribute significantly to viewers' sexual offending behaviour. For example, currently pornography is in use on a large scale and presents a way in which people are socialized towards particular sexual practices through the media. For some people, pornography serves as a model for sexually aggressive behaviour that encourages them to engage in behaviours depicted in pornographic images that they viewed.

Before media's meddling with the subject of sexuality, the traditional Indian society permitted sexuality to be handled at an appropriate stage by the elders, grandparents, aunts and uncles. Boys were educated on sexual matters before their marriage by their married friends or uncles and the girls by their mothers or aunts who educated the girls about menstrual hygiene and the secrets of sex life.[4] This form of sex education used to help prepare young people for their sex life. However, in contemporary society, the traditional methods of sex education are no longer enough, and flooding of information has made younger people vehemently explore newer methods that are easily available, accessible and affordable with preserved anonymity. Due to its easy availability and affordability, pornography has made the world a highly sexualized culture,[15] and the increased frequency and explicitness of sexual content in mainstream media in recent times has impacted the sexual behaviour greatly.[16], [17] Triple theory by Cooper, Delmonico and Burg[18] attributes the phenomenon to affordability, anonymity and accessibility. Viewing pornography online maintains anonymity; a person's status remains unknown to others and may not have the same impact as it does in the face-to face world. Regardless of status, wealth, race, gender, age or other characteristics, everyone starts on a level playing field. This lack of hierarchy on the Internet has its advantages; however, it is disadvantageous for populations that are equally exposed, such as children. In our society, hierarchies are maintained for certain behaviours, including the division between adults and children, that can be easily downplayed in the online world.

The role of pornography is implicated in the aetiology of sexual harassment as well. Cross-cultural studies correlate the use of pornography in the general population and the incidence of sexual crimes. Some studies have examined the effect of these materials on normal individuals in the laboratory and the effects of these materials on sexual harassers. Some studies[19] have compared the similarities and differences between sex offenders and other males.

Viewing pornography is quite common among college students who have reported the highest levels of pornography use.[20] This may be due to the fact that students are at a crucial stage in life where they are making choices that affect their sexuality. Exposure to pornography among students begins as early as 10 years of age, with a highest exposure being between 16 years and 18 years. In a study, pornography viewing was reported among students with 96.3 per cent of respondents exposed to some forms of pornographic material. A small percentage (5%) of respondents was exposed to it on a daily basis. [21] Studies also reveal that pornography is instrumental in moulding the sexual behaviour of many people. The majority of habitual users (men) between 18 and 34 years of age viewed at least one pornographic website a month and many of them attempted to incorporate the actions they witnessed in pornography into their own sex lives. There have been multiple meta-analyses to establish a link between pornography and sexual aggression.[22] Meta-analyses of the 1990s suggested no association between pornography and rape-supportive attitudes in non-experimental studies.[23] However, a meta-analysis by Hald, Malamuth and Yuen[17], [22] establishes a link between the viewing of violent pornography and rape-supportive attitudes in some groups of men, particularly when moderating variables were taken into consideration.[24]

In the sexually violent pornography, women are often shown in helpless, humiliating or degrading situations portrayed as the victims of forced or coerced sexual interactions. Sexually violent pornography has immense impact on the attitude of the viewer towards women and internalizes myths about rape to develop prejudicial, stereotyped or false beliefs about rape, rape victims and rapists. These attitudes and beliefs are often false but widely held, which deny or justify male aggression against women.

Repeated and regular watching of sexually aggressive pornography increases hostility towards women, accepts rape myths, decreases empathy and compassion for victims with increased acceptance of physical violence towards women. The women depicted in pornography as desiring and enjoying both sexual activity and degradation reinforces the attitude of violence in the viewers.

Child pornography is another type of pornography that plays a role in the aetiology of sexually harassing behaviour. Some individuals use child pornography to internalize aggressive behaviour as acceptable and adopt it into their own behaviour.

7.2. Sociocultural Issues and Sexual Harassment

Early childhood experiences contribute immensely to shaping the adult behaviour of an individual. Children who become victims of sexual abuse during their early lives grow into sexually harassing adults. While sexual harassers have a stronger history of childhood sexual abuse than people in the general population, all those abused sexually during their childhood do not become sexual harassers. Moreover, women who were abused as children did not turn into sexual harassers as adults.

However, a significant percentage of sexual harassers does report the experience of being sexually abused as children. This experience influences their learning responsible for their harassing adult behaviour.

There are certain variables that determine whether or not sexually deviant behaviour will manifest in adult life. They also determine the patterns of behaviour. Childhood experience of sexual abuse gets internalized as a normal or pleasurable experience likely to adopt a belief system that is favourable to sexually harassing behaviour in his adult life. Different thought patterns about early life abuse may lead to the development of sexually abusive behaviours in victims in later life. The internalization of sexual abuse as a normal or pleasurable experience in response to one's own abuse is likely to grow into an adult who views sexually harassing acts as less harmful and more pleasurable to the victim.

There are certain other factors that link childhood sexual abuse and later sexually harassing behaviours. These factors include the age of victimization in childhood, the relationship between the perpetrator and the child victim, the type of sexual act inflicted on the child and amount of force used, the duration of the abuse and the number of perpetrators. The younger the victim, the more violent and intrusive the sexual acts in adult life, the longer the duration of abuse and the greater the number of perpetrators, the more sexually deviant behaviour will develop in such victims in adult life.

Historically, in societies where sexual coercion of women was common, certain social factors played a significant role which promoted sexual violence against women. There were high levels of sexual assault on women in societies characterized by patrilocality and high levels of feuding. A number of social variables have been identified with a positive correlation with sexual assault frequency in tribal societies. Some of these variables are as follows:

- Raiding other groups for wives
- Interpersonal violence among two tribes

- Belief in male toughness and its link with inflicting violence against women
- Ideology of female inferiority, lack of power and their submissive nature and dependence on males
- Negative attitude towards women contributes immensely for violence against women

Social instability due to war or other social unrest often leads not only to sexual aggression in tribal communities but also in modern societies where aggression against women manifests in various forms during the times of social turmoil. Although stranger's assault has received attention historically, assaults and aggression within families and against friends and acquaintances have only recently become a topic of interest and focus. Various factors have contributed to this changing scenario, which include pressure from a number of advocacy groups, particularly women's groups, which describe male sexual aggression as a part of the social process that maintains the system of sexual stratification.[25]

Sociologists believe that sexual harassment behaviour is a social and not a natural phenomenon, prevalent only in certain type of society and not by an external immutable human nature. In India, at the time of partition of the country, when Hindu–Muslim riots occurred, sexual assault on women manifested at a large scale in which the women of one community were sexually assaulted by the men of another, asserting their identity and humiliating the other by sexually assaulting their women. The heinous violence—disfigurement, mutilation, castration, branding, slashing the breast—were the expressions that were countable in a continuum with sexual harassment.

Deep-rooted cultural and psychological reasons have played a role in sexual coercion of the women. Prejudice and deep-seated hatred latent in peacetimes erupted with extreme virulence during the community conflict, making women their targets.[26]

Cross-cultural studies of sexual aggression suggest certain social variables related to the relative positions that men and women hold in their societies. Feminists have held the view that sexual intimidation through assault or harassment plays a role in maintaining the relationship of social power. According to Brownmiller,[27], [28] sexual intimidation is simply the ultimate exercise of power by men over women. Rape in slavery and rape in wartime are two overt examples. But rapists also operate within an emotional setting or a dependent relationship that provides its own hierarchical, authoritarian structure that weakens a victim's resistance, distorts her perspective and confounds her will.[29]

In certain societies, gender norms are quite liberal and sexual acts of a mild nature are ignored as a normative expression. It is an indicator of the permissiveness of a society towards sexual harassment. These societies view sexual harassment by males as manly behaviour which women could expect from males and women who object to such expressions are considered, in fact, oversensitive and troublemaker. Blaming the victim and minimization of the consequences of sexual assault have been variously described throughout professional and scientific literature. Psychoanalytic studies[30] have long emphasized women's unconscious masochistic wishes to be raped or sexually assaulted.

For social philosopher Margaret Crouch,[31] sexual harassment of women is intended to keep them in their prescribed social place in male-dominated public spaces. According to her, pinching, pawing, staring, leering, whistling, sexual remarks, unsolicited touching with one pretext or the other and sexual assault are ways of communicating; women are open games for gazing, speaking, touching—they are powerless to stop it. These behaviours not only limit women's freedom of movement but also prevent them from availing opportunities at educational institutions, at work and in politics. The male behaviour deprives them of their fundamental right to freedom.

It makes them feel powerless, which is amplified when the behaviour is anonymous—no name, no face, to accuse. It is thriving online due to the anonymity the Internet provides to harass women in current times.[32]

Jan Crosthwaite and Graham Priest[33] define sexual harassment as a behaviour that limits the prospects of self-development, realization of goals and material success in women. This explains how male behaviour typically affects the victims to experience their powerlessness, which causes sexual harassment. Gender class subjugation is the fundamental feature of sexual harassment.

7.3. Workplace Environment and Sexual Harassment in Social Context

Isolated and infrequently trodden places provide a fertile ground for the perpetrators to harass a woman where the possibility of witnessing or intervention by others is minimum and the perpetrator can fearlessly express his conduct for his vicarious gratification. Lonely places embolden the perpetrator not only for the lack of being witnessed but also for the non-availability of possible help the victim can get from others.[34] Incidents of sexual harassment are more frequently experienced by women working in offices where the majority are men with male-dominated leadership and where the typical job or occupation is considered atypical for women.[35]-[37] In particular, the higher the extent of male domination at the workplace, the more incidents of sexual harassment will occur. In a study on the effect of gender equilibrium in the workplace, when comparing women who work in gender-balanced working groups (i.e., equal numbers of men and women in the working group) with those who work with almost all men, researchers reported that women in the latter category had 1.68 times more sexual harassment.[24], [38], [39]

Domestic care workers, hotel waitresses, housekeepers and agricultural workers, who often work in isolated spaces, report higher incidents of sexual harassment than average rates.[40] In India, where the agricultural labour force constitutes mainly women from the lower strata of rural society, these women often become victims of sexual assault of landowners and their men. It is common for landlords to sexually exploit these women without much resistance.[5] Educational institutions, particularly universities and professional colleges, where students depend heavily on their guides and mentors who are often males, for their professional and academic enhancement, female students become targets of sexual harassment by their teachers and seniors. According to National Domestic Workers Alliance and the University of Chicago,[40], [41] 36 per cent of live-in workers surveyed had been harassed, threatened, insulted or verbally abused in the previous 12 months.

Most cases of sexual harassment in India's educational institutions go unreported because of various reasons and the cases that come to light represent only the tip of the iceberg. According to the National Violence Against Women Prevention Research Center (NVAWPRC), 40 per cent to 60 per cent of female students and working women in educational institutions reported having experienced sexual harassment.[42], [43] The perceived lack of organizational sanctions against sexual harassment heighten the risk of sexual harassment perpetuation. Lack of organizational initiative in addressing the problem is perceived in three different forms. These are as follows: (a) the complainant will be at the risk of being targeted, (b) there will be no punitive action against the offender and (c) the complaints will not be taken seriously.[44] In environments where sexual harassment is perceived to be more permissive, women are more likely to be harassed directly[37], [45] and to witness harassment of others.[24] A meta-analysis that combined data from 41 studies with a total sample size of nearly 70,000 respondents found perception of organizational tolerance to be the most reliable predictor of workplace sexual harassment.[38] In a recent national survey of 615 working men,[45] it was revealed that the organizations without guidelines against sexual harassment had more cases of sexual harassment.

Social situations in which sexist views are modelled can enable, facilitate or even encourage sexually harassing behaviours, while, conversely, positive role models can inhibit sexually harassing behaviour.[46] Women working in occupations that focus on traditionally male-oriented tasks may be especially vulnerable to harassment and assault. In a survey from the early 1990s, close to 6 in 10 women working in the construction business, where their number was lesser than that of men, reported being touched inappropriately or asked for sexual favours.[47] In another study, 3 in 10 women construction workers reported experiencing sexual harassment daily or frequently. A 2014 study in the military estimated that 26 per cent of active duty women had experienced sexual harassment or gender discrimination in the past one year, including 5 per cent having experienced one or more sexual assaults.[48] The National Academy of Sciences recently documented high levels of harassment of women faculty and staff in academic institutions in science, engineering and medicine, with women in academic medicine reporting more frequent gender harassment than their female colleagues in science and engineering.[49]

In one study, male teachers of a college having intention to harass women were found more likely to indulge in sexual exploitation of female trainees.[50] Viewing a sexist movie enhanced the tendency among even the less sexist men to perform actions amounting to sexual harassment. In another experiment, men who viewed sexist TV programme excerpts were more likely to send women unwanted sexist jokes and to profess a willingness to sexual coerce, compared to men who watched programmes showing young, successful women in professional domains such as science, culture and business.[51] Sexual harassment is less likely if such behaviours are deemed unacceptable by authority figures. So while social situations may not quite function as triggers for existing tendencies to sexually harass, they can act as a force encouraging or discouraging sexual harassment, demonstrating the power of practised social norms.

7.4. Working in Power Differentials

Power differentials within hierarchical organizations enhance exploitation of the vulnerable. Hierarchical work environments, as seen in the armed forces, where the authority of those in power is not questioned, tend to have higher rates of sexual harassment than organizations with less power differential between organizational levels, like the private sector organizations.[52] A recent incident illustrates this fact when an army court-martial recommended the dismissal of a decorated major general in Indian Army after a woman army captain accused him of sexually harassing her when posted together in a remote area.[53] Such situations make women highly vulnerable to sexual harassment. Organizations with lax working conditions permitting the use of intoxicants on duty are other breeding grounds for exploitation. Organizational tolerance of alcohol use at the workplace increases the chances of sexual harassment. Environments that allow drinking during work breaks and have permissive norms related to drinking are positively associated with higher levels of gender harassment of women.[54] Such behaviour patterns have existed historically as well as have prevalence in current times.

Sexual harassment is almost always about power, about an individual controlling or threatening another individual and monopolizing all the resources available at the place of work. In most cases, it is an abuse of power by the resourceful at the cost of one who is deprived of resources.[55] The supervisor–employee dyad best characterizes a legitimate unequal distribution of power that gives the supervisor the capacity to reward and coerce a lower ranking employee who may at times be exploitative and violative of the subordinate's rights. The resources that most employees want and deserve, such as favourable performance evaluations, salary increases, promotions, better furnished cabins and the like, are often withheld and the less powerful individual is at the mercy of the powerful. However, there are situations where power dynamics may have no role and sexual harassment still occurs. For example, equal ranking colleagues do not have formal power differences in the organization, but they too can sexually harass female colleagues at times, though they engage in less severe forms of harassment than supervisors or those invested with power and authority.[56] They use the mechanism of withholding information, cooperation and support in teamwork, which is clearly a form of gender harassment. The withholding of information or refusing cooperation by the colleagues can exert power over the female colleagues. Women supervisors can be subjected to sexual harassment from male employees. Although the dyadic power differential is reversed in such a case, this is achieved by the employee devaluing the woman by highlighting traditional gender stereotypes, such as helplessness, passivity and lack of career commitment that reflect negatively on the woman in power.[57], [58] The male employee may engage in such behaviour in order to gain some power over the female supervisor or to minimize power differences. Although most victims of sexual harassment are women, there are instances of women in positions of power harassing male employees.[59]

7.5. Social Impact

7.5.1. Reduced Opportunities for Learning

In many occupations and with most training programmes in educational institutions, acquiring skilled expertise is an essential component of work. One has to depend on training instructors and mentors for gaining work experience. Learning opportunities for women trainees get restricted because of sexual harassment.[60] A recent study found that women pursuing training in professional colleges, such as engineering and medicine, had an adverse effect on their career advancement due to sexual harassment. Many of them had to give up tenure opportunities, drop out of major research projects or step down from leadership opportunities to avoid the unwanted and inappropriate conduct of the principal investigators as perpetrators.[61]

7.5.2. Forced Job Change and Cost to Organization

Because of unhealthy interpersonal relations due to sexual harassment, staff turnover may be affected at a workplace, and the employer may lose talented workers due to hostile work environment. Other than the victims, their colleagues and the witnesses may also find it difficult to continue working under such circumstances and decide to leave the workplace in order to prevent their own victimization.

Victims of sexual harassment undergoing emotional turmoil often stay away from their workplace to avoid harassers. The frequent absence of such a women employee is quite common, and the employer has to suffer costs due to the absence of working hands, sick leave, health benefits, monetary damage awards to victims and legal expenses. Due to the absence of employees, the work output of the establishment also suffers adversely in terms of work productivity and financial gains. The prestige of the organization gets tarnished due to the litigation process and unhealthy work environment.

Victims who quit work due to sexual harassment may face unemployment before finding another job. According to a recent study in this regard, there is a definite relationship between job change and sexual harassment. In this study, 80 per cent of women who experienced sexual harassment changed their job to different establishments within two years of the incident compared to 50 per cent who had no case of harassment. In addition to earnings and career attainment difficulties, the long-term consequences of frequent job change due to sexual harassment resulted in significant financial difficulties. Even when women were able to find work soon after leaving their previous employment, harassment contributed to their financial strain since change of job meant change of place requiring extra money for commuting if the new place was far from their place of living.[62] Because of harassment, some women abandoned their field of work altogether to look for other avenues to earn money by sacrificing their earlier acquired skills.

According to another study, the practice of job change in victims was more frequent and regular when they found no hope of improvement in the situation.[63] The study also found that victims were 6.5 times as likely as non-victims to change jobs. Employee turnover caused employers to suffer greater economic costs than litigation-related costs. To get a substitute for a talented employee was more expensive; a meta-analysis of case studies of the cost of employee turnover found average costs of 16 per cent to 20 per cent of an employee's annual salary, rising to up to 213 per cent of salary for experienced managerial and professional staff.[64]

Organizations also suffer other costs, such as legal costs if there are formal legal cases in courts, and costs related to lower productivity from increased absence of workers from the work, lower motivation and commitment of the employees who continue to work and team disruption and unhealthy work environment. Costs of sexual harassment are definitely substantial and bring the organizations into deficits. Some of the economic burden of sexual harassment comes out of taxpayers' money. In India, there are no such documented estimates; however, a 1988 study by the US Army on the costs of sexual harassment reported annual costs of $250 million dollars, which was much higher in 2018. A U.S. Merit Systems Protection Board study from the 1990s onwards estimated the economic costs of sexual harassment in US government workplaces over a two-year period to be $327 million.[65]

In a 2003 study, in India, the economics and law of sexual harassment in the workplace, Kaushik Basu[66] argued that sexual harassment affected the victims in ways similar to exposure to excessive health hazards. This menace comes at a cost to public health. It intersects with caste and class as well as relatively empowered women are also vulnerable to sexual harassment. The informal economy is far worse affected. Dalit women working in landlords' fields, for instance, are prime targets.

Not only the organizations suffer the economic losses, the individual victims also undergo financial difficulties that vary from person to person depending on the targets' occupations and career trajectories. Those in higher paying occupations will lose more in terms of income than those in lower paying occupations. The impact, however, is significant regardless of the wages lost: both those with high and low incomes may rely on this money to meet basic needs of their families and achieve economic security. *Both the groups suffer equally due to sexual harassment.*

7.5.3. Legal Costs

It is difficult to reliably estimate the total legal costs related to sexual harassment; typically, the amount of financial payouts in settlements is kept confidential and does not come into the public domain. However, the US Equal Employment Opportunity Commission (EEOC), which publishes all financial settlements it reaches on behalf of employees, in the financial year 2017, obtained $46.3 million in monetary benefits for employees in relation to sexual harassment charges.[24] These costs underestimate the actual payouts made by employers in response to sexual harassment charges, because the EEOC litigates only a small number of all complaints it receives.[67]

7.5.4. Increased Absenteeism

Sexual harassment demoralizes victims, erodes their confidence and morale, and causes conflict and stress in the victim. The deranged emotional state leads to avoid confrontation with stress situation and thus causes frequent absenteeism from the workplace.

The 2015 analysis of the National Health Interview Survey found that those who reported having been harassed or bullied at work in the previous year were 1.7 times more likely to have had at least two weeks off because of incidents of sexual harassment than those who had not been subjected to such encounters.[68] In a 2016 Merit Systems Protection Board study,[69] it was found that close to one in six employees who experienced sexual harassment took sick or annual leave following their harassment at the workplace. These studies corroborate the observations that sexual harassment leads to work absence behaviour.

7.5.5. Reduced Productivity

Increased absence from work means lesser work output; victims may not be able to function at their normal pace under the stress of sexual harassment, hence lesser productivity. If harassers block victims from professional advancement for not submitting to their sexual advances within a company, the organization loses out because the best candidate for a given position may not have the opportunity to fill it. Additionally, dealing with sexual harassment incidents and their impacts can take time and energy away from management's time and resources to complete their other tasks. Overall, this will be at the cost of official work and organization's resources.

Research supports the association between reduced motivation and lower job satisfaction and withdrawal. Decline of interest in the victims has been reported as some of them leave their job or do not take interest in their work if they stay back. The negative impact also spills over to those who are witnesses or well-wishers of the victim; there is reduced team performance. The friends of the victim who identify with her may join the victim in protest to stop working. One study of 27 teams at a food services organization found that sexual hostility— a form of sexual harassment—is damaging for team processes and performance[70] per person working in a team.

7.6. Overall Challenges due to Sexual Harassment

In addition to causing health problems and financial losses due to unpaid leave that the victim may avail because of ongoing discomfort at the workplace, sexual harassment is socially damaging to the victims. Their character becomes questionable or they are labelled as a 'troublemaker'. Some victims may even face broader career repercussions, such as the loss of job references when they decide to leave their current position or employer to avoid a hostile work environment.

[10] PTI. *Adultery Law Must Apply Equally to Men and Women.* Available at https://www.rediff.com/news/2003/aug/12adultery.htm (accessed on 18 December 2020).

[11] United Nations. *Convention on the Elimination of All Forms of Discrimination against Women New York, 18 December 1979.* Available at https://www.ohchr. org/en/professionalinterest/pages/cedaw.aspx (accessed on 18 December).

[12] *The Hindu.* NCW Rejects Proposal to Punish Women for Adultery; 2006. Available at https://www.thehindu.com/todays-paper/tp-national/ NCW-rejects-proposal-to-punish-women-for-adultery/article15735459. ece (accessed on 18 December 2020).

[13] Supreme Court of India. *Vishaka v. State of Rajasthan 1997.* Available at https://indiankanoon.org/doc/1031794/ (accessed on 13 August 2019).

[14] Ministry of Women and Child Development, Government of India. *Sexual Harassment of Women at Workplace (Prevention, Prohibition and Redressal) Act, 2013.* New Delhi: Ministry of Women and Child Development, Government of India; 2013.

[15] American Psychological Association. *Report of APA Task Force on the Sexualization of Girls.* Washington, DC: American Psychological Association; 2007. Available at https://www.apa.org/pi/women/programs/girls/report (accessed on 18 December 2020).

[16] Straus MA. Prevalence of violence against partners by male and female university students worldwide. *Violence Against Women.* 2004;10(7):790–811.

[17] Hald GM, Malamuth NM. Self-perceived effects of porn consumption. *Archives of Sexual Behavior.* 2008;37(4):614–625.

[18] Cooper RA, Delmonico D, Burg R. Sexuality in cyberspace: Update for 21st century. *CyberPsychology & Behavior.* 2000;3(4):521–536.

[19] Ben-Veniste R. Pornography and Sex Crime: The Danish Experience. *Technical Report of the Commission on Obscenity and Pornography: Erotica and Behaviour,* Vol. 8; Washington, DC: US Government Printing Office; 1971.

[20] Brussel T. The effects of sophistication, access and monitoring of pornography in three technological contexts. *Deviant Behavior.* 2005;26(1):109–132.

[21] Wamathai A, Merecia AMS, Mwenje M. Prevalence and factors contributing to pornography viewing among male students in selected universities in Kenya. *Journal of Humanities and Social Sciences.* 2014;19(11):1–7.

[22] Hald GM, Malamuth NM, Yuen C. Pornography and attitudes supporting violence against women: Revisiting the relationship in nonexperimental studies. *Aggressive Behavior.* 2010;36(1):14–20.

[23] Allen M, D'Alessio D, Brezgel K. A meta-analysis summarizing the effects of pornography: Aggression after exposure. *Human Communication Research.* 1995;22(2):258–283.

[24] Fitzgerald LF, Drasgow F, Hulin CL, Gelfand MJ, Magley VJ. Antecedents and consequences of sexual harassment in organizations: A test of an integrated model. *Journal of Applied Psychology.* 1997;82(4):578–589.

[25] Lerner G. *Black Women in White America: A Documentary History.* New York, NY: Vintage Books; 1972.

[26] Jiloha RC. *A Case of Early Life Psychopathology* (Unpublished manuscript); 2020.

[27] Brownmiller S. *Against Our Will.* New York, NY: Simon & Schuster; 1975.

[28] Marshall LW, Laws DR, Barbaree HE. *Handbook of Sexual Assault: Issues, Theories, and Treatment of the Offender.* Berlin: Springer; 1990.

[29] Sarwer DB, Kalichaman SC, Johnson JR. Sexual aggression and love styles: An exploratory study. *Archives of Sexual Behavior.* 1993; 22(3):265–275.

[30] Critelli JW, Bivona JM. Women's erotic rape fantasies: An evaluation of theory and research. *Journal of Sex Research.* 2008;45(1):57–70.

[31] Crouch M. Sexual harassment in public places. In: John Rowan, ed. *Social Philosophy Today*, Vol. 25. Bowling Green, OH: Philosophy Documentation Center; 2009. pp. 13–22.

[32] Barak AZY. Sexual harassment on the Internet. *Social Science Computer Review.* 2005;23(1):77–92.

[33] Crosthwaite J, Priest G. The definition of sexual harassment. *Australasian Journal of Philosophy.* 1996;74(1):66–82.

[34] Elliott GC, Cunningham SM, Linder M, Colangelo M, Gross M. Child physical abuse and self-perceived social isolation among adolescents. *Journal of Interpersonal Violence.* 2005;20(12):1663–1684.

[35] US Merit Systems Protection Board (USMSPB). *Sexual Harassment in the Federal Workplace, 1994: Trends, Progress, Continuing Challenges.* Washington, DC: US Government Printing Office; 1995.

[36] Fitzgerald LF, Swan S, Mugley VJ. But Was It Really Sexual Harassment? Legal Behavioural and Psychological Definitions of the Workplace Victimization of Women. In W O'Donohue, ed. *Sexual Harassment.* Needham Heights, MA: Viacom; 1997. pp. 5–28.

[37] Jennifer BL. The sexual harassment of uppity women. *Journal of Applied Psychology.* 2007;92(2):425–437.

[38] Willness C, Steel P, Lee K. A meta-analysis of the antecedents and consequences of workplace sexual harassment. *Personnel Psychology.* 2007;60(1):127–162.

[39] Kabat-Farr D, Cortina LM. Sex-based harassment in employment: New insights into gender and context. *Law and Human Behavior.* 2014;38(1): 58–72.

[40] Sojo VE, Wood RE, Genat AE. Harmful workplace experiences and women's occupational well-being: A meta-analysis. *Psychology of Women Quarterly.* 2016;40(1):10–40.

[41] Burnham L, Theodore N. *Home Economics: The Invisible and Unregulated World of Domestic Work.* New York, NY: National Domestic Workers Alliance; 2012.

[42] National Violence Against Women Prevention Research Centre; 1998–2002. Available at http://www.musc.edu/vawprevention (accessed on 8 December 2019).

[43] Hulin CL, Fitzgerald L, Drasgow F. *Organizational Influences on Sexual Harassment.* Thousand Oaks, CA: SAGE; 1996.

[44] Glomb TM, Richman WL, Hulin CL. Ambient sexual harassment: An integrated model of antecedents and consequences. *Organizational Behavior and Human Decision Processes.* 1997;71(3):309–328.

[45] Patel JK, Griggs T, Cain C. We Asked 615 Men about How They Conduct Themselves at Work. *The New York Times*; 2018. Available at https://www.nytimes.com/interactive/2017/12/28/upshot/sexual-harassment-survey-600-men.html?hp&action=click&pgtype=Homepage&clickSource=image&module=photo-spot-region&region=top-news&WT.nav=top-news (accessed on 18 December 2020).

[46] Dekker I, Barling J. Personal and organizational predictors of workplace sexual harassment of women by men. *Journal of Occupational Health Psychology.* 1998;3(1):7–18.

[47] Shaw E, Hegewisch A, Hess C. *Sexual Harassment and Assault at Work: Understanding the Costs* (Briefing Paper, Access to Good Jobs, Health and Well-being Pay Equity Discrimination and Violence Safety). Available at https://ncvc.dspacedirect.org/handle/20.500.11990/1846 (accessed on 18 December 2020).

[48] Andrew RM, Schell TL, Cefalu M, Hwang J, Gelman A. *Sexual Assault and Sexual Harassment in the US Military Estimates for Installation and Command Level Risk of Sexual Assault and Sexual Harassment from the 2014 RAND Military Workplace Study,* Vol. 5. Available at https://www.rand.org/pubs/research_reports/RR870z7.html (accessed on 18 December 2020).

[49] The National Academies of Sciences Engineering Medicine. *To Prevent Sexual Harassment, Academic Institutions Should Go beyond Legal Compliance to Promote a Change in Culture; Current Approaches Have Not Led to Decline in Harassment.* Washington, DC: The National Academies of Sciences Engineering Medicine; 2018. Available at https://www.nationalacademies.org/news/2018/06/to-prevent-sexual-harassment-academic-institutions-should-go-beyond-legal-compliance-to-promote-a-change-in-culture-current-approaches-have-not-led-to-decline-in-harassment (accessed on 18 December 2020).

[50] Hitlan RT, Pryor JB. and Hesson McIntnis MS. Antecedents of gender harassment: An analysisi of person and situation factors. Sex Roles. 2009. https://doi.org10.1007/s11199-0069072-5

[51] Hesson-McInnis MS, Olson M. Antecedents of gender harassment: An analysis of person and situation factors. *Sex Roles.* 2009;61:794–807.

[52] Maass A, Cadinu M, Galdi S. Sexual Harassment: Motivations and Consequences. In: M. K. Ryan & N. R. Branscombe, ed(s). *The SAGE Handbook of Gender and Psychology.* London: SAGE; 2013. pp. 341–358.

[53] Pryor JB, LaVite CM, Stoller LM. A social psychological analysis of sexual harassment: The person/situation interaction. *Journal of Vocational Behavior.* 1993;42(1):68–83.

[54] *The Times of India.* Major General Faces Sack Over Sexual Harassment; 2018. Available at https://timesofindia.indiatimes.com/india/major-general-faces-sack-over-sexual-harassment/articleshow/67223015.cms (accessed on 18 December 2020).

[55] Bacharach SB, Bamberger PA, McKinney VM. Harassing under the influence: The prevalence of male heavy drinking, the embeddedness of permissive workplace drinking norms, and the gender harassment of female co-workers. *Journal of Occupational Health Psychology.* 2007;12(3):232–250.

[56] Greenberg J. *Behavior in Organizations,* 10th ed. Upper Saddle River, NJ: Prentice Hall; 2011.

[57] George JM, Jones GR. *Understanding and Managing Organizational Behaviour,* 5th ed. Upper Saddle River, NJ: Prentice Hall; 2008.

[58] Freeman J. *Women in the Workplace: Wages, Respect, and Equal Rights.* New York, NY: Rosen Publishing Group.

[59] Reeves ME. *Women in Business: Theory, Case Studies, and Legal Challenges.* New York, NY: Taylor & Francis; 2011.

[60] Powell GN. *Women and Men in Management.* Thousand Oaks, CA: SAGE; 2011.

[61] Bimrose J. Sexual harassment in the workplace: An ethical dilemma for career guidance practice? *British Journal of Guidance and Counselling.* 2004;32(1): 109–121.

[62] Mathews M, Bismark MM. Sexual harassment in the medical profession: Legal and ethical responsibilities. *Medical Journal of Australia.* 2015;203(4):189–192.

[63] Mclaughlin H, Uggen C, Blackstone A. The economic and career effects of sexual harassment on working women. *Gender & Society.* 2017;31(3):333–358. Available at https://journals.sagepub.com/doi/full/10.1177/0891243217704631 (accessed on 18 December 2020).

[64] Rizzo T, Stevanovic-Fenn N, Smith G, Glinski A, O'Brien-Milne L, Gammage S. *The Costs of Sex-based Harassment to Businesses: An In-depth Look at the Workplace.* Washington, DC: International Center for Research on Women; 2017.

[65] Khubchandani J, Price J. Workplace harassment and morbidity among US Adults: Results from the National Health Interview Survey. *Journal of Community Health.* 2010;40(3):555–556.

[66] Faley RH, Knapp DE, Kustis GA, Dubois CLZ. Estimating the organizational costs of sexual harassment: The case of the U.S. Army. *Journal of Business and Psychology.* 1999;13(4):461–484.

[67] Basu K. The economics and law of sexual harassment in the workplace. *Journal of Economic Perspectives.* 2003;17(4):47–75.

[68] U.S. Equal Employment Opportunity Commission. *Select Task Force on the Study of Harassment in the Workplace: Report of Co-Chairs Chai R. Feldblum & Victoria A. Lipnic;* Washington, DC: U.S. Equal Employment Opportunity Commission; 2017.

[69] Ali SRO, Zakaria Z, Zahari ASM, Said NSM, Salleh SM. The effects of sexual harassment in workplace: Experience of employees in hospitality industry in Terengganu, Malaysia. *Mediterranean Journal of Social Sciences.* 2015;6(2):17–22.

[70] U.S. Merit Systems Protection Board Office of Policy and Evaluation. *Update on Sexual Harassment in the Federal Workplace.* Washington, DC: 2018; U.S. Merit Systems Protection Board Office of Policy and Evaluation. Available at https://www.mspb.gov/MSPBSEARCH/viewdocs.aspx?docnu mber=1500639&version=1506232&application=ACROBAT (accessed on 18 December 2020).

CHAPTER 8

Sexual Harassment of Women from Special Groups

Relationship between victims' experiences of harassment and their race, ethnicity, class and other social positions is understood through intersectional studies. Sexual harassment and gender discrimination among particular population involve special dynamics, which has remained largely unexamined and often ignored. Since women from certain populations are more vulnerable to sexual harassment in comparison to women, in general, they need to be studied separately to understand the dynamics, psychopathology and preventive measures in these populations.

There are several issues which influence the victim–perpetrator dynamics where victims come from racial or cultural minority groups.

Historically, sexual exploitation of women can be linked to Black feminism and critical race theory, which makes visible intersecting axes of oppression. It contributes to power hierarchies within a social structure related to race, ethnicity, gender, sexuality and class. Although there is no empirical certainty, many factors have been identified as contributing to the complexity of the discriminatory experiences of African–American women by perpetrators of their own race or by

Caucasian predators. In fact, the modern story of sexual harassment began with the discriminatory attitude that African–American women faced at their workplace in the USA and other parts of the world.

Social stereotypes linked to a particular race, religion or caste encourage harassers to view women belonging to these groups in a highly sexualized and non-professional way. This type of objectification of the socially marginalized women has been witnessed in almost all societies, and they are often perceived as deserving and inviting harassment and discrimination. In the case of African–American women, there are stereotypes portraying Black women as promiscuous, hypersexual, 'hot' and easily appropriated by white men.[1] On similar lines, stereotypes of Dalit women in India include features of exotica, passivity, and submission to upper-caste men. They are easily available too, without much resistance.[2] The *chamars* or shoemakers in India's socio-economic life, members of the Dalit community, have traditionally been the subjects of injurious and funny reflections and their daughter is objectified: '... when she has just attained puberty, is as graceful as an ear of millet ...' And at the harvesting time when summoned to work in the fields, she was often sexually exploited by the zamindar.[3] Stereotypes of minority women as maids living in affluent households contribute to their perception as low-skilled workers, who are easily available for sexual favours to their rich employers. Other contributory factors include low-pay positions, cultural and economic marginality, numerical minority or token status within workgroups without a protective mechanism to redress their grievances. Their own sexual laxity could be a contributory factor. All of these variables constitute high-risk factors for sexual harassment and discrimination as well as provide limited possibilities for redress.[1] Some special groups worth discussing are as follows.

8.1. African–American Slave Experience

Racial discrimination with its unreasoned and illogical feeling of self-superiority by certain races and spread of hatred and contempt for the others has no place in the modern society, but it continues to exist despite opposition from the civil society of modern times. Racial and gender discrimination prevails despite its rationality being often questioned; women are the worst sufferers of racial and gender discrimination. The tradition of sexualizing racial discrimination is characteristic of the African–American slave experience witnessed at the workplace. There are several features of this experience some of which are described as follows[4]:

- As a racial group, Black women share the oppression of the race, in general, and thus occupy a disadvantageous position in the social hierarchy.
- Traditionally, Black women have remained the objects of exploitive sex by White men. During the period of Industrialization, when the Black women came out to work in the factories to meet their financial needs, they were exploited by the employers for the job benefits in the form of 'quid pro quo'.
- Rape of women is often employed as a weapon of terror by the powerful as directed against the entire Black community for punishment and to instil fear.
- When Black men are prevented through social taboos and violence from defending their own women, the oppression of all Blacks is heightened and institutionalized.
- When Black men are oppressed economically to an extent that they cannot secure steady employment at decent wages, many Black women are deprived of the support of a male breadwinner and must take on additional economic and psychological burdens.

An institutionalized system of racism in case of Blacks includes restricted access to resources and sexual exploitation of the women. Devaluation of the relationships between men and women is an inevitable consequence. This combination of sex and racial discrimination applies to other racial and ethnic minority groups as well making it difficult for the victims to determine the difference between gender discrimination and sexual racism. A feeling of helplessness prevails. The victims feel lack of protection, a lack of credibility and a lack of value in comparison with the White women which makes them far more likely not to report the injustice to authorities as they believe they won't be heard. They find it difficult to voice their plight and to bring the attention of others to their situation and to advocate for better working conditions for themselves. They may socially withdraw themselves from mainstream life activities, limiting their interpersonal contacts with White men at work, in order to avoid discriminatory behaviours. Such an attitude may exclude them from career-enhancing relationships and further growth in their professional life. Inhibition is the self-restriction of career patterns which often overpowers these women. Evans and Herr[5] present evidence that African–American women alter their career patterns in order to escape harassment and discrimination and choose protected fields that serve their community needs, such as law, health care, social service and education. How extensive this self-limiting of career pathways to avoid discrimination is among other minority groups remains to be examined by the researchers.

If a member of the same racial or cultural minority as the victimized woman perpetrates the sexual harassment, additional factors may be activated, causing the perpetrator to expect protection and support from his community and the woman to suppress her complaint. If the perpetrator is advancing in the workplace and can be seen as a successful role model for that particular race members, the pressure on the aggrieved woman to suppress her complaint and not speak out against one of her own race is exacerbated. Many minority communities follow the tradition of:

- Male leadership in all public affairs
- Community representation by men in all outdoor activities
- Traditional gender stereotype role for men as a breadwinner for the family

If the aggrieved woman and the perpetrator are members of the same ethnic or religious minority, their social community may criticize the victim for filing a formal complaint and exposing their own community to public scrutiny and adverse publicity, rather than settling the matter confidentially within the community circles. For example, Anita Hill[6] was criticized for reporting Clarence Thomas and thus diminishing the chances for an African–American to sit on the Supreme Court. Victim's legitimate complaint may even be viewed by the community people as a racial or ethnic slur. Same ethnic or racial minority group victims, sometimes, themselves are personally reluctant to expose their perpetrator. Among Hispanics and other cultures that accept traditional, rigidly polarized sex roles, aggrieved women may be viewed as dishonoured, no longer pure, an embarrassment to their family or all of these. Similar is the attitude prevalent in almost all traditional societies where virginity of an unmarried woman is highly valued. A sexually harassed virgin is considered corrupted and slurred by the community and often branded as a woman of questionable character.[2]

In these situations, community advocacy against racism takes priority over advocacy against sexism. Bell[7] has described an old boys' club within the African–American community, which may protect perpetrators for these reasons. Cultural and religious values favouring modesty, virginity and domestic-centred roles for women may also discourage aggrieved women from complaining to avoid discussion in the public domain and seeking help from someone outside the community. As a result, these women often suppress their anguish with an exposure to psychological vulnerabilities to suffer mental health problems silently with no accessible community redressal mechanism available to address their grievances.

Empirical data regarding sexual harassment involving racial minorities are almost non-existent in the literature except for the case reports, which are often quoted in various texts. However, the available data focuses primarily on African–American and Hispanic groups, and the inference drawn from these reports goes contrary to most theoretical hypotheses of higher prevalence and low complaint rates. Barak[8] has reviewed the cross-cultural data and found no significant differences in incidence rates between Caucasian and Black women with regard to sexual harassment. On the contrary, Gruber and Bjorn[9] and Koss, Gidycz and Wisniewski[10] found the prevalence of sexual harassment against White women higher as compared to Black women. Harassment of White women was reported to be perpetrated by the men of the same Caucasian race and not the Blacks. Culbertson, Rosenfeld and Booth-Kewley[11] found no support for the hypothesis that Black women respond less assertively to sexual harassment than do White women. Black women were found to be equally assertive while protesting against sexual harassment. However, the results of these available studies might be suffering from minority women's underreporting of sex discrimination, labelling their situations racism rather than sexism or segregating themselves into low-risk work environments. The current data is inconclusive and more research with larger study populations is needed to reach an authentic conclusion. As the diversification of the workforce intensifies, adequate study and understanding of these interactions will become even more important.

8.2. India's Dalit Women

The traditional caste system in India divides people of the Hindu religion into social groups with their predetermined civil, cultural and economic rights as per divine ordinance. Hindu religious scriptures provide a regulatory mechanism to enforce social and economic organizations through the instruments of social ostracism and segregation.[12] In this arrangement, the Dalits or the erstwhile *Shudra* (lowest of the four in the Hindu caste-order), at the bottom of the caste pyramid, suffer the most from an anti-social spirit of the caste system, the *varna vyanvatha* (caste-system). They suffered from the notion of 'untouchability' and were subjected to physical and social segregation, deprivation of equal access in various resources of social life, cultural activities and economic pursuits.[13] Although the caste system is outlawed in independent India, and all the citizens of the country are accorded equal status, its lingering effect is continuing, and the worst affected are the women.

Dalit castes, known as SCs and STs, in an official lexicon, constitute one-sixth of India's population protected by certain safeguards in Article 341 for the protection of their fundamental rights and to prevent any further discrimination on the basis of their caste origin. However, despite these safeguards in operation for the last 70 years of Independence, their control over resources of the country is still less than 5 per cent compared to their population being more than 16 per cent. Close to half of them live below the poverty line, and even more (62%) are illiterate. In the agriculture sector, they are just landless labourers where their women are exploited the most.

To prevent discriminatory practices and ensure social and economic empowerment to Dalits, several laws have been enacted which include the Untouchability Offences Act, 1955 (renamed as the Protection of Civil Rights Act, 1976), and the Scheduled Castes and Scheduled Tribes Prevention of Atrocities Act, 1989, which aim to prevent crimes and atrocities. Permanent national commissions have been set up to safeguard their rights for both SCs and STs as well as for women.[12] In addition to legal protection, equal access to and participation in various spheres of life have been ensured.

Although the practice of caste discrimination has been theoretically outlawed, practically many of the behaviours, norms and values persist which overtly or otherwise induce discrimination at all levels. By the reason of their historical background, Dalit women, who constitute almost 100 million of India's population and three-fourths of them living in rural areas, face systemic oppression, social exclusion and structural violence from the male members of their own community as well as from upper-caste landlords and the employers.

They suffer from several fronts, including the patriarchal system organized according to the caste norms. The discrimination due to their being both a Dalit and a woman makes them a choice target of violence and sexual exploitation. This endemic intersection of gender and caste discrimination is the inevitable outcome of severely imbalanced social, economic and political power equations for Indian Dalit women.

Another aspect of Dalits life, particularly in the rural areas, is that they are forced to live in separate locations with poorer living conditions and away from the main village, face discrimination when accessing services, receive lower wages and face discrimination in the marketplace and other places of social interaction. This way, the Dalit women suffer a triple burden of discrimination, namely economic, patriarchy and caste. The religious practice of *devadasi* (temple prostitution) which still continues in certain parts of the country results in their sexual exploitation.[12], [14]

In the urban areas, many women organizations have been voicing their concern on gender issues since the early 1990s regarding the uneven distribution of gains of progress. However, out of all the women in the country, the Dalit women are at the margin and need more attention than others. The Dalit women show significantly low progress in human development indicators as compared to women from the upper-caste group.[15] Calling with profane names depicting their low-social origin or otherwise harassing them sexually while at work has been a regular feature of their work-environment, particularly in the agricultural fields and construction sites. Many landlords, their men and the contractors in the construction business consider it as a matter of their right to avail sexual services from these helpless women.[16]

The tradition of sexualizing caste discrimination in India is characteristic of the Dalit women's experience, which includes the following several features[12], [16]:

- They suffer multiple forms of discrimination, which is related to caste, class and gender.
- Rape of Dalit women is employed as a weapon to terrorize the entire Dalit community in the rural areas and to show them their place in reference to the traditional social order.
- When Dalit men are prevented through terror and violence from defending their own women, the oppression of all Dalits as a community is heightened and institutionalized.
- When rural Dalit men are oppressed economically to the extent that they cannot secure steady and well-paid employment, many of their women are forced to work in the landlords' fields and thus dependent on waged labour.
- Dalit women are subjugated by patriarchal structures, both in general and within their own family. Violence against them, such as sexual assault, rape and parading naked in public places, serve as a social mechanism to maintain Dalit women's subordinate position in the society.
- Crime against Dalit women is mostly committed with impunity. In most of the cases, they are denied of their right to seek legal and judicial aid.

Experiences of urban Dalit women differ from the experiences of their upper-caste counterparts. The preconceived notion of purity and pollution and their entry into educational institutions and white-collar jobs on the clutches of reservations make them the subjects of hatred, ridicule and discrimination. As domestic help, they do work in upper-caste houses only to clean the toilets or sweep the floor.

Failure of the upper-caste feminist movement to recognize caste as a form of social privilege isolated Dalit women from the mainstream women's movement. Mainstream movement of women was challenged by the Dalit women in the early 1990s as their experience of subtle hatred and covert discrimination, which drained their self-confidence and added to their stigmatized presence at the workplace, were not incorporated in the larger feminist movement. In fact, Dalit women had been left outside the mainstream feminism for their unrecognized and trivialized depth of caste disability. Gender exploitation of Dalit women by their own men was another issue, which prevents them from asserting their choices and participate in decision making in both the community and the family. They suffer from not only gender discrimination and economic deprivation but also discrimination related to prescribed customary provisions in the institution of caste and untouchability.

The Dalit women's movement is built around issues of access to livelihood and social needs, patriarchal high-handedness, caste-based discrimination at workplaces and impunity for violence against them.[13], [17] The contemporary Dalit women definitely have common problems with non-Dalit women with respect to gender, economic empowerment and patriarchy, but they also recognize access to education and opportunities in employment, caste-related violence and atrocities and sexual exploitation through institutions such as the *devadasi* system as their important concerns.[13], [18] The economic and social disparities and violence directed specifically against Dalit women is reflected in the National Sample Survey Office,[17] the Census of India, the National Crime Records Bureau and the National Family Health Survey-2 and 3.[18], [19]

The incident of gang-rape of a potter woman came to light when the state of Rajasthan took an indifferent stand to protect her as an employee of the government, from the perpetrators as she tried to prevent child marriage in a powerful landowning family of the village. Later taken up by an NGO, this case is known as Vishaka case of sexual harassment of a woman carrying out her assigned government duty. The Supreme Court had to intervene to formulate guidelines against sexual harassment at the workplace, known as Vishaka Guidelines.

From the beginning of the 21st century and more so after 2012, several groups of Dalit women, big and small, have come up across the country, asserting their identity and openly talking about the intersection of caste and gender. However, still, there is no mechanism for their protection and safeguard, particularly for those working as agricultural labourers in the fields of the landlord where their exploitation goes unreported and even unrecognized.

In the educational institutions where their presence irritates the majority of students and teachers, they find it difficult to get assimilated in the mainstream academic culture. The following case illustrates the plight of Dalit women students in higher educational institutions[20]:

A 27 years old Dalit scholar at Indian Institute of Technology Roorkee was sexually harassed by two professors. IIT authorities refused to take any action against the perpetrator dons despite her repeated complaint. She had to approach the police for redressal of her grievances.

Their ordeal continues even after the complaint is lodged, which generally goes unheard. The redressal mechanism often fails to protect the complainant, which is evident from the following case[21]:

A 23-year-old Dalit college student was dragged by her hair by a 38-year old powerful Brahmin and her head was smashed with a stone because she refused to withdraw a sexual harassment complaint against him which she had lodge. The incident occurred in broad daylight when the girl was walking to her College.

This incident speaks volumes of how the powerful and the influential perpetrator could easily make the Dalit women suffer from impunity.

With the advent of the spread of education among Dalit women, many of them have acquired positions of respect both in the government and private sector of the workplace. However, their plight of sexual intimidation continues because of their social background. The following case highlights the difficulties the working Dalit women face at the workplace[22]:

A senior woman Dalit scientist at a responsible position was mentally and sexually harassed by her superior for one year. She had to approach the National Commission for Scheduled Castes when the department failed to redress her grievances. Acting on the complaint, the Commission has issued notice to the state chief secretary and the DGP seeking action taken report within a fortnight.

In her case there was manipulation of inquiry and the witnesses before the Complaints Committee spoke in favour of the accused under the pressure of FSL director. Witnesses were threatened of dire consequences if they came forward in favour of the aggrieved woman....

The victims still fail to get justice despite the Act to protect them against sexual harassment. They have to look for other avenues for their grievances to be addressed.

8.3. Ethnic Minorities

There has been considerable focus on the violence against women in India during recent years. The essence of this focus is largely on the possible violence when there is conflict or tension between two ethnic groups, and women of one community are sexually assaulted by the men of the other in an overt assertion of their identity and a simultaneous humiliation of the other by dishonouring their women. The cultural groups in the society with lesser numerical representation, may respond to sexual harassment by other groups differently as compared to the larger society.[23]

During the Hindu–Muslim riots at the time of India's partition in 1947, the deep-rooted cultural conflict surfaced in the country, which in addition to other psychological reasons, played an important role in bringing out inter-community hatred between Hindus and Muslims. Deep-rooted prejudice hidden during peacetime erupted with extreme virulence during the community conflict. Violence against women during riots was explicitly familial forms of sexual violence indicator of the place that women's sexuality occupies in an all-male patriarchal arrangement of gender relations, between and within religious or ethnic communities. Women from minority groups remain vulnerable to harassment from males of larger social groups[24].

Indian society, a house for several minority socio-religious groups, often witnesses such situations at the workplace where women from minority status may be teased, bullied and sexually harassed. Workplaces scantily represented by the women members of a particular minority social group often provide a fertile ground for sexual harassment of such women. A recent episode illustrates the fact[25]:

A 22 year old Muslim girl from Meerut was harassed by inebriated class-mates during their college trip to Agra. The trip was organised by the college authorities with the teachers who accompanied the group. The girl in question was the only Muslim student out of the 55 students, she became an easy target of misbehaviour and harassment for the male students. '… they tried to touch me in an indecent manner …' she tweeted.

This incident explains how a male-dominated workplace can contribute to sexual harassment, particularly when the victim hails from ethnic, religious or caste minority group. In such cases, the victim may suffer psychologically with internalizing negative self-concepts after discrimination which get compounded by previously existing internalized negative racial stereotypes. Often, minority women are unsure whether to label their experience sex discrimination or ethnic minority discrimination. Racial and ethnic stereotypes characterizing women of certain groups as promiscuous or highly libidinous may target these women for increased sexual harassment or may result in their being blamed for any harassment that occurs. In cases of employment discrimination based on ethnic factors, it is even more likely that a person from such a subgroup who is being harassed will be at the very bottom of the work power hierarchy and thus perceived as less valuable to the organization than the harasser is.

Homosexual men and women victimized by same-sex harassers may fear that a complaint will expose their sexual orientation or will result in adverse criticism from the gay community for complaining about one of their own or bringing adverse publicity to the community.[6], [26]

Heterosexual men vary in their vulnerability to harassment sequelae. They are harassed much less frequently than women. Their harassers are much less likely to be in a superior position or to be able to impact their work status, and men often perceive the harassment as flattering and mutual, rather than humiliating and devaluing. Nonetheless, they are vulnerable to negative sequelae when their harasser is in a position to harm them at work or when the event is humiliating and devaluing. Studies suggest that as women become more successful and prominent in their profession at the workplace, the harassment of men may increase as an expression of abuse of power. Street et al.,[27] noted that in one organization characterized by a high number of female employees, the male members faced embarrassing moments quite frequently.

8.4. Domestic Workers

Domestic workers are the employees who carry out household errands for an individual or a family. They provide services ranging from care for children[1] and elderly, cleaning and household maintenance, cooking, laundry and shopping for food and other household items. Traditionally, women are employed as domestic workers barring few exceptions where services of men are needed. It was much harder to work for the domestic workers before the Industrial Revolution[2] and particularly before the labour-saving devices came in use. In some cases, domestic workers live with their employers to provide full-time services while others work on a part-time basis providing services in either one or multiple houses while living in their own home; they are referred to as a live-out domestic worker. In some cases, the skills of domestic workers, whose work encompasses complex management tasks in large households, are highly valued. Since domestic work falls under the domain of the unorganized sector, in many jurisdictions, it is poorly regulated, and the employees are subjected to serious abuses. Although legislation protecting domestic workers is in place in most of the countries, it is often not extensively enforced.[28], [29]

A significant share in the global workforce is held by domestic workers, and they are among the most vulnerable groups for sexual harassment. Although they constitute a big workforce, they are often

[1] https://en.wikipedia.org/wiki/Child_care
[2] https://en.wikipedia.org/wiki/Industrial_Revolution

unclear of their status, they are unregistered and are excluded from labour legislation.[28] That is the reason, they are sometimes called the 'invisible workforce'.

There are around 67 million domestic workers worldwide, excluding children, 80 per cent of all domestic workers are women, constituting 4 per cent of the global woman workforce.[30]

The exploitation of domestic workers within the households is quite common; often hidden from the public view, it has garnered increased attention in recent years. In their working life, domestic workers face multiple challenges, often receive very low wages without benefits of leave or medical care, work for long hours without legal and social protection, rarely have days off and always exposed to the risk of sexual abuse.[27] They are often abused by employers and labour agents in several ways, including physical, psychological and sexual; they suffer forced confinement in the workplace, face non-payment of wages and work excessively long working hours without a rest day.

The workforce of domestic workers, which primarily comprises women for the gendered norm surrounding housework, generally receives no value similar to ascribed to women's work in their homes. Even when the domestic work at an employer's house is a paid work, it has given no value in the larger context of work.[29] It is often undervalued and accorded an inferior status, both in their own minds and in the society. Moreover, women and girls caught up in situations of forced labour or trafficked into forced domestic work, land up like slaves for their employers.

India has around 4.2 million domestic workers out of the world's 67 million, without any protection under provisions such as social security and working conditions, and they cannot have any unions. India is one of the few countries who have not ratified the International Labour Organization's Domestic Workers Convention.[30] This work should be projected in the larger context of patriarchy and the subjugated role of women. The Sexual Harassment Act, 2013, could include domestic workers under its provisions only after the extensive campaigning of women activists. Since they come from an unorganized sector of the workforce, their complaints of sexual harassment are received by LCC.

However, most of the domestic workers are unaware of such a committee, and not all districts have initiated the constitution of LCC. Although the domestic workers are covered under the Act, the mechanisms to ensure a safe working environment for them needs more teeth.[31]

Increased awareness about the plight of domestic workers has not been matched by concerted government action. Provision of weaker laws and poorly enforced regulations leave employers enjoying virtual impunity to exact excruciatingly long hours of work for grossly inadequate wages.

However, some NGOs have begun fighting for domestic workers' rights to see a change in the system. NDWM is one organization that works to set up unions for domestic workers. NDWM under the Bombay Public Trust Act, 1950, has championed the rights of domestic workers, children in domestic work and migrant domestic workers since 1985.

NDWM supports the empowering of and the campaign for the labour rights of domestic workers through solidarity, participation and leadership training, seeking dignity and justice for them. It involves negotiating with the government to pass comprehensive legislation for protecting domestic workers' rights. It also works for creating a stronger public awareness to enable them to achieve a healthy recognition in the society. Over 30 years, NDWM has achieved several gains for them spread across 17 states of India, involving nearly 200,000 domestic workers in major cities, towns and villages.

The primary focus of NDWM is not on sexual harassment but on getting the children of domestic workers into schools and keeping them in schools as most of them tend to drop out. It also helps with health issues and access to medical facilities. Although sexual harassment is not its main concern, it takes up cases when needed.

There are other organizations which support domestic workers through social security schemes and provide insurance, pensions, etc.

In the USA, domestic workers have taken to '#MeToo' movement to share their grievances related to sexual harassment and make their voices heard in its domain, but in India, this movement has impact mainly among the women working in the organized sector and student community of elite colleges. It has resonated with the educated middle-class women who are employed, who dare to speak, and who are fighting for their space and are active on social media.[32] Needless to say, they have access to the internet. As Poo[28] puts it, 'What is so powerful about #MeToo movement is the way that we are speaking to each other, like a call and response between women across so many different experiences, communities and industries.'[33] Males should be included in the campaigning of sexual harassment awareness.[34] Since the victims are lacking sufficient support, there should be an accessible helpline for domestic workers to call. They could organize a WhatsApp group among their community to raise awareness and campaign.[35]

For domestic workers, an incident of sexual harassment in the workplace could be a minor difficulty, and even if they wanted to use social media to put across their experiences, many cannot, as only 30 per cent of the internet users in India are women and most of the domestic workers have no access to the internet. It is beyond the reach of most of them.

Domestic workers often remain silent about their sexual harassment out of fear of not being believed, being further victimized and many other reasons. While victims go through an intense emotional turmoil and battle, for the most part, fighting themselves against their morbid emotions, the perpetrators face no repercussions for their actions; community support can be of great help for them to open up.

There have been positive changes seen among the domestic workers in India to pick up courage and speak up their grievances. Although it is just a beginning, the trend has already set in. The following news item illustrates the fact[36]:

> ... second in command at the naval airbase was booked after his domestic help lodged a complaint for attempting to molest. While his family was out he found her alone and in the attempt he tore her clothes.... 46 years old was booked for the crime under Section 354.

Domestic workers are particularly more at risk when there is no other woman at home but in the presence of predatory males.

References

[1]   Adams J. Sexual harassment and Black women: An historical perspective. In: O'Donohue W, editor. *Sexual Harassment: Theory, Research and Treatment.* Boston, MA: Allyn and Bacon; 1997, 213–225.

[2]   Carstairs GM. *Death of a Witch: A Village in North India 1950–1981.* London: Hutchinson; 1983.

[3]   Risley H. *The People of India.* New Delhi: Oriental Books Reprint Corporation; 1969.

[4]   Lerner G. *Black Women in White America: A Documentary History.* New York, NY: Vintage Books; 1972.

[5]   Evans KM, Herr EL. The influence of racism and sexism in the career development of African American women. *Journal of Multicultural Counselling and Development.* 1991;19(4):130–135.

[6]   Hill A. *Speaking Truth to Power.* New York, NY: Knopf Doubleday Publishing Group. 2011;53.

[7]   Bell EL. Myths, stereotypes and realities of black women: A personal reflection. *Journal of Applied Behavioural Science.* 1992 Sep;28(3):363–376.

[8]   Barak A. Cross cultural perspectives on sexual harassment. In: O'Donohue W, editor. *Sexual Harassment: Theory, Research and Treatment.* Boston, MA: Allyn and Bacon; 1997, 263–293.

[9]   Gruber JE, Bjorn L. Women's responses to sexual harassment: An analysis of sociocultural, organizational, and personal resource models. *Social Science Quarterly.* 1986 Dec 1;67:814–826.

[10] Koss MP, Gidycz CA, Wisniewski N. The scope of rape: Incidence and prevalence of sexual aggression and victimization in a national sample of higher education students. *Journal of Consulting and Clinical Psychology.* 1987 Apr;55:162–170.

[11] Culbertson AL, Rosenfeld P, Booth-Kewley S. Assessment of sexual Harassment in the Navy: Results of the 1989 Navy-wide Survey. Navy Personnel Research and Development Centre, 1992. Available at: https://apps.dtic.mil/dtic/tr/fulltext/u2/a248546.pdf (accessed on 28 December 2020).

[12] Jiloha RC. *Native Indian: In Search of Identity.* New Delhi: Blumoon Books; 1995.

[13] Ambedkar BR. Philosophy of Hinduism. In: Moon V, editor. *Dr. Babasaheb Ambedkar: Writings and Speech.* Mumbai: Education Department, Government of Maharashtra; 1987.

[14] Briggs GW. *The Chamars: Religious Life of India.* Kolkata: Association Press Calcutta; 1992.

[15] Bhasin K. *Understanding Gender.* New Delhi: Kali for Women; 2000.

[16] Nidhi S, Sabharwal A. Caste and social exclusion: Concept, indicators, and measurement. In: Kumar AK, Rustagi P, Subramanian R, editors. *India's Children: Essays on Social Policy.* New Delhi: Oxford University Press; 2015, 774–392.

[17] Government of India. National Sample Survey Office (NSSO). Available at: http://mospi.nic.in/NSSOa (accessed on 28 December 2020).

[18] Crime in India. National Crime Records Bureau. Census of India. Government of India, 2011.

[19] National Family Health Survey-2 and 3. Available at: http://rchips.org.nfhs

[20] Susheel T. Two IIT-R Profs Booked for 'Sex Harassment'. *The Times of India*, 2018. Available at: https://timesofindia.indiatimes.com/india/two-iit-r-profs-booked-for-sex-harassment/articleshow/67186264.cms (accessed on 28 December 2020).

[21] Press Trust of India. Dalit Student Stoned to Death for Not Withdrawing Sexual-harassment Case in MP. *Hindustan Times*, 2019. Available at: https://www.hindustantimes.com/india-news/dalit-student-stoned-to-death-for-not-withdrawing-sexual-harassment-case-in-mp/story-Wdi1d-IJn2qpQ32vgEyKOEI.html (accessed on 28 December 2020).

[22] Yadav S. Gurugram: Scientist 'Harassed' by FSL Boss, Panel Notice to Government. *The Times of India*, 2019. Available at: https://timesofindia.indiatimes.com/city/gurgaon/scientist-harassed-by-fsl-boss-panel-notice-to-govt/articleshow/69779610.cms (accessed on 28 December 2020).

[23] Cortina LM, Berdahal JL. Sexual harassment in organizations: A decade of research in review. In: Barling J, Cooper CL, editors. *Handbook of Organizational Behaviour. Micro Approaches*. Thousand Oaks, CA: SAGE Publications; 2008, 469–497.

[24] Jiloha RC. *A Case of Early Life Psychopathology*. New Delhi: Century Publications, 2020.

[25] Rai P. UP Muslim Girl Harassed for Not Wearing BJP Cap. *The Times of India*, 2019. Available at: https://timesofindia.indiatimes.com/city/meerut/muslim-girl-harassed-for-not-wearing-bjp-cap/articleshow/68729339.cms (accessed on 28 December 2020).

[26] Menon PM. Lacking Support, Male Rape Victims Stay Silent. *The Times of India*, 2013. Available at: https://timesofindia.indiatimes.com/city/chennai/Lacking-support-male-rape-victims-stay-silent/articleshow/18524668.cms (accessed on 28 December 2020).

[27] Street AE, Gradus JL, Stafford J, Kelly K. Gender differences in experiences of sexual harassment: Data from a male-dominated environment. *Journal of Consulting and Clinical Psychology*. 2007 Jun;75(3):464–474.

[28] Poo A. Out from the Shadows: Domestic Workers Speak in the United States. Open Democracy, 2017.

[29] Newsclick Report. Govt Says Policy for Domestic Workers in Progress, but Activists Are Demanding Legislation Instead. News Click, 2018. Available at: https://www.newsclick.in/govt-says-policy-domestic-workers-progress-activists-are-demanding-legislation-instead (accessed on 28 December 2020).

[30] Mehrotra S. Domestic Workers: Conditions, Rights and Responsibilities. JAGORI, 2010. Available at: http://www.jagori.org/wp-content/uploads/2006/01/Final_DW_English_report_10-8-2011.pdf (accessed on 28 December 2020).

[31] International Labour Organization. Sexual Harassment at Work. Declaration on Fundamental Principles and Rights at Work. International Labour Office, 2015. Available at: https://www.ilo.org/wcmsp5/groups/public/---ed_norm/---declaration/documents/publication/wcms_decl_fs_96_en.pdf (accessed on 28 December 2020).

[32] Varghese A. The Sexual Harassment of Women at Workplace Act and the Unorganised Sector. Women in Informal Employment: Globalising and Organising, 2018. Domestic Workers: Size, Contributions and Challenges, WIEGO. Available at: http://www.wiego.org/informal-economy/occupa

[33] Dhillon A. India's #MeToo Moment Is Still about the Struggle to Survive. The Sydney Morning Herald, 2018. Available at: https://www.smh.com.au/world/asia/india-s-metoo-moment-is-still-about-the-struggle-to-survive-20180330-p4z750.html (accessed on 28 December 2020).

[34] Stites J. Beyond Hollywood: Domestic Workers Say #MeToo. Available at: https://inthesetimes.com/article/beyond-hollywood-domestic-workers-say-metoo (accessed on 28 December 2020).

[35] Farrell, M. Sexual harassment in the Indian workplace: An exploratory study in civil society organisations. *Madhya Pradesh Journal of Social Sciences*. 2013;18(1). Available at: https://www.questia.com/library/journal/1G1-412800303/sexual-harassment-in-the indian-workplace-an-exploratory (accessed on 28 December 2020).

[36] Sequeira N. Naval Officer Booked for Molesting His Maid. *The Times of India*, 2019. Available at: https://timesofindia.indiatimes.com/city/goa/naval-officer-booked-for-allegedly-molesting-his-maid/articleshow/67978860.cms (accessed on 28 December 2020).

CHAPTER 9

Physical and Mental Health Consequences

Women's sexual harassment was recognized as a social problem during the civil rights movement of the 1960s in the USA, and soon, it turned into a legal issue related to an individual's civil rights. EEOC considered sexual harassment both as an ethical and a legal problem. In the subsequent years, its adverse effects on the victims and the organizations were widely recognized and extensively studied.[1], [2]

Prevalence studies on the magnitude of sexual harassment since the 1970s have confirmed that it is a widely occurring phenomenon across workplaces, generally ignored or trivialized for various reasons. However, its adverse impact on workplace productivity is evident from various studies. Academicians and researchers from the fields of business management and economics explored its negative economic and productivity aspects and gathered sufficient empirical evidence related to adverse effects on productivity. As a result, it has become a matter of serious concern for the managers and the owners of the establishments who run into losses in their business due to sexual harassment at their establishments.[1]

Effects are limited not only to the financial losses and the lower productivity, but sexual harassment also causes most harming and ubiquitous barriers to career success and job satisfaction of the employees. The recent focus of research on the individual victims, an area which was largely ignored till recently, reveals a wide range of health effects on the victims of sexual harassment. Initial reports showed several disparities in occurrence of these effects because of multiple intervening variables, but lately, the evidence has clearly emerged that sexual harassment does carry an adverse impact on the health of the aggrieved woman.[2]

Conceptual models drawn from other forms of gender-based abuse and expressed in terms of developmental-identity paradigms and stress-trauma paradigms are utilized to understand and predict adverse sequelae.[3]

Sexual harassment may create an unpleasant environment with disturbed interpersonal relations. Research studies provide ample evidence that sexual harassment inflicts negative effects on victims' job satisfaction, stress levels and mental well-being. Victims are more likely to become disinterested in their work, withdraw from the workplace activities and colleagues, frequently stay absent or reach the office late, avoid certain tasks or situations where there is a risk of further victimization or look for another job free from sexual harassment.[4] Some victims develop negative attitudes towards their supervisors and co-workers for not getting their support and stop interacting with them, which leads to their further social withdrawal from others. Those who witness sexual harassment, regardless of their own victimization, being members of a work group in which sexual harassment occurs and find the work environment unhealthy with disturbed interpersonal relations at the workplace.[5]

Sexual harassment has been recognized as a major public health problem with long-term health effects in terms of physical and mental health consequences for the victims. Victims belong to all races, ethnic groups and socio-economic backgrounds who suffer from somatic and psychological symptoms with a wider impact on their social and professional life. Mental health literature regarding the health consequences of sexual harassment is relatively new and has appeared in a fragmented and sporadic fashion, while physical health effects are consistently documented and well recognized. Clinicians working with the victims of sexual harassment have reported case histories with symptom manifestation, related stress factors and the attempts at intervention. Retrospective surveys giving information on the symptomatology also add to the information regarding the health effects of sexual harassment. Another source of information available is from those theoreticians who work in the areas of women development, cognitive functioning and gender-based traumas, such as rape and childhood sexual abuse. They have generated a parallel body of relevant information applying their theories to the field of sexual harassment.[6], [7]

The United States Merit Systems Protection Board,[8] in a self-report survey, found thousands of female employees experiencing detrimental effect on their emotional or physical health due to sexual harassment. Subsequent studies have recognized sexual harassment a serious risk to employees' psychological and physical well-being warranting not only therapeutic intervention, but also these studies emphasized a strong need for preventive measures.[9]

Physical health and emotional well-being are closely interrelated; an individual having physical ill-health will have an unhealthy state of mind and vice versa. A woman under the stress of sexual harassment, experiencing morbid emotions, is likely to have physical symptoms, such as poor appetite, weight fluctuations, headache and sleep problems. Such a wide spectrum of physical and mental health effects with a greater proportion of the population is probably seen only in sexual harassment than other forms of discrimination.[10] A large population of women suffers from sexual harassment; therefore, many women suffer from physical and mental health symptoms. National Intimate Partner and Sexual Violence Survey, carried out in 2017,[11] found one-third of the surveyed women suffering from some form of sexual violence, which resulted in their compromised health status. They reported negative health effects such as staying fearful (62%), pre-occupied with safety issues (57%) and symptoms of PTSD (52%). Several other studies corroborated the findings of this study that victims had increased risk for developing PTSD and the severity of harassment predicted the levels of PTSD symptoms.[12] Physical health of the victims remains exposed to the risk of various ailments such as asthma, irritable bowel syndrome, frequent headaches, chronic pain, interrupted sleep and restricted daily activities. Jina and Thomas,[13] in their review, have listed commonly occurring medical conditions in response to sexual harassment, which include gastrointestinal symptoms, nausea, vomiting, pain in the abdomen, diarrhoea, cardiopulmonary and neurologic symptoms such as difficulty in breathing, irregular heart rate, pain in the chest, hyperventilation, numbness, weakness, sleep difficulties, fatigue, genital and reproductive symptoms such as bleeding from the vagina, irritation in genitals, pelvic pain, urinary tract infections, painful sexual intercourse and lack of sexual pleasure.[14]

A particular focus of some studies has been on the etiological and empirical perspective of sexual harassment which highlights the negative psychological consequences. Some others have focused on emotional and stress-related aspects from a historical and a treatment perspective. There are few other studies which have discussed consequences of treating victims in relation to cultural, racial and progressive symptom stages context. Sexual harassment has also been studied in relation to the diagnosis of PTSD and other psychological consequences.[9]

As already discussed, workplace sexual harassment stems from hierarchical power dynamics, and the majority of complaints come from subordinate position victims. Miller[15] first described the psychological impact of women's subservient role in society, later elaborated on the importance of maintaining attachments and avoiding conflicts in experiencing anger and power. Carmen et al.[16] discussed women's subordinate status in the workplace hierarchy in relation to their mental health status. Moscarello[17] explored these features in gender-based abuse and their implication in a treatment setting. Regardless of the level of power, women's victimization, irrespective of the place it occurs in, results in higher levels of depression, anxiety and eating disorders on a long-term basis. In the following pages, the impact of trauma and traumatic experience of sexual harassment is discussed under three sub-headings:

1. Impact of trauma on the mind
2. Early life exposure to sexual trauma and later psychopathology
3. Immediate and long-term consequences of sexual harassment at the workplace

9.1. Impact of Trauma

Human beings react cognitively to every incident, and sexual harassment is no exception. It causes a tremendous impact on the mind of the victim. Most of the victimized women suffer tormenting thoughts about the incident and often hold themselves guilty for someone taking liberty with them. Some of them also accuse themselves of their believed to be inviting behaviour that provoked the harasser to feel free to make sexual advances. This pattern of retrospection makes a victim morally responsible to be constantly vigilant. The traumatic event and the distressing thoughts disturb the homeostasis and dysregulate the normal coping mechanisms of the victim. In order to cope with the increasing threat, several defence states emerge such as hypervigilance (freeze-alert), flight or fight, tonic immobility (freeze-fright), and collapse. The memory of the event and associated stimuli are inadequately processed and get stored in an isolated memory network and have its effect on both short-term and long-term memory of the victim.[18]

9.1.1. Brain and Trauma

The sympathetic nervous system prepares the body to be ready for a 'fight or flight' response to the traumatic event.[19] There is an increased heart rate and respiration rate, which prepare the body to attack or transition into a state of immobility. In the brain, amygdala, an early warning system, regulates the basic drives and emotions, analyses stimuli, enhances attention and increases heart rate and muscle tension.[20] The victim becomes hypervigilant, the amygdala and insula react to fearful stimuli together, and the prefrontal cortex inhibits the amygdala's reactivity to fear.[21] A network, responsible for impairment of the regulation of fear responses and hypervigilance to threat-related stimuli, is formed by these structures. Abnormal reactivity from the amygdala and its communicating structures during sexual harassment is depicted in radiological findings in which inadequate regulation from the prefrontal cortex resulting in hyperarousal and inability to suppress exaggerate fear responses to trauma-related stimuli.[22] Structural plasticity of the amygdala and fluctuating levels of cortisol cause disbalance between amygdala excitation and inhibition, which results in extensive dendritic growth and increased firing rate of the amygdala and chronic hypervigilance. A defensive response may trigger if the environment is not free from potential threats when there is a chronic hypervigilant state.[23]

In response to the stress of sexual harassment, amygdala of the victimized woman activates the hypothalamus which is connected with it through the limbic system.[24] Hypothalamus regulates physical and behavioural activities of the individual through autonomic nervous system. It controls the release of certain hormones and regulates emotional states. The limbic system comprises amygdala and hippocampus, which keeps track of spatial location and encodes memories and emotional state. Experiences and expression of emotions is regulated by the intimately connected limbic system to the hypothalamus and pituitary gland. In response to sexual harassment, the hypothalamic-pituitary-adrenal axis is activated through the amygdala, wherein the hypothalamus sends a signal to the pituitary gland, which activates the adrenal glands which in turn release hormones, including glucocorticoids and catecholamines. These hormones help the body respond to trauma and stress.

To cope with the extremely severe stress, for the fight or flight, the body gets energy from glucocorticoids such as cortisol catecholamines such as norepinephrine and epinephrine.[22] The sympathetic nervous system facilitates blood flow to the lower extremities in order to prepare the body to flee; it is the body's inherent response to cope with the stress. In case the body responds to fight, the sympathetic nervous system enhances blood flow to the upper extremities to prepare the body for that purpose. The release of hormones, no doubt, helps in flight or fight response; their high level impairs cognitive functioning in the prefrontal cortex by inhibiting working memory important for facilitating reasoning, decision-making and behaviour in the event of a stressful situation. Because of the excessive release of cortisol and norepinephrine, rational thought, reasoning, planning and organization become limited during the exposure to sexual harassment, and the victim may not be in a position to decide.[18]

The release of high levels of glucocorticoids and catecholamines[17] activates the amygdala, which affects encoding, consolidation and retrieval of memory.[18] Catecholamines and non-genomic glucocorticoids have rapid but short-lasting effects, whereas long-term effects are observed with genomic glucocorticoids.[25] During emotional arousal due to sexual harassment, the release of catecholamines and non-genomic glucocorticoids augments the encoding processes through the strengthening of synapses in the hippocampus.[26] Administration of glucocorticoids soon after the traumatic experience of sexual harassment consolidates memory by suppressing the learning and processing of competing information not related to the trauma. Studies by Roozendaal et al.[27] and Roozendaal and McGaugh[28] substantiate these findings which show impairment of memory consolidation after glucocorticoid was removed. In experimental animals, increased memory consolidation can be seen after administration of a glucocorticoid receptor agonist in the amygdala in rat models. This brain activity shift, supporting memory encoding and consolidation, has opposite effects on retrieval of memory. Buchanan[29] found high levels of glucocorticoids like cortisol in women when they undergo increased stress during sexual harassment, which results in memory retrieval impairment. However, persons who develop memories in conditions of high emotional intensity have enhanced encoding, which enables them to develop more salient memories of their trauma.[30] Traumatic events of high emotionality are often better recalled with the critical details of the experience retained for a long time.[31]

The brain is almost re-wired to focus only on the traumatic event and its associated emotions, and the event is constantly on repeat in the brain. When this occurs, the individual re-experiences the trauma because the sounds, smells, images and feelings are not adequately processed and stored in the brain's memory system. However, the empirical studies of these mental health effects are preliminary, limited and still devoid of any hypothesis testing of etiologic models. The empirical evidence in support of this should be available to formulate an etiologic model, which is yet to be generated.[32]

9.1.2. Psychology of Trauma

In the occurrence of sexual harassment, there is a complex interaction between individual, interpersonal, societal and institutional factors, which create individual psychopathology expressed in the context of mind–body interactions. Psychological stress in the victim is described in relation to the environment that is appraised by the victim as being taxing or exceeding her resources and endangering her well-being.[33] The severity of the psychological impact depends on the seriousness of the episode as a stressor, the situational context in which the stress occurs and the pre-existing individual and psychological characteristics of the victim. Response to the psychological stress due to sexual harassment depends on the following factors.[34]-[36]

- **Stimulus factors:** These include the objective aspects of the harassment experience, such as frequency, duration, intensity, predictability and ambiguity.
- **Contextual factors:** These are like organization's tolerance, the importance of the organization to victim's career or financial stability, availability of effective complaint channels, retaliation, the power differential to directly affect the victim's well-being, the quality of the victim's relationship with the perpetrator and co-worker responses.
- **Personal factors:** These are prior exposure to gender-based trauma, high commitment to work for personal or economic reasons, personal resources available, the impact of the experience on deeply held beliefs, values and sense of self and the personal losses incurred.

Generally, sexual harassment consists of a cumulative series of escalating experiences involving gender-based devaluations and inequities, sexual behaviours or any combination of these. The experiences can be the result of a single perpetrator, a group of people at the workplace or institutional policies and communications. In the case of institutional policy, there is usually an individual in immediate authority who is responsible for the cumulative experience of all employees or students within the particular work or academic environment. The accumulation of sexual harassment experiences often results in a chronic level of stress and affective arousal. This is in contrast to the acute, intense level of arousal that is commonly associated with experiences like rape, where a single, unexpected attack is accompanied by an immediate fear of death. Intense arousal is also a characteristic of:

- Sexual harassment involving violent and humiliating sexual assault or the realistic possibility of such assaults

- Other discriminatory experiences that threaten physical boundaries of legitimate control over the work environment or financial viability
- Experiences that reactivate memories and responses to previous sexual trauma

To begin with, these situations exhibit intense arousal, followed by more chronic stress and arousal if the victim continues to remain in the harassing environment and there is repeated exposure to harassment, or the harassment is chronic.

For evaluating the severity of stress in the victims of sexual harassment, Hamilton et al.[37] used Holmes's Social Adjustment Scale meant to measure the severity of life crisis in psychosocial perspective.[38] They found a life change score of 161 commonly associated with sexual harassment experiences. This score brings harassment into the range of a mild life crisis. In this category of victims of sexual harassment, about one-third of them had adverse health effects manifesting in physical and psychological symptoms.

The stress of severe harassment is comparable with the stress of a divorce or a major illness. The impact of a harassment experience is classified by Loy and Stewart[39] as mild, intermediate and severe. These stressors correlate to the following experiences.[14]

- **Mild:** Comments with a sexual tinge, whistles, gestures and staring
- **Intermediate:** Unsolicited physical contact of a non-sexual nature
- **Severe:** Unwanted physical contact of a sexual nature and sexual assault

American Psychiatric Association[40] categorizes stressful experience as traumatic for the victim or the witness. This experience may be due to actual or threatened death, serious injury or threat to the physical integrity of self or others, and then, the individual responds with intense fear, helplessness or horror. Traumatic experiences result in a variety of serious psychological sequelae and psychiatric illnesses like PTSD. This observation has been corroborated by Avina and O'Donohue[41] in their study that sexual harassment can produce

PTSD symptoms in many victims. Sexual harassment may act as abrupt disruption in significant attachments, followed by characteristic emotional reactions. Sexual harassment has been associated with multiple acute relational disruptions at home and work.

Dansky and Kilpatrick[42] elaborate on the cognitive behavioural aspects of the stress–trauma paradigm and apply 'classic cognitive models' to explain the negative internal psychological sequelae of sexual harassment. There is significant psychological distress due to shattering of values and assumptions regarding the self as worthy and invulnerable to serious harm, others as honest and fair and the world as just, rational and predictable. These values are often imbibed during the course of development.

To restore her internal equilibrium, the victim attributes a benign motivation to the harasser or trivializes the event in order to safeguard her assumption of personal safety by creating explanations for the event. Such explanations could be ultimately detrimental to her health. Sometimes, the victim may blame herself for getting sexually harassed, rather than seeing her harasser as unfair or experience the work organization as irrational in its approach. If these attempts at cognitive coping fail, the victim will remain symptomatic, experiencing intrusions of the traumatic event and its associated negative emotions when exposed to any stimuli similar to those present during the event (classical conditioning) and constricting her behaviours to avoid these triggers (instrumental conditioning). Her core assumptions need to be altered to accommodate the reality of the event to become symptom free. However, if her beliefs assimilate the discriminatory event in unhealthy ways, like 'all bosses are untrustworthy' or 'my personal judgment regarding co-workers is always erroneous,' she may remain symptomatic indefinitely. The model of learned helplessness is used to explain negative altered assumptions arising from uncontrollable situations. If the victim cannot correct her situation, she will develop assumptions that bad outcome is inevitable, regardless of effort, and thus acquires learned helplessness.[43]

The psychological sequela of the stress is the rapid loss of high-value resources of the victim. This sequela is explainable on the 'conservation of resources model'. Hobfoil[44] suggests the following five reasons for the rapid loss of resources occurring as a result of a traumatic stressor:

- It disrupts basic values.
- It is unexpected.
- It demands more from victims' systems than they are equipped to handle.
- No previous resources or coping strategies were developed prior to the event.
- The stressor results in the creation of negative mental images that can be triggered by other cues.

The internal negative cognitive changes are not the only problem the victim faces, but stress-associated adverse effects in work and academic performance also diminish the self-esteem and internal security. Due to difficulty in cognitive assimilation of the harassment experience and cognitive readjustment, there is internally generated high level of stress. This adverse effect combines negatively with the external economic, vocational and interpersonal sources of stress created by the sexual harassment. Negative and defensive cognitive attributions and physical symptomatology are the common manifestations.

'Stress–trauma model' explains the negative psychological consequences reported in sexual harassment with mild or more transient reactions falling into the spectrum of stress reactions.

The more severe and chronic reactions occur which cause post-traumatic reactions involving, intrusive cognitive flooding, affective numbing, avoidance behaviour and affective hyperarousal. Anxiety disorders, depression, substance-abuse disorders, adjustment disorders, and mental health conditions associated with sexual harassment can be observed as fallout from the initial trauma. These disorders are related to traumatic losses, traumatic disruptions of attachments, and attempts at self-treating trauma-related affective arousal via tobacco smoking, drinking alcohol and abusing drugs. Drug-abuse behaviour is quite common; due to regular and excessive consumption, the victim may become dependent on alcohol or drugs to fight the stress. The higher prevalence of drug abuse and alcohol intake in the victims of sexual harassment is to get relief and to cope up with the unbearable and agonizing experience of pain due to sexual harassment. Well-controlled studies of recent years provide information about a broad range of psychological symptoms and psychiatric diagnoses corroborate these findings.[7]

The commonly seen psychiatric disorders in the victims are depression, anxiety, PTSD and drug addiction and alcohol dependence. Persistent psychological distress is noted even two years after the event. Studies indicate depression to be the most common psychiatric diagnosis, and about 10 per cent of victims have symptoms of PTSD. In addition to disabling physical and mental health symptoms, they often experience work withdrawal, career instability and job dissatisfaction. They also experience the damage to their self-identity because of the:

- Destruction of deeply held beliefs and values relating to people's fairness and work ethics
- Shattering of assumptions and expectations

The psychological impact of sexual harassment is conditioned in part by the victim's vulnerability to harassment. In the case of chronic stressors or lack of sufficient resources to buffer stressful life events and circumstances, some women are particularly more vulnerable to the psychological impact of pathological nature.[9] The experience of sexual harassment presents a significant challenge to a woman's sense of herself. Her self-concept is eroded due to the unexpected trauma. Its resolution becomes difficult, especially if she is preoccupied with other significant issues in her personal life, such as marriage prospects, impending divorce, pregnancy, parenthood and career development. The aggressive behaviour that may manifest because of sexual harassment can disrupt important and valued relationships in the workplace and at home with friends leaving the aggrieved woman vulnerable to blaming and devaluing herself or assuming an overly conciliatory and under-assertive role in her approach to address the situation. The victim's anger may further damage her sense of herself, her self-esteem, especially if she is viewed by others as 'characterless' or a 'troublemaker' or otherwise negatively labelled by co-workers, family members and friends. If she expresses her grievances in the form of a complaint, negative or retaliatory behaviours from others is even more likely to occur, and she may lose or destabilize valuable relationships with mentors or the co-workers at the workplace or in the academic institutions.

9.2. Early Life Trauma and Later Psychopathology

Depression in adulthood may be the consequence of the long-term effect of early life harassment or sexual trauma. Traumatic events of early childhood increase the risk of later life psychopathology. Painful events of childhood manifest across the life course, and those who experience early life sexual trauma are more likely to experience sexual trauma again during their adult life.[7] Later-life depression in those who had traumatic childhood is more common in those who have gone through subsequent experiences of sexual harassment. Experiences of incest, sexual abuse, rape and lack of necessary mentoring relationships during the early developmental period make many working women experience:

- Low self-esteem
- Self-doubt about their abilities
- Excessive reliance on the opinions of others, they carry external locus of control
- Difficulties with self-assertion and coping with the situations
- Empathic concern for others at the expense of their own needs
- Blurred sexual boundaries and other traits, which increase their risk for further sexual harassment and abuse

Early exposure to sexual harassment contributes to poor long-term mental health, irrespective of harassment in adulthood. Several cases of depression reveal their childhood sexual traumas linked to their current psychopathology. Compromised mental health increases the risk of exposure to social stressors and the occurrence of depressive symptoms, which could, in turn, increase the risk of sexual harassment and depression in adult life. Early life sexual harassment may also affect later-life depressive symptomatology through diminished resources. As already discussed, sexual harassment is associated with work withdrawal, job turnover and career instability,[8] all of which can threaten adult socioeconomic status and increased severity of depression, which may culminate further into suicidal behaviour. Such patients may be vulnerable to sexual harassment.

Several individual characteristics moderate the psychological impact of sexual harassment, which include prior sexual harassment and prior mental health status. Many researchers[14], [15] have noted a strong relationship between harassment and discrimination, rape, battering, sexual exploitation in professional relationships, childhood sexual abuse and incest.

Those who have a history of sexual harassment may react more negatively to the current event of harassment than first-time victims because past experience diminishes one's ability to cope with the fresh experience of similar nature.[10] Stressful experiences create a generalized vulnerability to stress so that stressors have stronger effects on mental health for those who experienced earlier life stressors.[6] Because of the poor tolerability, chances of developing a psychiatric illness are more. If sexual harassment occurs repeatedly, the negative impact is more deleterious to mental health, as the accumulation of workplace stressors may exert larger effects than a single isolated incident.[12] This may be especially true when the perpetrator is someone who works with the victim at the place of work. Facing each other throughout the day itself may be a stressful experience. Victims may feel ashamed, dirty or scared, withdraw from friends, family members and the society; underlying depression or anxiety[1] can worsen and can result in suicidal risk.[13]

According to a WHO 2002 report, a woman who had been exposed to sexual trauma during early life is 3 times more likely to suffer from depression, 6 times more likely to suffer from PTSD, 13 times more likely to abuse alcohol, 26 times more likely to abuse drugs and 4 times more likely to contemplate suicide. They are more vulnerable to mental health abrasions in comparison to the women never had the experience of sexual trauma in their childhood.

9.3. Trauma: Immediate and Long-term Effects

A wide range of literature is available on long-term effects of sexual harassment, which can be used to design treatment for the victims.[45] Studies related to psychological and physical consequences of sexual harassment are mostly descriptive, citing empirical survey results and

---

[1] https://www.health.com/condition/anxiety/19-natural-remedies-for-anxiety

case reports. The available literature on the health consequences can be divided into the following categories:

1. Physical and psychological symptoms and psychiatric disorders
2. Problematic coping responses
3. Disruptions in interpersonal relationships and vocational functioning
4. Psychological reactions related to loss and grief

9.3.1. Physical and Psychological Symptoms and Psychiatric Disorders

Women who experience sexual harassment repeatedly and have no outlet to talk about and share their difficult experience are most vulnerable to suffer from physical and psychological symptoms. They develop symptoms of disorders such as depression, anxiety and PTSD. Harassment could be especially dangerous for those women who have pre-existing mental health disorders that may be triggered or exacerbated by the stress of sexual harassment.

Chronic and ongoing sexual harassment becomes a threat to one's identity and may lead to failure in achieving the desired goal at the workplace or in the academic institution where one is pursuing one's studies. The failure in work pursuits or academic enhancement may further add to symptom manifestation. It puts the targeted victim under physical and mental stress in her day-to-day work activities immensely affecting her routine life.

As a stressor, sexual harassment produces an involuntary physiological response which can cause adverse effects[2] on blood pressure, cortisol release, pulse rate and heart rate. At times, this biological response persists even beyond the removal of the threat and precipitate mental disorders.[3] To cope with the situation, the victim may acquire unhealthy behaviours such as substance and alcohol use and smoking of tobacco, which are commonly seen in the victims of chronic and ongoing sexual harassment.[22]

[2] https://pubmed.ncbi.nlm.nih.gov/18950922/
[3] https://psycnet.apa.org/record/2003-06685-007

As already discussed, biological pathways for depression in victims of sexual harassment lead to increased secretion of corticotropin-releasing factor (CRF) from the central nervous system circuits, which leads to anxiety and depressive symptoms. Hartline, Owens and Nemeroff[46] found that harassed women had more CRF-like immune reactivity in cerebrospinal fluid compared to non-victim women. Animal model studies have found chronic stress associated with continuous sensitivity of pituitary, adrenal and autonomous stress response. Enhanced pituitary reactivity to stress among women who have experienced sexual harassment may result in vulnerability to and the onset of stress-related psychiatric disorders.[47]

There is an increased risk of workplace accidents in a dangerous job situation if workers get distracted while working.[48] Unwanted accidents have negative effects, which often lead to significant costs for both mental and physical health services. Common physical symptoms in sexual harassment are as follows[49]:

- Gastrointestinal symptoms such as nausea, diarrhoea, dyspepsia, loss of appetite, binge eating, weight loss and weight gain
- Jaw tightening
- Teeth grinding
- Dizziness
- Tics, muscle spasms, fatigue, neck pain, back pain, pulse changes, headaches, increased perspiration, cold feet and hands and decreased sexual desire
- Sleep problems, ulcers, irritable bowel syndrome, migraines, eczema and urticaria
- Increased respiratory or urinary tract infections

The relationship between physical symptoms and the sexual harassment experience generally remains un-noted by both the clinician and the victims.

Several 'psychological symptoms' reported in victims include:

- Persistent sadness, crying spells, low mood, decreased self-esteem and self-confidence, feelings of humiliation, helplessness and negative outlook

- Irritability
- Lability of effect
- Anergia and hypergia
- Mood swings
- Impulsivity
- Emotional flooding, anxiety, fears of loss of control
- Excessive guilt and shame
- Fantasies
- Compulsive thoughts and obsessional fears
- Persistent anger and fear and self-doubt
- Decreased concentration
- Anhedonia, vulnerability and alienation
- Feeling betrayed and or violated, loss of confidence and self-esteem, withdrawal and isolation, suicidal thoughts or attempts, which may culminate into suicide

Common psychiatric disorders associated with sexual harassment are as follows.

- **Anxiety disorders:** Especially generalized anxiety disorder, PTSD, acute stress disorder and dissociation disorders and panic attacks are commonly seen in cases of sexual harassment. Among the most debilitating conditions is PTSD which virtually paralyses the victim's routine activities. Vietnam War victims who suffered sexual harassment in addition to war trauma suffered from PTSD not because of the war itself but largely due to sexual harassment.[47], [48]
- **Somatization disorders:** Adult women with neurological and abdominal symptoms, which are functional in nature, may have a history of sexual harassment. Childhood sexual abuse also manifests with somatic symptoms of a wide variety during adult life. The intervening processes that link harassment to bodily symptoms are yet to be identified; however, they are unlikely to be the part of general illness-orientation.[49]
- **Sleep disorders:** Various studies have found an association between sexual harassment and sleep problems. Commonly seen problems are nightmare-related distress and increased nightmare frequency, sleep paralysis, nightly awakenings, restless sleep and tiredness during nights. Difficulties in sleep onset and impaired

sleep efficiency are other sleep problems seen in victims. There are several limitations in these studies and to overcome them, future researchers should use standardized and objective measurements of sleep in follow-up or longitudinal studies. There should be larger sample sizes, adequate comparison groups and comparison groups with other forms of discrimination.[50]

- **Sexual dysfunction disorders:** In a study, 72 per cent of the victims were found having sexual dysfunction of various forms.[4] As the severity of the harassment increased, the desire, arousal, lubrication, orgasm[5] and satisfaction during the sexual act significantly declined with their spouses or partners.[51] Repeated and chronic exposure to sexual harassment renders many victims frigid and disinterested in sex.

- **Eating disorders:** Due to impaired appetite after going through a traumatic event, the victim may lose weight. Weight gain may also occur as they either restrict or binge to hide their feelings of shame, hopelessness and fear. They tend to self-medicate and inflict non-suicidal self-injury such as wrist slashing and other forms of self-mutilation in order to release feelings of guilt and anger. Self-destructive behaviours are used to maintain control while distancing oneself from the pain of the trauma. Clinicians often fail to recognise that the patient tries to bury her disturbing emotions through the eating habits to the point that she may completely forget why her eating disorder began in the first place. Eating disorders in cases of sexual harassment is a significant association observed commonly. In a study, 50 per cent of anorectic and bulimic patients were linked to sexual harassment while only 28 per cent of them were found in the control population.[52]

- **Psychoactive substance use disorders and alcohol use disorder:** There is an increased frequency of drinking alcohol in the victims of sexual harassment. They have escapist motivations for heavy drinking and drink to intoxicate themselves. They use prescription drugs such as sedatives and antidepressants, and smoke cigarettes to relieve their

---

[4] https://www.sciencedirect.com/topics/medicine-and-dentistry/sexual-dysfunction

[5] https://www.sciencedirect.com/topics/medicine-and-dentistry/orgasm

anxiety. In prolonged cases of sexual harassment, there is an increased quantity of alcohol consumption on a regular basis.[53]

- **Depressive disorders:** Victims experience a multitude of negative emotions such as embarrassment and fear of others questioning their ability as a competent employee. Depression is common, particularly in those cases who have suffered ongoing sexual harassment. Suicidal thoughts and suicidal attempts are reported in cases of severe and chronic nature.[54]

- **Adjustment disorders:** When a sexual harassment event acquires excessively negative reaction with a chronic course, the victim may have adjustment disorder, typically manifesting with anxiety,[6] difficulty moving forward, and reckless behaviour. In some severe and chronic cases of sexual harassment, there is significant impairment in social, occupational or academic functioning and adjustment disorder often brings on depressed mood, anxiety or inappropriate conduct or other maladaptive reactions such as problems at work and physical complaints. There is an increased risk of suicidal[7] behaviour and substance abuse, as well as the prolonging of medical disorders or interference with medical treatment. When it persists, it may progress into a more severe condition such as major depressive disorder.[28]

There is also an increased risk of workplace accidents. While the employees are working in dangerous job situations at their workplace, they often get distracted by the incidents of sexual harassment which may result into an accident[55], [56] causing significant costs for both mental and physical health services.[57]

According to Equal Rights Advocates in the USA,[58] most of the victims suffer from some debilitating stress reaction, including anxiety, depression, headaches, sleep disorders, weight loss or gain, nausea, lowered self-esteem and sexual dysfunction. There is a loss of $4.4 million in wages and 973,000 hours in unpaid leave each year due to sexual harassment in the USA.

---

[6] https://www.psychologytoday.com/intl/basics/anxiety
[7] https://www.psychologytoday.com/intl/basics/suicide

In an Ethiopian study among college faculty and staff member, 82.2 per cent had experienced at least one episode of workplace abuse within the past 12 months with a similar pattern of distribution amongst academic and administrative staff.[59] About 50 per cent of the study population suffered sexual harassment, and in comparison to non-harassed women, they suffered from depression eight times more. From developing countries, most of the studies indicate a majority of women experiencing bullying in some form or the other; however, very few studies connect experiences of sexual harassment and workplace abuse with mental health effects and monetary losses.

Although there are no systematic studies on financial losses, it can be concluded from Equal Rights Advocates study[58] that sexual harassment causes significant monetary loss in any society due to adverse health effects.

9.3.2. Problematic Coping Responses

Unproductive coping methods are often used by the victims; unhealthy practices are generally adopted in those situations where there is the absence of appropriate and timely channels for resolution of the stress caused by the harassment. Validation support to the victim from others varies. Some may support the genuineness of her plight while others may label it her attention-seeking behaviour. Some others may be overtly neutral, but their unconscious negative cognitive attributions may further worsen the situation and complicate the problem for her. Use of unhealthy practices to cope with the crisis may become the cause of her being discredited or blamed for her experience of sexual harassment, and she is isolated from the supports. Denial is a common long-standing coping response and leads to the continuance and exacerbation of discrimination. Denial can result in an emotional crisis, in which the accumulated pain or rage related to the discrimination gives rise to emotional flooding and injurious disorganized behaviour. This, in turn, diminishes the victim's credibility and inhibits her ability to formulate an effective plan of action.[60]

Coping responses involving impulsive withdrawal from the workplace or academia lead to diminished credibility, economic losses, career derailment and exacerbation of family or work conflicts. Many women interpret discriminatory experiences as signals that they do not belong in the workplace and should be at home, caring full time for their families, including children. Coping through internalization of responsibility and blame for discrimination can lead the victimized woman to self-doubt, lowered self-esteem, diminished self-confidence, poor morale and lowered career aspirations which may adversely affect her work performance. As already mentioned, the prevalence of depression in the victims of sexual harassment is quite common, and such a coping mechanism may further add to the severity of depression, making it difficult to treat.

The victim experiences an ongoing ambivalence between outward anger toward the perpetrator and inward self-doubt, which can lead to stalemates in work or academic performance. Displaced anger can result in alienation of neutral or supportive figures, such as family members, friends, colleagues and mentors. Unprocessed surges of anger can lead to injudicious confrontations or impulsive litigations that are not in the victim's best interest. She may not be able to talk about her traumatic experience because of feelings of guilt or shame, which may lead to her isolation, reduced exposure to supports, and limited access to ideas for more productive coping options. Obsessional fears or images or retaliation can render her incapable of investing in new people or in work that can be more potentially productive. Use of psychoactive substances, smoking tobacco and intake of alcohol are the usual but unhealthy coping methods.

9.3.3. Disruptions in Interpersonal Relationships and Functioning

For the victims, the experience of sexual harassment could be a profound disillusionment with previously respected teachers, mentors, supervisors, health professionals, clergy, godman and other authority figures who either perpetrated the harassment or did not support them in appropriate redress of their grievance. As a result, the victims may develop a generalized mistrust for the people and experience evaporation of inhibitions in dealing with the important authority figures in the future. Many potentially useful male mentors and well-wishers who are sensitized to the current climate of political correctness regarding harassment in the workplace may avoid engaging with promising female students or workers because of anxiety and uncertainty regarding acceptable personal and work boundaries. Personal and professional relationships with co-workers are often disrupted, especially when a victim takes legal action or files a formal complaint. Colleagues and co-workers often fail to validate a victim's experience and to support her in speaking out because of their own limitations and fears. They may collude with the harasser and the organization out of fear or in hope of being rewarded for not siding with the complainants and upholding the dignity of the organization. Complainant is often ostracized and branded as a troublemaker at the workplace where all the workers are expected to tolerate one-another to maintain a harmonious work environment. Hamilton et al.[37] described a complainant as one whose work was devalued by her supervisor and was subsequently given to another woman colleagues who then received credit for its true value. The relationship is also disrupted with co-workers who confide the truth privately and show their sympathy with the victim but will not speak out publicly and with female supervisors who defend the institution or the harasser and neither validate the woman's experience nor provide her with provisions for appropriate redress. In order to protect the reputation of the institute, the supervisors often deny any cases and, in turn, blame the complainant for creating a mountain of a molehill. Disappointing reaction from female mentors or co-workers who deny the occurrence of discrimination or are pessimistic themselves, further encourage the occurrence of harassment at the workplace.[61]

The lack of trust in the working relationship with the colleagues, the organization or the institution and the leadership may have a direct effect to inhibit work functioning. In addition, anxiety and depressive symptoms may have an adverse effect on the productivity of work output because of decreased energy, self-confidence, motivation and concentration. Missed work time during the disturbed days and due to sickness related to emotional or physical health further diminishes work capacity. Avoidance reactions and diminished communication with individuals of key importance to work are also common. The work time spent in dealing with the adverse effects of sexual harassment significantly reduces work performance, efficiency and output. The professional relationship with the therapist may be compromised if he fails to appreciate the gravity of harassment or his assessment implies that the victim was at the wrong footing and there was no case of sexual harassment as such.

Relationships with family, friends and community people get complicated in unique ways. Husbands, boyfriends and male family members may identify with the harasser's point of view. In some cases, they may insist upon the victim filing a complaint or may intrude into her workplace to personally deal with perpetrators. Irritability, depression, sexual dysfunction or any other morbidity of the behaviour of the victim may further widen the marital relationship or a relationship with a lover. Parents of victims may feel guilty for not adequately preparing their daughters to be more assertive and bolder. A victim daughter may feel reluctant to tell her parents that she has been accused of being 'characterless' or incompetent in her work. A high-achieving father may take discrimination toward his daughter as a personal insult to his power and integrity and may insist upon intervening for his daughter.

In those societies or cultures where traditional sex roles are valued, the victimized woman may be viewed as a dishonour to her family for being the focus of public scrutiny in a sexual matter. A woman who is ambivalent about combining work and family roles may view harassment experience as proof that her place is in the home or as punishment for neglecting her family. Families supporting traditional roles for women may only exacerbate this viewpoint and further damage the victim's well-being. Family members may not even appreciate the psychological injury the victim has suffered, and they may not even believe that she needed some kind of help or support. Families unaware of the negative health and psychological consequences may even criticize the victim for neglecting housework or nurturing duties. Financial crisis precipitated by the loss of the job, diminished income, or high litigation costs may cause family strain in the interpersonal relations. The extra time that must be devoted to litigation or complaint procedures can be equivalent to another part-time job and can disrupt time with the family.

9.3.4. Psychological Reactions to Loss and Grief

The victim generally suffers both internal and external losses even when sexual harassment experience is ultimately resolved in her favour. The internal losses that the victim suffers include the loss of a sense of self as a competent and relational person; loss of faith in people around whether colleagues or superiors, institution and its policy and standards of fairness and equity on the part of the redressing mechanism and loss of a sense of enjoyment and commitment to work. External losses include the loss of a job, loss of income, loss of economic security, loss of important opportunities for career development, loss of important mentoring relationships, deterioration in interpersonal relationships, loss of opportunities for specialized training and education, loss of seniority or expected promotions and adverse effect on marriage prospects if the victim happens to be an unmarried person and about to get married. The victim grieves and mourns when she becomes fully aware of the impact of these losses. The victim's grief is seldom acknowledged and supported by others, and often, it is denied by the women themselves who are around her. This is especially true if they have received a positive outcome to formal complaints or litigation. Such denial can lead to unresolved mourning, severely complicating the victim's adjustment in the post-complaint workspace.[62]

There are many unresolved areas requiring further research in this area. Some of these are as follows:

- Longitudinal and prospective studies linking gender discrimination with other forms of gender abuse
- Studies linking gender discrimination with specific psychiatric disorders

A specific model for treatment intervention based on the conceptual models and targeting the common groups of sequela is needed for the victims.

References

[1] Equal Employment Opportunity Commission. 2006. Available at: http://www.eeoc.gov

[2] Roberts BS, Mann RA. Sexual harassment in the workplace: A primer. *Akron Law Review.* 2006;56:607–631.University of Akron.

[3] Fitzgerald LF, Drasgow F, Hulin C, Gelfand MJ, Magley VJ. Structural equation models of sexual harassment: Longitudinal explorations and cross-sectional generalizations. *Journal of Applied Psychology.* 1997;84:14–28.

[4] Glomb TM, Munson LJ, Hulin CL, Bergmen ME, Drasgow F. Antecedents and consequences of sexual harassment in organizations: A test of an integrated model. *Journal of Applied Psychology.* 1999;82:578–589.

[5] Willness CR, Steel P, Lee K. A meta-analysis of the antecedents and consequences of workplace sexual harassment. *Personnel Psychology.* 2007;60:127–160.

[6] Sundaresh N, Hemalatha K. Theoretical orientation to sexual harassment at workplace. *Journal of Business Management and Social Sciences Research.* 2013;2(4):75–81.

[7] Fitzgerald LF, Ormerod AJ. Perceptions of sexual harassment. *Psychology of Women Quarterly.* 1991;15:281–294.

[8] US Merit Systems Protection Board. *Sexual Harassment of Federal Workers: Is It a Problem?* Washington DC, WA: US Government Printing Office; 1989.

[9] Vincent-Höper S, Adler M, Stein M, Vaupel C, Nienhaus A. Sexually harassing behaviors from patients or clients and care workers' mental health: Development and validation of a measure. *International Journal of Environmental Research and Public Health.* 2020 Jan;17(7):2570.

[10] Lawson AK, Wright C, Fitzgerald LF. The evaluation of sexual harassment litigants: Reducing discrepancies in the diagnosis of post-traumatic stress disorder. *Law and Human Behaviour.* 2013;37(5):337–347.

[11] CDC. *The National Intimate Partner and Sexual Violence Survey 2010–2012 State Report.* Atlanta, GA: Centres for Disease Control and Prevention, 2017. Available at: https://www.cdc.gov/violenceprevention/pdf/nisvs-statereportbook.pdf (accessed on 29 December 2020).

[12] Millegan J, Wang L, Mann CA, Miletich D, Street AE. Sexual trauma and adverse health and occupational outcomes among men serving in the U.S. military. *Journal of Traumatic Stress.* 2016 Apr;29(2):132–140.

[13] Jina R, Thomas LS. Health consequences of sexual violence against women. *Best Practice & Research Clinical Obstetrics & Gynaecology.* 2013;27(1):15–26.

[14] DeLago C, Deblinger E, Schroeder C, Finkel MA. Girls who disclose sexual abuse: urogenital symptoms and signs after genital contact. *Pediatrics.* 2008;122(2):281–286.

[15] Miller JB. *Toward a New Psychology of Women.* Boston, MA: Beacon Press; 1987.

[16] Carmen EH, Russo NF, Miller JB. Inequality and women's mental health: An overview. *American Journal of Psychiatry*. 1981;138:1319–1330.

[17] Moscarello R. Victims of violence: Aspects of the victim-to-patient process in women. *Canadian Journal of Psychiatry*. 1992;37:497–501.

[18] Baldwin DV. Primitive mechanisms of trauma response: An evolutionary perspective on trauma-related disorders. *Neurosciences Bio-behavioural Review*. 2013;37(8):1549–1566.

[19] Purves D, Augustine G, Fitzpatrick D, Hall W, Lamana AS, White L. *Neuroscience* (5th ed). Sunderland, MA: Sinauer Associates; 2012.

[20] Gray P. *Psychology* (6th ed). New York, NY: Worth Publishers; 2011.

[21] Ochsner KN; Bunge SA; Gross JJ and Gabrieli JD. Rethinking feelings: An FMRI study of the cognitive regulation of emotion. *Journal of Cognitive Neurosciences*. 2002;14(8):121.

[22] Southwick SM, Vythilingam M, Charney DS. The psychobiology of depression and resilience to stress: Implications for prevention and treatment. *Annual Review Clinical Psychology*. 2005;1:255–291.

[23] Roozendaal B, McEwen BS, Chattarji S. Stress, memory and the amygdala. *Nature Review of Neurosciences*. 2009;10(6):423–433.

[24] Groeneweg FL, Karst H, deKloet ER, Joels M. Rapid non-genomic effects of corticosteroids and their role in the central stress response. *Journal of Endocrinology*. 2011;209(2):153–167.

[25] Katsuki H, Izumi Y, Zorumski CF. Noradrenergic regulation of synaptic plasticity in the hippocampal CA1 region. *Journal of Neurophysiology*. 1997;77(6):3013–3020.

[26] Cahill L, Alkire MT. Epinephrine enhancement of human memory consolidation: Interaction with arousal at encoding. *Neurobiology of Learning and Memory*. 2003;79(2):194–198.

[27] Roozendaal B, Bohus B, McGaugh JL. Dose-dependent suppression of adrenocortical activity with metyrapone: Effects on emotion and memory. *Psycho-neuroendocrinology*. 1996;21(8):681–693.

[28] Roozendaal B, McGaugh JL. Glucocorticoid receptor agonist and antagonist administration into the basolateral but not central amygdala modulates memory storage. *Neurobiology of Learning and Memory*. 1997;67(2):176–179.

[29] Buchanan TW, Tranel D, Adolphs R. Impaired memory retrieval correlates with individual differences in cortisol response but not autonomic response. *Learning and Memory*. 2006;13(3):382–387.

[30] Rubin DC, Boals A, Berntsen D. Memory in post-traumatic stress disorder: Properties of voluntary and involuntary traumatic and nontraumatic autobiographical memories in people with and without posttraumatic stress disorder symptoms. *Journal of Experimental Psychology*. 2008;137(4):591–614.

[31] Christianson SA. Emotional stress and eyewitness memory: A critical review. *Psychology Bulletin*. 1992;112(2):284–309.

[32] Gilligan C. *In a Different Voice: Psychological Theory and Women's Development*. Cambridge, MA: Harvard University Press; 1982.

[33] Lazarus RS, Folkman S. *Stress, Appraisal, and Coping.* New York, NY: Springer; 1984.

[34] Fitzgerald LF, Swan S, Mugley VJ. But was it really sexual harassment? Legal, behavioural and psychological definitions of the workplace victimization of women. In: O'Donohue W, editor. *Sexual Harassment.* Needham Heights, MA: Viacom; 1987, 5–28.

[35] Lenhart SA. *The Psychological Impact of Sexual Harassment and Gender Discrimination in the Workplace.* New York, NY: Guilford Press; 1996.

[36] Avina C, O'Donohue W. Sexual harassment and PTSD: Is sexual harassment diagnosable trauma? *Journal of Traumatic Stress.* 2002;15(1):69–75.

[37] Hamilton JA, Alagna SW, King LS, Lloyd C. The emotional consequences of gender-based abuse in the workplace: New counseling programs for sex discrimination. In Braude M, editor. *Women, Power and Therapy.* New York, NY: Haworth; 1987, 155–182.

[38] Holmes TH. Life, situations, emotions and disease. *Psychosomatics.* 1978;19:747–754.

[39] Loy PH, Stewart LP. The extent and effects of sexual harassment of working women. *Sociological Focus.* 1984;17:31–43.

[40] American Psychiatric Association. *Diagnostic and Statistical Manual of Mental Disorders* (5th ed.). Washington DC, WA: American Psychiatric Publishing; 2013.

[41] Avina C, O'Donnohue W. Sexual Harassment as diagnosable PTSD. *Psychiatric Times.* 2006;23(1):61–62.

[42] Dansky BS, Kilpatrick PG. The effects of sexual harassment. In: O'Donohue W, editor. *Sexual Harassment Theory, Research and Treatment.* Boston, MA: Allyn and Bacon; 1997. pp. 152–172.

[43] Horowitz MJ. *Stress Response Syndromes.* New York, NY: Jason Aronson; 1986.

[44] Hobfoil LE. Traumatic stress: A theory based on rapid resource loss. *Anxiety Research.* 1991;4:187–197.

[45] Shrier DK. Sexual harassment and discrimination. Impact on physical and mental health. *New Jersey Medicine: The Journal of the Medical Society of New Jersey.* 1990;87(2):105–107.

[46] Hartline KM, Owens MJ, Nemeroff CB. Postmortem and cerebrospinal fluid studies of corticotropin-releasing factor in humans. *Annals of the New York Academy of Sciences.* 1996;780:96–105.

[47] Gulley LR, Nemeroff CB. The neurobiological basis of mixed depression-anxiety states. *Journal of Clinical Psychiatry.* 1993;54:16–19.

[48] Coplan JD, Andrews MW, Rosenblum LA. Persistent elevations of cerebrospinal fluid concentrations of corticotropin-releasing factor in adult non-human primates exposed to early-life stressors: Implications for the pathophysiology of mood and anxiety disorders. *Proceedings of the National Academy of Sciences of the United States of America.* 1996;93:1619–1623.

[49] Reilly J. Somatization disorders. *Psychological Medicine.* 1999;29(2):399–406.

[50] Stein IM, Harvey AG, Krystal JH. Sleep disturbances in sexual abuse victims: A systematic review. *Sleep Medicine Reviews*. 2012;16(1):15–25.

[51] Mohammad GF, Hashish RK. Sexual violence against females and its impact on their sexual function. *Egyptian Journal of Forensic Sciences*. 2015;5(2):17–22.

[52] Tice L, Hall RC, Beresford TP, Quinones J, Hall AK. Sexual abuse in patients with eating disorders. *Psychiatric Medicine*. 1989;7(4):257–267.

[53] Judith L, Rospenda KM. Sexual harassment and alcohol use. *Psychiatric Times*. 2005;22(2):12–16.

[54] Nauert R. Mental Disorders Often Follow Sexual Abuse. Mayo Clinic, 2018.

[55] David S, Degioanni S, Drummond A, Philip P. Workplace bullying and sleep disturbances: Findings from a large scale cross-sectional survey in the French working population. *Sleep*. 2009;32(9):1211–1219.

[56] Cruz F. Women and accidents: The need to separate gender database. *Procedia Engineering*. 2016;145:662–669.

[57] Lauren S. #MeToo in Traditionally Male-dominated Occupations: Preventing and Addressing Sexual Harassment. Chicago Women in the Trades, 2018. Available at: http://womensequitycenter.org/wp-content/uploads/2017/10/CWIT-MeToo-in-Male-Dominated-Jobs-003.pdf (accessed on 29 December 2020).

[58] Equality and Human Rights Commission. What constitutes sexual harassment. Available at: http://www.equalityhumanrights.com/en/foradvisers/EocLaw/eoclawenglandwales/Sexualharassment/Isthereasexualharassment claim/Pages/Whatconstitutessexualharassment.aspx McGolgan, A. (2004, June).

[59] Marsh J, Patel S, Gelaye B, Goshu M. Prevalence of workplace and sexual harassment among female faculty and staff. *Journal of Occupational Health*. 2009;51:314–322.

[60] Lilia M, Cortina S, Wasti A. Profiles in coping: Responses to sexual harassment across persons, organizations, and cultures. *Journal of Applied Psychology*. 2005;90(1):182–192.

[61] Boyle KM. Sexual assault and identity disruption: A sociological approach to posttraumatic stress. *Society and Mental Health*. 2017;7(2):69–84.

[62] Border T. Disenfranchisement and ambiguity in the face of loss: The suffocated grief of sexual assault survivors. *International Journal of Applied Family Studies*. 2017;26(2):17–19.

CHAPTER 10

Treatment of Sexual Harassment

Sexual harassment of women at workplace involves a complex interaction between the victim and the perpetrator(s) having social, economic, legal and public health implications. The victim undergoes a morbid emotional experience with adverse psychological and physical consequences, and the workplace suffers from the hostile environment with adverse productivity, economic losses, disturbed interpersonal relations and frequent absenteeism and employees' mobility. The perpetrator's behaviour is by no means desirable and appropriate in the interest of the organization and requires therapeutic intervention. We need to treat the behaviour of the harassers as well as the adverse effects on the victims caused by the harassers' behaviour. Both the victim and the harasser require treatment that is highly complex and often challenging with limited information on the efficacy of the available therapies, which have ample scope for further improvement. Although in India, it is completely a new experience at present, in times to come, the relevance of such treatments cannot be denied. Based on the available published research, the treatment is framed in the following two groups:

- Treatment of the victims who suffer sexual harassment
- Treatment for perpetrators who inflict sexual harassment on women

10.1. Treatment of the Victims Who Suffer Sexual Harassment

Reaction to the trauma of sexual harassment often begins with 'shock', moving on to denial, followed by a feeling of victimization with a direct effect on self-esteem and the working capacity of the victim. In many cases, the victim may have endured the trauma for a long time silently, attempting first to handle it on her own before realizing the need for help from outside sources. Immediate and timely intervention helps the victim greatly. Intervention should create a safe and reassuring environment for open communication about the incident without judgment and criticism.

Victims enter treatment programme under different situations, and many of them may be unaware that the psychological problems they are suffering from are a primary or at least a contributory cause of their distress due to sexual harassment. Some of the victims are already involved in the litigation or complaint process before they contact the clinician for the treatment, which may exacerbate symptomatology to a serious level. Some victims may come for the treatment for some different problems such as marital discord and unresolved grief, which are the aftermaths of sexual harassment event. Therefore, the clinical history of every victim patient is required, in details, to understand the entire situation. Physicians, generally, do not explore work history in details; they may be unaware of the workplace or the academic institution trauma that has transpired during the episode of sexual harassment. The patient may not tell about the sexual harassment in the initial interview; it is for the clinician to explore the possibility of such a traumatic event. The treating physician may be the first contact in whom the victim confides her distress; he/she should explore work history in every individual patient in order to understand the cause and the nature of the distress. Common situations under which the victim presents before a physician are:

- Different stages of harassment experience, which may require different intervention styles and focuses
- Different levels of insight and motivation, requiring a variety of alliance-building techniques

- Diverse and variable symptom complexes of varying degrees of severity, requiring a broad range of treatment modalities, including psychotherapy, cognitive behaviour therapy and pharmacotherapy

The treating physician, while evaluating the severity of psychological distress should, particularly, focus on the following[1]:

- Nature of the harassment experienced
- The context in which it occurs
- The pre-existing physical and mental condition of the victim with regard to both external and internal resources and vulnerabilities such as socially isolated, financially strapped, past history of sexual abuse and belonging to a minority social group, traditional rural background or the Dalit community.

If the victim is psychologically healthy and economically stable with a supportive family and co-workers, the experience will be milder. Earlier accounts focused primarily on economic and productivity losses while the more recent accounts address medical and psychological consequences from multiple perspectives.[2]-[6]

Emotional and psychological trauma, when left untreated can result in mental health problems such as major depressive disorder, PTSD, brief psychotic disorder and generalized anxiety disorder. The pain of the trauma can lead the victim to attempt suicide. Suicide is not uncommon in severely traumatized victims (already discussed, in details, in the previous chapter).

There is limited research devoted to the treatment of victims of sexual harassment. The literature on the treatment of psychological trauma and other forms of sexual assault, such as incest, rape, sexual exploitation and battering, can be valuable in conceptualizing treatment approaches for sexual harassment, which is challenging in nature. Treatment is unique for each victim and needs to be tailored according to the individual requirements. Victims need to be helped before the occurrence of new symptoms in order to avoid complications. Early intervention is key to an effective resolution of the crisis. Some frequently used intervention techniques are as follows:

- Cognitive behavioural therapy with a particular focus on the harassment event
- Eye movement desensitization and reprocessing
- Somatic experiencing
- Psychotherapy with a focus on PTSD

There is a paucity of research literature on the treatment of sexual harassment, and the concept of its treatment has been borrowed from related literature available on treatment of incest, rape, sexual exploitation and battering.

A multidimensional approach is needed to treat cases of sexual harassment, which comprises the following factors[2]:

- The existing literature on the treatment of sexual harassment
- Relevant pre-existing literature on psychopharmacology, psychodynamic therapy, cognitive behavioural therapy, group therapy and trauma and grief therapies
- The experience of clinicians in dealing with such cases

One of the related therapies is the practice of osteopathy[1] which began in the USA in 1874 to encourage self-healing with personal inner resources. This system of medicine focuses on promoting health and preventing disease, often used for the treatment of the victims of sexual harassment. In fact, victims approach osteopathy physician for bodily symptoms and, during the course of treatment, reveal the event of sexual harassment. However, these patients are, generally, not interested in preventive treatment. The focus of treatment in osteopathy for the cases of sexual harassment remains on the lasting psychological and physical symptoms caused by the event. The osteopathic approach to medical care involves 'touch' as an important component; the victims may not be comfortable with this approach because of their historical reasons. In the event of sexual harassment,

---

[1] https://en.wikipedia.org/wiki/Osteopathy

she might have experienced an inappropriate touch, and the bitter memories of the event may invoke fresh discomfort. A detailed history is of great therapeutic value for the osteopathic physicians to understand the victim's suffering. Generally, immediately after the episode, the victim is interviewed to know the details of the event when the glucocorticoid and catecholamine levels are still high in the brain interfering in cognitive functioning; the victim's recollection of the event is fragmented and not clear. Fragmented memories can be misinterpreted as inaccurate information; therefore, the victim should be given time and space for her memories to solidify before obtaining the detailed and accurate history.

The physician evaluates the victim's state of health by palpating her skin, muscles, bones, joints and the viscera. Structural dysfunction is determined with the tactile memories of palpation. This procedure may be retraumatizing for the victim as the touch and palpation could possibly revive the old memories of harassment. Trauma-informed care and practice is a method to provide treatment to the survivors of sexual trauma such as rape and other forms of sexual assault.[7] The same procedure is applicable to the cases of sexual harassment, considering a close link between serious sexual crimes and sexual harassment. Osteopathic medicine uses a manipulative technique of touch for examination and treatment.[8]-[10]

Trauma-informed care and practice is one way of treating the victims of sexual harassment used by the practitioners of osteopathic medicine. At present, there is no empirical evidence to support the validity and effectiveness of this method, and sufficient data needs to be generated to authenticate this procedure.

There have been attempts to use other approaches to treat the victims of sexual harassment, of which one comprehensive approach is conceptualized by the extensive work by Sharyn Lenhart.[1] The author has meticulously designed the sequential steps, flexible and adaptable to the wide variation of victims, nature of the problem, stage at which the victim enters the treatment and the constant changes in status with which clinicians deal. The Lenhart's approach comprises nine steps: the initial three steps relate to alliance building, evaluation, validation, support and treatment of immediate symptoms. Next three steps include emotional ventilation, re-establishment of a sense of autonomy and assessment of potential personal losses the victim has suffered. The remaining three steps relate to the identification and appropriate mourning of loss, restoring the pre-existing status and attention to long-term therapy.

This approach incorporates new data and experiences appropriate to sexual harassment. It provides illustrative and related information necessary for proper case management, such as available resources, modes of resolution, relevant legal issues, types and severity of presenting symptomatology, appropriate therapeutic stance for the therapists and formats for initial evaluations.[3]

Following are the nine steps outlined by Lenhart[1] in this approach of treatment divided into three groups.

10.1.1. Alliance Building

Alliance building is an essential component of the treatment plan. It is carried out in the following steps.

10.1.1.1. Handling the Referral

The first contact for which the physician, generally, refers the victim for psychiatric evaluation and treatment is when the symptoms remain unresolved despite the physician's intervention. At times, the victims are referred from courts for a variety of reasons, which are as follows:

1. Treatment of psychiatric symptoms which are developed after the incident of sexual harassment
2. Management of the stress involved in litigation
3. Forensic assessment
4. Expert testimony

Sometimes the referral may come from the employer of the victim on the development of psychiatric symptoms. In such cases, there can be attempts by the employer to intrude upon the treatment with institutional goals, like discouraging litigation. In instances where the treating psychiatrist is an employee of the workplace or the academic institution where the incident occurred or when the evaluation or treatment is mandated or financed or both by that institution, the potential for a conflict of interest and the misuse of the clinician's role is further heightened unless the boundaries of confidentiality and disclosure are established at the beginning itself with both the victim and the institution. The treating expert has to be careful and cautious about these issues. There is always a possibility of exploitation by the employer for the institutional gains and protection of the organization rather than to protect the rights of the victim.

In India, at present, the clinical aspects of sexual harassment are not well recognized, and the problem is viewed more as a social menace where a clinician's role is limited. Moreover, clinicians are often ill-equipped to provide effective therapeutic intervention in such cases because of their poor exposure to the problem during their training programme. Sometimes, courts refer cases of sexual harassment for forensic evaluation and to give an expert opinion; however, the role of treatment is still unrecognized in India.

10.1.1.2. Clinician's Role and Treatment Boundaries

To promote the therapeutic alliance and to get the victim's informed consent for the treatment, it is necessary to address the issues such as conflicts of interest and limits to confidentiality. How much information could be shared with other stakeholders needs to be discussed with the victim (patient), and there should be a mutual agreement between the therapist and the patient on the confidentiality issue. The clinician should keep the treatment record in a concise medical and legal mode and avoid speculations.

In some cases, the victim is already involved in litigation before seeking psychiatric help. In such cases, the clinician should insist that the victim's lawyer obtains a separate forensic evaluation by another professional. The treating psychiatrist should avoid playing forensic psychiatrist.

If the victim is referred by the organization where the sexual harassment occurred, or the treatment is finance by that organization, the clinician should discuss and clarify the following issues with the victim:

1. Purpose of the referral
2. The type of reporting contract the clinician is expected to have with the organization
3. The purpose of any mandated reports
4. Clinician's relationship and obligation to the institution, whether the clinician is an employee of the organization or the academic institution

The victim and the clinician can agree to mutually discuss the contents of any reports, records or other communications with the institution prior to their disclosure and afterwards. If the victim is too distressed to fully appreciate these issues, they should be reviewed again when she has stabilized. In case of conflict of interest, the clinician should refer the victim to another therapist for proper treatment and management.

10.1.1.3. Therapeutic Stance

A strong therapeutic alliance is needed for an effective outcome of the treatment. An empathic validation of the incident of sexual harassment is the most important therapeutic strategy on the part of the therapist for an actively supportive and educative therapeutic alliance during the initial sessions of interacting with the victim or the patient. She will respond favourably and gladly if the clinician makes her believe that[11]:

1. Her perspective is valid, and she has not fabricated a story to teach the perpetrator a lesson or to defame the organization or to hide her own inadequacies at the place of work.
2. She deserves help; her case is genuine.
3. She is not 'a troublemaker', as others often brand her, and that any initial symptoms and impairment in her functioning are more likely the result of her real experience of sexual harassment than caused by any other pathology.
4. She has suffered retaliation in some form if she has filed a complaint or taken legal action.

Since it is a sensitive matter to deal with an emotionally hurt woman, there is a possibility of secondary traumatization and exacerbation of symptoms, if the clinician's behaviour is unfriendly, indifferent or emotionally cold. The clinician should be careful about[12]:

1. Having disbelief in the victim's statements and should avoid vigorous questioning of her report and credibility. The clinician should not sound like an interrogator or detective agent.
2. Preoccupation with whether the victim's experience meets legal criteria for discrimination, rather he/she should focus on the victim's distress, symptoms and misery.
3. Undue focus on the incident of sexual harassment; the clinician should not fail to elucidate other forms of discrimination which the victim has experienced.
4. A rigid analytic stance that often fails to acknowledge the significance of real external events, that overemphasizes the contribution of internal psychological issues and implies that the victim is to blame for her distress.
5. Minimizing the importance of harassment event and attempt should be made to identify other issues as the focus for the treatment. The clinician should judiciously choose the areas of exploration without offending the victim.

After the alliance has been satisfactorily established, the clinician should assess whether the victim is distorting the events or exhibiting inappropriate or self-destructive behaviours and motives that are contributing to her suffering. Some women may distort, exaggerate or engage in provocative or other destructive workplace behaviours because of:

- Earlier sexual traumas which may get activated during the adult life
- Other characterological or affective pathology in the background could be a reason behind such a behaviour
- A psychotic delusional state which may be the part of her psychopathology and mental illness

The above factors may be responsible for such behaviour. In the delusional state, the victim may believe that the perpetrator in question is stalking her, controlling her activities or sexually harassing her. Psychosis needs to be ruled out during the process of interview and examination.

The clinician should identify and treat such conditions in a supportive and timely manner. At the initial stages of treatment, the woman's effectiveness in coping with her situation should be enhanced, and she should be prevented from taking inappropriate steps toward resolution. Later in the treatment, she should be helped to avoid future distress and vulnerability to fall back on drugs, alcohol or smoking. The victim can and should be asked if she feels that other psychological or external factors are contributing to her distress, but this should be done in a manner that communicates a wish to target all sources of stress, as opposed to questioning the validity of her perceptions.

Countertransference may influence the formation of a good therapeutic alliance between the victim and the clinician. The clinician should be careful about certain behaviours which may adversely affect the establishment of the therapeutic alliance. The behaviours such as overidentification with the perpetrator's or the institution's viewpoint should be avoided by the clinician. The lack of awareness of the prevalence of events on the part of the clinician can also lead to some therapeutic errors, which are as follows:

1. Denial or disbelief regarding the abuse of power and irrational stereotyping inherent in these situations
2. Overemphasis of the victim's pathology and ignoring the other aspects
3. Undue preoccupation with the institution's reputation and minimizing the victim's injuries
4. Failure to identify the detrimental effects of lack of support from friends, co-workers, family and the work/academic institution

Overidentification with the victim by the clinician can also be detrimental and can result in[13]:

1. Failure to address the victim's contributing behaviours, ineffective coping strategies or any underlying pathology.
2. Failure to assist in avoiding premature action, based upon incomplete processing of anger and other effects. The therapist should be

aware of any personal gender stereotypes and conflicts of interest that is coming in the treatment.

The victims, in great distress, should be provided with a cognitive framework for treatment to help in forming an alliance. This way the therapist assists in altering negative cognitive attributions with the modulation and the processing of effect. The therapist also assists the victim in identifying the unconscious meaning of the trauma and in developing strategies to contain the trauma without resorting to maladaptive or avoidance behaviours.

10.1.2. Immediate Crisis: Assessment and Intervention

10.1.2.1. Assessment and History Taking

After the formation of a therapeutic alliance, the clinician should assess the nature of the immediate crisis in terms of:

1. Safety of the victim from suicidal attempts or otherwise self-harming behaviour should be ensured. Appropriate measures should be taken to prevent impending self-harm.
2. Threats to employment or academic status of the victim, any possible adverse effect on studies or her work should be explored and addressed accordingly
3. The severity of presenting somatic and emotional symptoms should be evaluated in view of therapeutic intervention.
4. Disruptions in important relationships at the workplace, family and personal life are possible. This area of information should be explored carefully without hurting the sentiments of the victim and should be taken care of accordingly.
5. Threats to financial viability should also be taken into consideration and should be addressed accordingly.

This assessment helps the clinician to ascertain areas of stress and structure an appropriate course of treatment and support. This also encourages the victim to realize the reality of her external situation rather than denying it. It also helps the victim to mobilize her coping responses and problem-solving skills. The victim should be explained that the following detailed information will be needed to plan treatment:

1. This information may include a detailed account of the events, the context, circumstances under which it took place, the place of occurrence and the reasons to be there and the presence of others at the time of incident whether the colleagues or others and the reasons for their presence.
2. Victim's developmental, scholastic, family, marital, sexual and work-related history is important for understanding various aspects of the problem. Peer-relations prior to the event should also be explored.
3. Past medical and psychiatric history is important to understand the current problem. Family history of mental illness, suicide or any deviant behaviour in any of the family members may be relevant.

A detailed mental state examination of the victim should be conducted with an emphasis on assessing the severity of the immediate crisis so that appropriate preventative interventions are instituted regarding extenuating external circumstances and debilitating symptomatology. Physical examination may also be relevant and important in cases of sexual harassment where physical assault is reported.

10.1.2.2. Exploration of Cultural and Economic Factors

It is essential for the treating clinician to be familiar with the victim's relevant cultural background and economic status in order to collaborate effectively in the preliminary assessment of her circumstances. The following factors are important to explore at this stage of the inquiry:

1. Most women work for economic reasons to meet their domestic requirements. Circumstances that led the victim to get into the job need to be explored to understand the importance of the job she is doing. In several instances, the woman may be the only breadwinner for the family.
2. Majority of women at the workplace are in junior or lower-status positions, and their perpetrators are likely to have some authority

or status advantage over them in the work hierarchy. If a woman holds a higher-status position, she is likely to be outnumbered by male peers who might identify with the perpetrator or minimize the significance of her experience or high position.

3. If a woman rejects a harasser's advances, she is challenging his masculinity, manhood and authority. If she tactfully ignores him, she may be mistaken as being coy, which may encourage the perpetrator to enhance his efforts for further harassment. If she challenges his behaviours, she may be labelled a troublemaker. If she chooses to be silent, she may lose any opportunity for promotion, salary enhancement, expert mentoring and other benefits. She has to suffer silently.

4. Traditionally, women are encouraged to internalize misconduct. They are socialized to accept nurturing subordinate roles and to internalize responsibility for maintaining relationships, even when those roles are discriminatory.

5. For most of the women, families come first before jobs and may interpret sexual harassment as a reminder that they should be at home with their families, even if they are working out of economic necessity.

6. Sexual harassment reinforces the low self-confidence and impaired judgment regarding one's own abilities as a result of negative stereotypes one is taught at an early age.

7. In educational institutions, the female students may depend heavily on the perpetrator for educational and training experiences, evaluations and references and opportunities for career advancement. Informal blackballing instigated by the perpetrator can be difficult to combat under the academic environment. The student may be a loser if she protests.

8. Those victims who are in highly specialized positions or those who are specially trained in some particular field and those women who are in significant financial needs and have minimal work or educational backgrounds cannot easily get a transfer or change jobs. In these situations, the victim may be forced to deal with the stress of sexual harassment or suffer severe educational, economic, job and career-development losses.

9. Victims hailing from ethnic, racial, religious or caste minority groups may be subjected to the withdrawal of support or community sanctions because of cultural mandates as follows:

   a. In a particular sociocultural group, a woman victim of sexual harassment at work is asked by her community members not to speak publicly about sexuality as the cultural norms in certain social groups prohibit the victim from doing so publicly.

   b. The community directs such issues to be settled privately within the community rather than speak out publicly against one of her own community people.

   c. The community norms assert to value domestic roles over work roles in the offices.

   d. Community norms also direct its members to give advocacy against racism priority over advocacy against sexism.

   e. In traditional Indian society, a low-caste woman harassed by a high-caste man in the villages is often not taken seriously, and most of such cases go unreported and even unnoticed, and the victim suffers silently without opening her mouth in protest.

10. A woman may already be suffering from some stressors, and the stress of sexual harassment may further complicate the situation, adding to her psychopathology.

11. The support from family, co-workers, superiors and friends plays a crucial role in contributing to treat psychological symptoms and resolution of harassment event.

12. Several victims with previous histories of sexual traumas are more vulnerable to severe symptom manifestation and flooding of repressed memories into the consciousness.

13. Resolution of sexual harassment may be complicated by the presence of other forms of gender discrimination, which the victim might be facing.

14. When one victim complains of sexual harassment, there is a possibility of others facing a similar problem but reluctant to complain. The institute or the workplace may blame the complainant of incompetence in work or academic performance which is likely to have been adequate or superior prior to the event. The longer her problem has persisted, the more likely her performance has deteriorated.

15. Occurrence of sexual harassment may cause disruption and conflict in significant relationships with spouse, family members, friends, co-workers, mentors and others. Disturbed relations are common and highly significant sequelae of sexual harassment.

Assessment of victim's cultural and economic background and other related issues helps both the victim and clinician to know the severity of the problem and the challenges the clinician is likely to face during the treatment of the victim. The assessment also helps to identify special areas of stress which need to be addressed during the therapeutic intervention. This also helps both of them to avoid the following countertransference errors common at this stage of management:

1. It is not appropriate to devalue a victim for an initial inability to take action.
2. The clinician should avoid erroneously supporting the victim in taking immediate or impulsive action that may be ineffective or not in her best interest.

At this stage, the clinician should be able to identify those victims who have minimal symptomatology, healthy coping skills and good support and may require little or no treatment. They may be referred to a self-help group.

10.1.2.3. Guidelines for Effective Individual Responses

The following are the guidelines for effective individual responses:

1. The victim should be clearly able to identify and define the problem as sexual harassment requiring treatment. She should also conceptualize her experience as sexism, skewed group behaviour or micro-inequity. The victim should also evaluate and document the severity of impact and its lasting effect on her personal and professional life.
2. The victim should also assess her emotional status, whether it is depression, psychosomatic illness, anxiety disorder, panic state, rage reactions or post-traumatic reactions. Is she using problematic

defensive reactions such as displaced anger, withdrawal from people, self-blame, isolation, chronic ambivalence and lowered goals? If so, try to contain these developments and work on a more effective response.

3. The clinician should ensure that the victim does not isolate herself from the rest; she should discuss her situation with a trusted friend, a colleague, a peer or a mentor to find an effective solution to the problem.

4. The clinician should enable the victim to define her goals in working out a solution for the problem she is facing.

5. The victim should examine her responsibilities within her institution and should list all possible strategies for dealing with her situation and the potential risks and benefits of each situation. What back-up strategy she could use if her first strategy fails should also be explored.

10.1.3. Evaluation and Treatment of Immediate Symptoms

Victims of sexual harassment present physical and psychological symptoms of varying severity and intensity, which exacerbate at different stages of treatment. The victim deals with prolonged litigation, faces traumatic confrontations, bears significant losses in the form of friends and opportunities, experiences withdrawal of support and other commonly associated stresses. If the victim is in crisis at the time of the initial evaluation or has endured a prolonged experience, it is likely she will have some configuration of debilitating symptoms, requiring the immediate attention of the therapist. Some victims may experience suicidal or homicidal ideas depending on internalization or externalization of her aggression.

The therapist should identify the immediate problems that require urgent intervention, which can be done by focussing on patients complaints and immediate concerns.

The victim should be made aware that her symptoms could change or exacerbate as she experiences stress and changes over the course of treatment. Common symptoms to review include distractibility, psychomotor agitation or retardation, appetite change, insomnia, hypersomnia, decreased libido, hypersexuality, impaired functioning (social or occupational), disorientation, memory loss, phobias, obsessions, compulsions, ruminations, hallucinations, delusions, racing thoughts, dysphoria, apprehensive expectations, anxiety, dyspnoea, palpitations, chest pain, choking sensations, vertigo, feelings of unreality, paraesthesia, sweats, fainting, trembling, suicidal or homicidal ideation, re-experiencing traumatic events (flashbacks), constricted affect, difficulty concentrating, hypervigilance, avoidance, psycho-physiologic symptoms, exaggerated startle response, irritability, detachment, pessimism, social withdrawal, crying, depression, logorrhoea, indecisiveness, guilt, feelings of worthlessness and inadequacy, loss of interest or ability to enjoy life, loss of energy, crying spells, drug and alcohol abuse, headaches, diarrhoea, muscle spasm, nausea, panic attacks or dyspepsia.

Some of the most common psychological problems requiring treatment include:

1. Anxiety disorder or PTSD, along with depressive and substance use disorders.
2. Psychosomatic symptoms and complaints.
3. Victims going through trauma may use restricted or binging behaviour to cope with their shame, guilt and frustration. There may be an occurrence of eating disorders.
4. Victims often self-medicate or inflict non-suicidal self-injury, which includes cutting of wrist and other forms of self-mutilation in order to release feelings of guilt and anger.

Anxiety disorders, depression and PTSD can be treated effectively with adjunctive psychotropic medications selected on the basis of symptom manifestation. There are not many controlled studies on these clinical conditions occurring due to sexual harassment in comparison to other traumatic stress disorders; they provide some guidelines regarding the choice of medication. Several approaches have been recommended to deal with the situations:

- Low-dose anti-anxiety medications can be helpful for daytime anxiety, panic and agitation, provided that they do not trigger dissociative states.

- Selective serotonin reuptake inhibitors are used preferentially, but tricyclic and monoamine oxidase inhibitor antidepressants are also prescribed which can reduce depression, mixed depression and anxiety and obsessive ruminations, generally, experienced by the victims of sexual harassment.
- Mood stabilizers alone or in combination with antidepressants can be effective in patients complaining of hostility, irritability, agitation and hyperactivity.
- Sleep medications are helpful for transient uncomplicated insomnia which can be gradually withdrawn when sleep stabilizes.
- Meditation or a variety of behavioural relaxation techniques may also help in combination with pharmacotherapy.

If the victim trivializes her situation or is simply unaware of the connection between her physical symptoms and her harassment experience, the clinician should explore further to find out the association between the two. The victim should be asked specifically about suicidal ideation and destructive feelings toward themselves, especially if they are depressed and guilt ridden. Homicidal ideation should also be elicited as some victims harbour strong hostility towards the perpetrator. These behaviours are rare but do occur especially in victims with previous sexual traumas. Interventions for symptom relief should be placed in the context of enabling the victim to function optimally so that she can maintain credibility at work and devise the best strategy for resolution.

10.1.4. Emotional Ventilation, Exploration of Negative Perceptions and Formulation of Outcome Goals

After a treatment alliance is formed and the initial debilitating symptoms or external crises are stabilized, the clinician should assist the victim in formulating her plan for dealing with the harassment experience. This is done to re-establish her sense of autonomy and internal control. The victim is assisted in identifying a plan that best suits her needs, goals and style and best protects her against retaliatory actions and the losses she has suffered. The role of the clinician is to provide a safe, stabilizing environment for the victim in view of her needs and goals and plan protective measures against any possible retaliatory behaviours that may result from her actions. This process usually involves the following three steps.

- **Emotional ventilation of feelings:** Emotional ventilation is an important step towards the release of pent-up emotions. Exploration of negative perceptions and formulation of outcome goals should be expressed.
- **Review of the pros and cons:** A review of possible responses to the discrimination, as well as the formulation and enactment of a realistic plan of action involves the second step.
- **Assessment of potential losses:** Assessment of retaliatory behaviours and opportunities lost should be done.

A victim of sexual harassment undergoes a wide variety of experiences which include intense feelings and related cognitions, such as anxiety, fear, confusion, disbelief, guilt, shame, anger, sadness, disillusionment, self-blame, and self-devaluation.[14] This wide spectrum of emotional responses is common and usually unfolds in progressive stages.[12], [15] Full exploration and ventilation of these feelings are not only to relieve the distress but also to prevent the adverse outcomes, which are as follows:

- Impulsive actions that are not in the victim's best interest and do not lead to effective resolution
- Emotional displays in the workplace, which can lead to decreased credibility, termination of employment or exposure of the victim's vulnerabilities to unsupportive people.
- Displacement of negative affect onto potentially supportive individuals, such as spouses, mentors, treating clinicians and the lawyers.

Emotional ventilation and exploration of negative perceptions can be described as follows.

10.1.4.1. *Stages of Reactions*

The first reaction to the experience of sexual harassment could be a feeling of confusion and disbelief often related to a wish to believe that the harassment did not happen at all or will stop soon or that it is not detrimental to her. However, a well-informed victim who knows the factual realities at work will face her problem effectively in a reality-oriented manner. Her knowledge to deal with the sexual harassment will help to 'normalize' the experience and prevent the development of a sense of isolation or narcissistic injury, which can be problematic later.

The emotional ventilation will help to clarify the fear, anxiety and occasionally paranoia related to threats of physical injury, job loss, economic ruin, derailment from crucial career and educational pathways, loss of key relationships and supports and retaliatory actions from the perpetrators. Emotional ventilation also stabilizes the victim and prevents her from impulsive withdrawal from the workplace or abruptly changing the career, prepares her for developing a plan of action that will minimize and protect her from future trauma. Paranoia in response to sexual harassment is often seen in the victims and should not be assumed as indicative of more severe pathology like psychosis or personality disorder. Anxiolytic medication or relaxation therapy can be useful to control severe anxiety reactions.

The uninterrupted emotional ventilation of shame, guilt and self-blame serves several important functions:

1. Emotional ventilation permits a realistic discussion and an adaptive resolution of any pre-existing concerns regarding intrinsic work or academic ability triggered by the experience of sexual harassment.
2. Shame regarding women's roles, sexual orientation or the public discussion of sexual issues, which could be a stigma in a particular culture, can be alleviated with emotional ventilation prior to the disclosure or complaint proceedings.
3. Imaginary and real concerns regarding the victim's contributions to her situation can be addressed, and appropriate action can be taken to rectify any inappropriate or contradictory behaviour on her part, like previously colluding with or encouraging the behaviour.
4. The public, in general, and most of the victims view sexual harassment as something the individual can and should be able to handle directly and assertively, despite empirical evidence to the contrary.

This viewpoint induces guilt in the victim and exposes her to direct and subtle blame from others.

5. In case, the clinician has discovered that the woman has lied, distorted or fabricated the event of sexual harassment, she can be discouraged from further action, and the motivations for her behaviour can be explored in the privacy and safety of her therapy.

6. The clinician should put the situation in proper perspective taking into consideration her work, family and other women's role conflicts aggravated by the situation. This will help in decreasing the chance of an impulsive and detrimental flight from the workplace based on guilt.

The victim may not express anger directly at the perpetrator or the institution, which could be detrimental for her. Impulsive expressions of anger through litigation, verbal confrontations and obsessional thoughts of revenge are generally destructive; the victim should be allowed ample opportunity to express her grievances, in detail, explore her anger and bring it into perspective before she takes any action. Some victims, out of anger, are unable to be properly assertive and take appropriate action. If the woman's anger is because of distortion of the event or a displacement from other issues, it cannot be effectively resolved via workplace complaints, which might correctly be identified as frivolous and therefore ultimately detrimental to her credibility and well-being.

Because of sexual harassment experience, the victim's belief system may get shattered, and there could be immediate or potential losses resulting in depression and disillusionment. The experience of being harassed, unsupported and devalued by powerful individuals should be resolved within the therapy so that these experiences do not interfere with the victim's energy and ability to assert herself on her own behalf.

10.1.4.2. Processing of Negative Perceptions

The victim experiences negative changes in the internal perception of self, others and the world, which accompany the victim's strong feelings in accordance with the progressive emotional stages. Negative internal cognitions may trigger, intensifying the impact of sexual harassment. Negative self-concepts due to sexual harassment include:

2. Incompetence and personal helplessness
3. Lowered self-esteem
4. Generalized self-doubt
5. Underrating one's own skills and abilities and talents
6. The belief that she has chosen the wrong job, profession or academic focus. She regrets her decision
7. Loss of faith in people in general and finds it difficult even to believe most trusted people
8. Disillusionment with mentors, superiors, institutions which she used to value before the event
9. Exacerbation of inner conflicts regarding home and work balance, accompanied by a belief that harassment is punishment for neglecting her family or proof that she belongs at home, rather than in the office
10. The belief that she only provoked the harassment for his sexual advances. She feels guilty about it
11. The victim may believe that if action against the perpetrator was taken on her behalf, it would be unfair or harmful to the perpetrator and his family members will suffer for no fault of theirs
12. Destruction of a sense of justice
13. She may develop a belief that hard work, ability, or loyalty will never be rewarded

The clinician should educate and caution the victim about the frequency of these reactions; the victim needs to self-monitor and openly discuss such changes with her treating clinician. These perceptions are often reinforced by the subtle and overt blame the victim faces in her work and social communications. Permanent and maladaptive changes in internal perceptions of the victim will occur if the clinician ignores these perceptions. There can be serious long-term consequences for the victim, like maladaptive coping responses. The most common maladaptive behaviours could be as follows:

- Impulsive confrontation and litigation.
- Impulsive withdrawal involving job, career or academic changes.

- Displacement of legitimate anger onto supportive or neutral people in the organization or at home.
- Internalization of the blame with self-punitive behaviours or persistent non-productive attempts to make the situation better.
- Isolation and secretiveness regarding the events, avoiding discussion with even the most trusted friends or family members.
- Ambivalent anger for the perpetrator and self-doubts about her work competence and career choices. There is erosion in her confidence.
- Denial of the seriousness of the situation and failure to act perceiving it to be a minor incident.

Intense feelings, negative cognitions and maladaptive coping responses may arise and recede at various stages of the treatment process, which requires continuous monitoring by both the victim and the therapist. Ventilation of emotions prepares the victim for developing a realistic and effective plan of action, free of emotional distortion. This process also educates her regarding common emotional reactions that may hinder her and allies her with her therapist in identifying and monitoring her affect as treatment progresses.

10.1.5. Restoring Autonomy and Control

The next step of treatment is regaining the sense of autonomy and control by developing effective coping strategies and formulating an effective plan of action.

After exploring and processing the feelings of the victim, she should be made to develop a plan for action. The clinician should refrain from recommending a specific course but should assist in developing her own plan, based on her individual needs and goals. Her independent decision will go a long way in helping her establish herself. By encouraging her to do so, the clinician re-establishes her sense of control to review her coping mechanisms and address any inappropriate responses in light of what she has learned about her feelings and perceptions—to review all possible options for resolution of the situation, along with the pros and cons of each and choose the option that best suits her own needs and goals, provided that they are realistic. It also helps her to proceed with her plan at her own pace and to develop protective measures against further discrimination or retaliation minimizing further losses.[1]

However, the clinician should be aware of the types of options and grievance formats to provide a cognitive framework from which the victim can construct her personal plan. There are following five approaches to resolve sexual harassment experiences:

1. Direct approach for response
2. Indirect approach for response
3. Formal complaint
4. Litigation/legal action
5. Special approach methods

The first four approaches routinely recommended by the organizational consultants include confrontation–negotiation and advocacy-seeking categories of victim responses. These externally directed assertive responses are effective in stopping sexual harassment behaviours; therefore, these are assumed to be the healthiest responses from a psychological point of view. From the clinical perspective, a healthy assertive response should include a response in which the victim, thoughtfully and without denial or avoidance, acts assertively to protect her own interests. She may initially utilize a special form of response to stabilize herself and then move on to utilize a more traditional plan of action.

All aspects of these approaches should be carefully examined. However, the clinician should not advise on legal matters and should refer her to a lawyer to assess the possibilities for litigation if she chooses to go for that.

For restoring autonomy and control the above mentioned five approaches are described, in detail, as follows.

10.1.5.1. Direct Approach for Response

The direct approach is generally through the institutional representative. It is an effective approach provided that the victim feels that the discrimination is not conscious and that the institutional representative is reasonable and supportive to her in the past, and his intervention will be in her interest.

Mary Rowe[14] has outlined the advantages of the direct approach, which are as follows:

1. Presence of the third person may polarize the views of the opposing person and discussion may help in clarifying some issues.
2. It provides a chance to defend those who are wrongly accused.
3. It gives a chance to those who are correctly accused to make amendments.
4. It gives an opportunity to provide evidence of the offence.
5. This opportunity can be used to give a fair warning to those perpetrators who don't understand what they have done or are doing.
6. It gives the victim a chance to get the harassment stopped without experiencing public embarrassment, damaging the organization's reputation or causing the offender to lose face.
7. It provides the victim with a way to demonstrate that all reasonable means to get the offender stop have been tried. This step may be convincing later to supervisors, spouses, and others who become involved.
8. It encourages ambivalent complainants to present a consistent and clear message.

Rowe also suggests a written approach to the perpetrator with concise and polite content. However, writing to the perpetrator could be risky and may adversely affect the victim.

10.1.5.2. Indirect Approach for Response

The indirect approach requires the victim to do the following[15]:

1. Identify a supportive third party or parties with formal authority or informal influence within the place of work
2. Request that the identified party or parties intervene on her behalf, either directly with the perpetrator or via the appropriate institutional representative
3. Maintain control over the process by requesting the third party to intervene in a specific or limited way

The victim may request the third party to communicate specifically with the perpetrator or a responsible authority in the work hierarchy to address the issue. A circular may be issued reiterating departmental policies and giving the offending experience as an example of a violation without naming the parties. The victim may distance herself and leave the third party to exercise its own discretion regarding intervention approaches. Informal channels can also be utilized to ascertain:

- If others in the workplace have complained or experienced similar problems
- The offender's status or vulnerability within the organization
- The organization's official stance and history of dealing with discrimination

Indirect approaches have several advantages, some of which are as follows:

- They eliminate the risks of individual confrontation.
- Confidentiality and privacy can often be maintained.
- Victim can effect resolution with minimal time and effort.
- Effort is focused on reconciliation, rather than on sanctions or confrontation.

In most of the cases, victims are more interested in resolving the problem than in ascribing blame and punishing individuals or institutions. In a significant number of cases, they only want discriminatory activities to stop without disrupting their work or academic activities and disrupting their work relations.

There are some disadvantages to the indirect approach include the following situations:

- The inability to maintain control of the process
- The risk that the third party will be unsympathetic
- The possibility that institutional policies may mandate that the third party institute formal complaint procedures, despite the victim's unwillingness

10.1.5.3. Formal Complaint

A formal complaint can be lodged with ICC within three months of the episode or within three months of the last episode of the ongoing harassment. If the ICC is satisfied that the conditions for the victim were so grave that made her unable to lodge her complaint in the specified time, she is granted a period of three months to lodge her complaint. The victim files a written complaint providing six copies of the complaint to the ICC. The ICC then conducts a formal investigation that commits to protecting the rights of any individuals accused, as well as those of the complainant, that is, protection against retaliation. A hearing is held to discuss the results of the investigation and to determine what sanctions will be applied if the accused individual or individuals are found responsible for sexual harassment of the complainant. Either side may institute an appeals process if it finds the outcome unacceptable. Because law mandates policies against discrimination, almost all institutions have policies against sexual harassment and discrimination. Many institutions are yet to have a policy against sexual harassment.

Disadvantages of formal complaint could possibly be as follows:

1. The procedure exposes the complainant to informal ostracization and negative labelling such as 'troublemaker', 'whistle-blower', 'seductress' or 'mental case'. Colleagues often criticize her rather than sympathizing. She is often labelled as 'attention seeker'.
2. The complainant has to collect and compile substantial evidence, which is often difficult if records and documentation have not been kept. For want of documentary evidence, many cases are dismissed, and the harassers go free with their routine activities of sexual harassment.
3. The process is time-consuming (gives ICC 90 days to complete the process), intimidating, exhausting and traumatizing. There may be repeated hearings by the ICC for reaching conclusion.
4. Co-workers' and superiors' support can be minimal, and their negative reactions intense and prolonged and may have adverse effects on the victim.
5. Sanctions may be minimal, especially if the accused is valuable to the institution and the victim a low-ranking employee.

10.1.5.4. Litigation/Legal Action

Sexual harassment behaviour may violate both civil and criminal laws, such as assault, intentional infliction of emotional distress, interference with a contract, defamation, breach of contract and negligent intent. Suits may be filed against an individual, an institution or both. Legal action can be effective as a means of empowerment or in obtaining monetary restitution. If the victim is no longer affiliated with the institution or has suffered serious economic or other losses that cannot be resolved by other means, litigation may be the only option. Legal proceedings allow women to expose and directly face the perpetrator or institution in a setting outside the institution, a setting where case law sets precedents and treatment can be more objective. This can be psychologically healing for those victims with unshakable determination to do everything possible to seek vindication for themselves and to improve the workplace for others.

The nearest police station can be approached to lodge an FIR registered as a 'zero FIR', in case the police station is not the one of appropriate jurisdiction which is transferred to appropriate jurisdiction, and hence, no complaint can go unaddressed. No FIR can be refused if the complaint does not relate to the area of the police station where the complainant has approached. There is a separate lady police officer at every police station to deal with cases related to women. If the lady police officer is not available, a lady constable can be approached. A complaint can be lodged with a telephonic call or by email as well. No sexual harassment[2] complaint can be refused to be lodged by the police officer since it is a cognizable offence. However, in case if the police officer still refuses to do so, one can complain to the district judicial magistrate under Section 156(3) and Section 190 of the Criminal Procedure Code with the help of a lawyer.

Legal suits may be costly, time-consuming and, at times, highly adversarial. Negative outcomes may result in a sense of profound loss and complicated mourning reactions. If the goals of litigation are unrealistic, even a positive outcome can be disappointing. Legal proceedings, especially involving professional women, can result in

[2] https://lawrato.com/criminal-lawyers

permanent blackballing within their fields via informal networks. Work efficiency is adversely affected by the institution.[1]

10.1.5.5. Special Approach Methods

The treating clinician should encourage the victims to generate options outside the standard procedures in order to maximize the chance of a positive resolution based on realistic goals, available resources and overall best interests (internal psychological health and external goals and needs). Some women choose to become active on an organizational or educational basis, joining women's groups and organizing workshops and work-gender issues committees within their institution rather than focusing on their specific case. These activities are inappropriate if they lead to avoidance or displacement regarding the individual's situation. However, they could be empowering if a woman feels that her organizational role mandates a broader response. A woman can also efficiently resolve a situation by minimizing contact with the problematic person, initiating a transfer within the institution, changing her reporting status. Some women create their own environment by starting their own businesses or professional practices or by partnering with other like-minded individuals. Sometimes a special approach is needed first to allow the victim time to stabilize emotionally, gather her resources and review her options, in order to move on to a more direct response aimed at the specific discriminatory behaviour.

10.1.6. Assessment of Losses, Retaliatory Behaviours and Administering Protective Measures

After the victim has developed an action strategy, the clinician should collaborate with her in assessing potential losses and retaliatory behaviours, which she has gone through, to prepare her for protective strategies as she begins to act upon her overall plan for future. Protective actions include:

- Identifying and neutralizing potential opponents documenting work quality
- Maintaining an impeccable attendance record to negate the claim of criticisers

- Meeting deadlines of the assigned tasks
- Identifying and utilizing supportive people and advocates within the workplace and maintaining a harmonious relationship with them
- Locating witnesses wherever they are
- Collaborating with other victimized people to gain their support
- Identifying possibilities for transfers or for changing supervisors

The victim should identify the most supportive among her family and friends and engage them in helping her as and when the need arises. Identification of unsupportive family members and friends is also important to neutralize them if possible. Professional and women's organizations can be useful sources of support and information. Friends' help also goes a long way in bringing the situation back to normal.

The clinician can help by guiding her in processing underlying feelings that might cause disappointments and frustrations like revenge as a major goal. Revenge is unlikely to bring satisfaction as it is often the result of unresolved anger and persisting bitterness against the perpetrator. The therapist can educate the victim about the common reactions of institutions, families, friends and workers, thus enhancing her ability to anticipate and cope with their problematic responses in a healthy and supportive manner. These disruptions in significant relationships are emotionally damaging and may lead to disturbed interpersonal relations. The therapist should also identify other potential risks of the victim's action plan and prepare for avoiding or coping with potential difficulties. The clinician should make the victim aware of these possibilities. The therapist should also provide information regarding the litigation and complaint processes and their consequences.

The clinician can assist the victim in protecting herself within her own environment or selecting the best environment for herself if she is considering either transferring locations within her workplace or leaving it for a new work where chances of sexual harassment are minimum.

10.1.6.1. Special Proactive Measures during Litigation

The risk of retraumatization and retaliation may be possible during the litigation process, and special assistance may be required in preparing protective measures. The clinician should implement the following steps:

- Expected impact of litigation on the therapy should be reviewed by the therapist with the confidentiality of the therapy in mind.
- The victim's lawyer should have a forensic expert other than the therapist (clinician) to testify clinical issues.
- The clinician can also help the victim in assessing the emotional, interpersonal and economic costs of litigation and in formulating realistic goals for the outcome.
- Exacerbations of symptoms and stressful experiences are likely to occur during the litigation process, and the clinician should be able to manage them.
- The therapist should enable the victim to maintain control over the litigation process.
- The victim should be encouraged to seek support from significant others within the office and family.
- The clinician should assist the victim in focusing her energy on restoring her life, independent of the litigation process.

The clinician should be aware of the purpose of litigation and discuss it with the victim. The purpose of litigation, at times, may not be clear or may be aimed at unrealistic goals, idealistic wishes for the resolution of truth and justice and a desire for financial gain,[16] which may not be a real accomplishment.

There should be a careful evaluation of emotional distress costs versus the benefits in litigation. The following issues should be considered during the process of litigation[1]:

- Interruptions in the psychotherapy process
- Exacerbation of somatic and psychosomatic symptoms
- Psychological retraumatization
- The victim may devote excessively on legality than on health issues

Potential benefits of ligation outcome include[17]:

- The victim may obtain genuine compensation for the harassment which she has experienced.
- There may be a big impact on procedures for dealing with sexual harassment or both.
- The victim may obtain a sense of support when others join her collectively in a lawsuit.
- A positive outcome in the legal battle will give a sense of satisfaction.
- There will be a feeling that the outcome of the legal battle will benefit others as well.

Retaliation is possible by the colleagues or supervisors during the process of litigation which may lead to polarization of opinion combined with an organized institutionalized stance against the complainants, which often results in feelings of ostracization and invalidation of her claim. There can be the withdrawal of support from those who previously shared similar concerns or experiences; they may refuse to come forward to support the victim and part ways with her. It could be because of fear of retaliation from others or the fear of antagonizing the authorities. The victim may feel betrayed if it was co-workers' encouragement that led her to proceed with her complaint. The management may pressure and reward other female employees to replace the victim or to speak out in support of the institution. This may prove more damaging psychologically for the victim. Poor performance evaluations, demotions, withdrawal of mentor support, adverse job transfers, dismissals, verbal threats and persona non grata status are common retaliations leading the victim to self-doubt, have diminished self-confidence, ambivalence about her career or job, disillusionment with the institution and the supervisors, mistrust and withdrawal. If the victim is able to garner support from co-workers or key authorities, the experience can be empowering, even when the legal verdict is unfavourable.[2]

The outcome of the lawsuit can disrupt the victim's personal relations, or it may strengthen them. Spouses may identify with the

harasser or may experience the episode of harassment with rage, guilt and shame that they were unable to protect their woman from the perpetrator. There can be turbulence in victim's family life, finances or sexual relations. They may be harassed for 'allowing' their wife to file a complaint. There could be fear and disruption for the children and distressed by the increased stress levels within the family. The victim's complaint could be a cause of embarrassment for her mothers who may experience guilt and a sense of responsibility for not properly warning and protecting her daughter. The daughter may identify with the mother's shame or become pessimistic about the workplace. If a victim receives constant support from significant people in her personal life, she can feel encouraged, confident and oblivious to the stress of the lawsuit.[16]

The clinician should discuss the possibility of career derailment or job loss and financial stress with the victim before she goes for litigation. If the victim wins the legal battle but loses the larger battle which can extend well beyond her immediate work institution, it may be more distressing for her. If the litigation is prolonged, it can disrupt her working and may be more distressing, and she becomes disillusioned with her institution, her mentors and the leaders in the organization or the professional fields who either perpetrate or collude with the perpetrators and the retaliators.

10.1.7. Mourning, Recovery and Reinvestment

Recovery from the bitter experience of sexual harassment is a complicated process that is often overlooked by both the clinician and the victim. Full recovery from the experience involves more than just getting back to the work that prompted the victim to seek help. To complete the process of treatment, the following three final steps are needed:

1. Identification and appropriate mourning of the inevitable loss
2. Starting everything afresh and investment in prior or newly formulated life goals and activities
3. Attention to other significant therapy and treatment issues

These steps are discussed, in detail, as follows.

10.1.7.1. Identification and Appropriate Mourning of Inevitable Loss

The victim suffers significant losses even when she has handled her situations well, and her plans of action had a positive outcome. These losses must be properly identified, evaluated and addressed before the victim reinvests energy in her life and moves forward in life as a productive member of the workplace or a contributing student of an academic institution. The losses may be very significant in the victim's life and can leave her alone to mourn as others may not be in a position to appreciate these losses. The victim should be encouraged to talk about what has changed for her as a result of the harassment and the ways to cope with it need to be suggested. Commonly experienced losses are of job, income, significant work or academic relationships, such as mentors, teachers, co-workers and superiors, career and job derailments, loss of time from personal and career development, loss of opportunities for specialized training, loss of motivation, self-confidence and enthusiasm for job or academic activities and loss of confidence in career or job choice.

Loss can be there in the victim's personal life—marital harmony, sexual function, family's co-operation or community support. Social ostracism, parenting conflicts, financial stress and disruption of friendships and family relationships are the commonly occurring losses. Financial difficulties due to loss of job, demotions, absentee-ism, treatment for physical and emotional adverse effects, legal costs, relocations and career changes may necessitate significant lifestyle changes.

There can be loss of trust in others, in work, institution and in value systems related to fairness and equality. Defensive or self-destructive attributes, such as self-blame, viewing the experience as bad luck, rather than as transient or addressable and expecting that the current experience will be repeated in any work or academic setting are other internal changes that are crucial to address in treatment.[12], [18], [19]

10.1.7.2. Starting Everything Afresh and Investment in Prior or Newly Formulated Life Goals and Activities

Specific cognitive behavioural approaches should be utilized to start everything afresh. These approaches are as follows:

1. Search for the meaning of the experience
2. Attempts to regain mastery and control and prevent reoccurrence
3. Efforts to promote self-enhancement and greater confidence, mature perspective, sensitivity and self-control

10.1.7.3. Attention to Other Significant Therapy and Treatment Issues

The therapist should provide emotional support to the victim going through a bitter experience. This is done helping her to:

1. Manage depression and other psychiatric symptoms
2. Make her properly utilize complimentary self-help supportive therapy
3. Apply cognitive behavioural interventions appropriately that will prepare her to reinvest in new life and work situations

10.1.8. Re-establishment of Investment in Pre-existing or Newly Formulated Goals and Activities

With effective treatment, the victim will develop a sense of stability and will spontaneously exhibit energy and motivation in her personal life and new work situation. She will reinvest herself in working to achieve old goals and commit herself to new goals, which she may have formulated during the course of this treatment.

In case the victim has not been able to reinvest her energies, the clinician should actively assist her. The unresolved issues should be identified by him and addressed adequately to bring the victim to normalcy. These issues might be residual depression, unresolved losses, negative cognitive attributions, the reactivation of old losses and early issues around self-esteem, assertion and entitlement. Previous sexual abuse or trauma might be revealed at this time and may be appropriately addressed in longer-term treatment. If there is no additional work to be done and the victim is asymptomatic and actively engaged in her life, the treatment can be terminated at this stage, with the understanding that treatment can be resumed if issues arise in the future. It is advisable that the victim remains in active contact with the clinician for future professional advice.

10.1.9. Long-term therapy and Other Therapeutic Issues

The treatment for sexual harassment may intersect with other treatment issues in several ways, which are as follows:

- The victim may enter treatment for sexual harassment, and in the process may uncover significant long-term issues that need to be addressed when immediate work or academic situation has been resolved
- The victim may encounter discrimination in the context of ongoing therapy focused on other issues.
- Several crises may be occurring at once.

It is unlikely for the victim to be able to focus on other issues when she is trying to cope with the crisis of her immediate problem of sexual harassment and protect herself from retaliation. The clinician can reassure her that other issues can receive attention after the immediate situation has been resolved. If several crises are occurring at the same time, that is, physical harassment in the marriage and sexual abuse at work, the situations need to be addressed in the order of priority based on the woman's safety and overall well-being. Motivating the victim to lodge a sexual harassment complaint may not be feasible with other ongoing issues such as marital discord and child's illness. The victim should be helped to minimize the stress of the work situation by avoiding the harasser and focus her energy on the more serious crisis. If the woman has a pre-existing history of another type of gender-related abuse or psychological trauma, her work or academic situation may precipitate a psychological crisis and might require a specialized approach. This will be true for a significant number of victims.[20]

10.1.9.1. Specialized Techniques for Pre-traumatized Victims

If a victim has a history of rape, incest, childhood sexual abuse, sexual exploitation or another trauma, she may have difficulty coping with even the mildest forms of sexual harassment because of her past painful experience. Significant symptoms, especially anxiety, depression, substance abuse and traumatic reactions are commonly present in such situations. Difficulties with self-esteem, self-assertion, self-confidence and confusion regarding the boundaries of power, authority and sexuality may also be present and will severely inhibit her capacity to resolve her current situation. She may have a prior history of difficulties with work or personal boundaries, including repeated injudicious workplace affairs. Previous problems with self-esteem, self-assertion and healthy entitlement may have already led to her placement in a low-level work position. All of these situations predispose her to be targeted for sexual harassment, gender discrimination or both. They will also inhibit her capacity to cope and reduce her credibility, placing her at risk of being blamed for any situations that occur. Often, the discriminating experience, especially if sexual in nature, will act as a precipitant for the depression caused by previously forgotten traumatic experiences. Being compromised in coping with her current situation, she must also deal with a new disorder, which is often misunderstood and may lead to her being labelled hysterical or oversensitive. In these instances, immediate intervention is needed, and the treatment plan should be reformulated to focus on short-term stabilization of symptoms. This can be accomplished with psychotropic medication, relaxation techniques and cognitive education aimed at helping the victim appreciate what is happening to her. Meditation and behavioural therapy and yoga can be utilized to help the patient control the flooding of memories. She may be unable to deal with her current situation until she has stabilized and may require either time off from work or special assignments involving minimal contact with the discriminatory situation, perpetrator or both.[21]

10.1.9.2. Short-term Stabilization

Short-term stabilization of symptoms can be accomplished with psychotropic medication, relaxation therapy and cognitive behaviour therapy aimed at helping the victim appreciate what is happening to her. Yoga and behavioural techniques can be utilized to help the victim control the flooding of memories of the unpleasant experience of sexual harassment. It won't be possible for her to deal with her current situation until she has stabilized.[1]

10.1.9.3. *Coping with the Current Sexual Harassment*

The victim should be assisted in dealing with her current situation by utilizing the earlier format. The clinician should help her to pace her plan of action so that she does not become overwhelmed with anxiety. The clinician should assist her to adequately protect herself from retaliation. Transferring or otherwise removing herself from the presence of the perpetrator may be advisable.

10.1.9.4. *Exploration of Previous Trauma History and Its Impact*

Long-term treatment, including elucidation of memories of abuse and its insidious effects, should only be undertaken when the immediate situation has been resolved, when the victim has established an effective relationship with her therapist and when she has both time and resources to complete treatment.[22]

If left untreated, sexual harassment can cause long-lasting negative changes in victim's perception and severely hinder her enjoyment of her abilities and deprive the workplace of her valuable and much-needed learned contribution. Appropriate clinical interventions can provide the victim to deal with the immediate work crisis, ventilate and process her feelings, monitor and contain symptoms, prevent maladaptive coping, develop an effective plan of action, protect against further negative consequences, and recover, and reinvest in life. The treatment model provides a sequential but flexible framework for the accomplishment of these tasks.[1]

10.2. Treatment for Harassers

There is very little research on the characteristics of men who sexually harass women. In many countries, there is a practice of psychiatric evaluation of the perpetrator, if the charge is proved, to be sent for treatment of sexual harassment behaviour and its correction before allowing to re-enter his workplace.[21] The treatment includes counselling and psychotherapy in the absence of any specifically defined treatment for sexual harassment. Indian courts generally don't refer to such cases for treatment, since there is no well-defined available treatment, and the problem is by and large considered law and order and management issue to be tackled otherwise.

Similarities between individual characteristics of sexual harassers and the perpetrators of other sexual offences, like rape, sexual harassment are often viewed along a continuum of behaviours that could result in sexual violence. Viewed this way, the treatment provided for offenders of serious sexual crimes can be applied to sexual harassers. There can be attempts to devise treatment programmes for the sexual harassers from the treatments for sex offenders.[21], [22] However, the treatments for sexual offenders of serious crimes are also not well defined and have their own limitations as little has been demonstrated about the efficacy and outcome of the available treatments for such subjects. The characteristic features of sexual harassers include problematic schematic fusions between power and sex, unfavourable attitudes towards women, poor empathy and have a tendency to blame their victims for their own actions which they try to justify in their own way.[23] In addition, some other research suggests that men who sexually harass women are lonely individuals who have problems establishing and maintaining intimacy in more appropriate ways, they don't trust others easily and find difficulty in establishing close intimacy.[24], [25] In view of these characteristics of harassers, therapeutic intervention can be designed accordingly.[26], [27] Moreover, research with sexual offenders also indicates that they exhibit problems with emotional regulation and coping with negative life events;[28] these characteristics could be of significant value in designing their treatment plans. They engage in sex-focused coping mechanisms which increase their probability to commit the crime of rape or other serious offences.[29] These findings are of great value for further research in designing treatment strategies for sexual harassers.

The only means of research so far is done by Pryor and Stoller[25], [30] who studied the underlying features of the sexual harassers to identify the likelihood of committing sexual harassment. Current research is mainly victim-focused and rarely interviews sexual harassers themselves to obtain information on the key factors facilitating sexual harassment; therefore, understanding of the basic typologies of men, who sexually harass, is required to formulate treatment plans.

Since sexual harassment is now recognized as a continuum of sexual violence,[29] the gap exists in the knowledge of how the harassers are similar to the culprits of serious crimes in their personality characteristics. Longitudinal follow-up studies of young sexual harassers are needed that could throw light on their individual characteristics to know who turns into serious sexual offenders and who does not. Identification of subtypes who may go on to commit serious forms of sexual aggression would increase the ability of professionals to formulate effective preventive treatment programmes for use with first-time sexual harassers. It will reduce sexual harassment and possibly more severe sexual crimes as well.

The cognitive styles of sexual offenders (socio-cognitive theories), their deficits in empathy and also their intimacy issues and attachment styles[30] need to be better comprehended and used in treatment designing.

Currently, there is no effective and well-tested treatment, and the lack of treatment programmes means the harassers, who are directed to receive treatment, would receive usual counselling or psychotherapy by an unaware professional and then be allowed to re-enter the workplace to continue his earlier behaviour. The victims of sexual harassment continue to face harassment, a situation that could be much improved were researched to examine the characteristics of sexual harassers more thoroughly and design effective treatment strategies on the basis of those characteristics ...

References

[1]   Lenhart SA. *Clinical Aspects of Sexual Harassment and Gender Discrimination.* New York, NY: Routledge; 2004.

[2]   Avina C, O'Donohue W. Sexual harassment and PTSD: Is sexual harassment diagnosable trauma? *Journal of Traumatic Stress.* 2002;15(1):69–75.

[3]   Esacove AW. A diminishing of self: Women's experiences of unwanted sexual attention. *Healthcare for Women International.* 1998 Apr 1;19(3):181–192.

[4] Fitzgerald LF. Sexual harassment: Violence against women in the workplace. *American Psychology.* 1993 Oct;48(10):1070–1076.

[5] Richman JA, Rospenda KM, Nawyn SJ, Flaherty JA, Fenrich M, Drum L, Johnson TP. Sexual harassment and generalized workplace abuse among university employees: Prevalence and mental health correlates. *American Journal of Public Health.* 1999 Mar;89(3):358–363.

[6] Schneider KT, Swan S, Fitzgerald LF. Job related and psychological effects of sexual harassment in the workplace: Empirical evidence from two organizations. *Journal of Applied Psychology.* 1997;82(3):401–415.

[7] Chila A. *Foundations of Osteopathic Medicine* (3rd ed.). Philadelphia, PA: Lippincott Williams and Wilkins; 2011.

[8] Raja S, Hasnain M, Hoersch M, Gove-Yin S, Rajagopalan C. Trauma informed care in medicine: Current knowledge and future research directions. *Family Community Health.* 2015;38(3):216–226.

[9] Scalzo TP. Rape and Sexual Assault Reporting Requirements for Competent Adult Victims. The National Centre for the Prosecution of Violence Against Women, 2006. Available at: http://www.ncdsv.org/images/Rape%20and%20SA%20Reporting%20Requirements%20%20-%20Scalzo%206.15.06.pdf (accessed on 4 January 2021).

[10] Machtinger EL, Cuca YP, Khanna N, Rose CD, Kimberg LS. From treatment to healing: The promise of trauma-informed primary care. *Women's Health Issues.* 2015;25(3):193–197.

[11] Hamilton JA, Jensvold M. Personality psychopathology and depressions in women. In: Brown LS, Ballou M, editors. *Theories of Personality and Psychopathology: Feminist Reappraisals.* New York, NY: Guilford Press; 1992, pp. 116–143.

[12] Shrier DK, Hamilton JA. Therapeutic interventions and resources. In: Shrier DK, editor. *Sexual Harassment in the Workplace and Academia: Psychiatric Issues.* Washington, DC, WA: American Psychiatric Press; 1996. pp. 95–112.

[13] Simon RI. The credible forensic psychiatric evaluation in sexual harassment litigation. *Psychiatric Annals.* 1996;26(3):139–148.

[14] Rowe Mary P. Dealing with sexual harassment. *Harvard Business Review.* 1981;59:42–46.

[15] Hughes JO, Sandler BR. In Case of Sexual Harassment: A Guide for Women Students. Washington, DC: Project on the Status and Education of Women. Association of American Colleges, 1986. Available at: https://files.eric.ed.gov/fulltext/ED268920.pdf (accessed on 4 January 2021).

[16] Berstein AE, Lenhart Sharyn A. *The Psychodynamic Treatment of Women.* Washington DC, WA: American Psychiatric Press; 1993.

[17] Gutek BA. Sexual harassment: Rights and responsibilities. *Employee Responsibilities and Rights Journal.* 1993;6(4):325–340.

[18] Lenhart SA, Schrier DK. Potential costs and benefits of sexual harassment litigation. *Psychiatric Annals.* 1996;26(3):132–138.

[19] Janoff-Bulman R, Frieze IH. A theoretical perspective for understanding reactions to victimization. *Journal of Social Issues.* 1983;39:1–17.

[20] Taylor SE. Adjustment to threatening events: A theory of cognitive adaptation. *American Psychologist*.1983;38:1161–1173.

[21] Sbraga TP, O'Donohue W. Sexual harassment. *Annual Review of Sex Research*. 2000;11. Available at: https://pubmed.ncbi.nlm.nih.gov/11351834/ (accessed on 4 January 2021).

[22] Brunswig KA, O'Donohue W. Relapse prevention, harm reduction, and sexual harassment: Confronting sexual mis-behavior in the workplace. Workshop presented at the 17th Annual Meeting of the Association for the Treatment of Sexual Abusers, Vancouver, British Columbia, Canada; 1998.

[23] De Judicibus M, McCabe MP. Blaming the target of sexual harassment: Impact of gender role, sexist attitudes, and work role. *Sex Role*. 2001;44(7/8):401–441.

[24] Brewer M. Further beyond nine to five: An integration and future directions. *Journal of Social Issues*. 1982;38:148–158.

[25] Pryor JB, Stoller LM. Sexual cognition processes in men who are high in the likelihood to sexually harass. *Personality and Social Psychology Bulletin*.1994;20:163–169.

[26] Reilly ME, Lott B, Caldwell D, DeLuca L. Tolerance for sexual harassment related to self-reported sexual victimization. *Gender and Society*. 1992;6(1):122–138.

[27] Cortoni F, Marshall WL. Sex as a coping strategy and its relationship to juvenile sexual history and intimacy in sexual offenders. *Sexual Abuse: A Journal of Research and Treatment*. 2001;13(1):27–34.

[28] Marshall WL, Marshall LE, Serran GA, Fernandez YM. *Treating Sexual Offenders: An Integrated Approach*. New York, NY: Routledge; 2006.

[29] Lucero MA, Middleton KL, Finch WA, Valentine SR. An empirical investigation of sexual harassers: Toward a perpetrator typology. *Human Relations*. 2003;56:1461–1483.

[30] Ward T, Hudson SM. A model of the relapse process in sexual offenders. *Journal of Interpersonal Violence*. 1998;13(6):700–725.

CHAPTER 11

Clinician's Role
in Addressing
Legal Aspects

Disciplines of medicine and psychology provide expert assistance in the court proceedings in the cases of sexual harassment.[1] An expert witness is often retained whenever the subject matter of a case is complex or of scientific nature so that the expert can better explain the technical issues to a jury, a situation which arises frequently in current times in the court proceedings. Ideally, expert witnesses should always work as an asset by adding evidentiary support to the case and increasing the possibility of a favourable outcome. Full and free disclosure of facts from witnesses, unhampered by fear of retaliatory lawsuits, is required for the proper administration of justice. The witness immunity doctrine is a concept which originated to encourage open and honest testimony without fear of a subsequent lawsuit related to the testimony. However, the accountability of experts is important because of the increasing use of experts in the legal system in recent times.[2] The risk of misuse of experts is always there.

Psychiatry as a body of knowledge is widely used, and help is often sought from its experts to determine various shades of abnormal behaviour, which come in conflict with the law within the ambit of the judicial framework. Psychiatrists are often summoned in the courts as an expert witness and some psychiatrists, by choice work, as forensic psychiatrists to deal with mental health issues related to the law; therefore, they possess legal knowledge required for dealing with psychiatric problems in relation to law. This requirement is not adequately met with during the medical training or during the residency programme; however, with regular exposure to court cases, they come to learn the legal implications of various psychiatric disorders. To become a forensic psychiatrist is both rewarding and challenging.

In some countries, sexual harassers are routinely referred for psychiatric evaluation and treatment by the courts. They are allowed to rejoin their work only after they have received adequate psychiatric treatment and become fit to work. Victims are also referred for psychiatric evaluation to determine the extent of mental health damage caused due to sexual harassment and also for a psychiatric diagnosis of the clinical condition. This practice helps not only to evaluate the damage and make a diagnosis but also in therapeutic intervention and designing the preventive programmes. In India, it is not a routine practice to refer them for psychiatric evaluation except in cases where there is overt evidence of mental health issues. However, psychiatrists are expected to be aware of the procedure and its implications.

11.1. Clinical Evaluation of the Victim

Since sexual harassment at workplace is long recognized as a public health problem, the clinical importance of the problem cannot be underestimated. The psychiatrists interested in the discipline of forensic psychiatry should have adequate training in a forensic work related to psychiatry, which is necessary for the clinicians to become forensic expert. They should know that clinical evaluations and reports are different from forensic evaluations and reports. They should also know the following relevant legal issues:

- Legal requirements in a psychiatric case
- Court proceedings
- Conducting forensic evaluations

- Interacting with the victim, lawyers and judges
- Writing forensic reports
- Making depositions and court testimonies.

Clinical evaluation of the victim must be done in person, in order to obtain an accurate mental status. Ideally, it should be performed in two stages, subject to the court's permission, to allow for corroboration, follow-up questions and additional information the victim may remember after the first interview. Additional information obtained subsequently is incorporated in the main body of the information obtained earlier during the first interview. The interview should be conducted in a neutral professional space, and the victim should be permitted breaks, as needed. The presence of third parties should be avoided, like lawyers or supportive individuals, so that the content of the interview is not distorted or influenced by the presence of third-party individuals. At the very beginning, before initiating the evaluation, the victim should be explained about:

- The purpose of the evaluation.
- Who has retained the clinician for her evaluation?
- Confidentiality cannot be promised as the clinician may testify in court regarding the contents of the evaluation. Confidentiality is often a big issue in forensic reporting, and it may come in conflict with the professional ethic.
- With the forensic evaluation, no treatment relationship exists, and no treatment is offered by the forensic psychiatrist. There is no therapeutic alliance between the victim and the forensic psychiatrist.
- The impact of the interview and evaluation on the victim's case may be positive, negative or neutral. It all depends upon the court's decision whether it is in her favour or against.
- The victim cannot be forced to answer questions, although refusals to answer a particular question will be noted by the forensic psychiatrist and documented in the record file.
- The plaintiffs may take breaks at any time during the interview when she feels unable to continue at a stretch or tired or in no mood to respond. The forensic psychiatrist should respect her sentiments and permit her the break.

All relevant collateral materials should be reviewed by the forensic psychiatrist, if possible, prior to the clinical interview. After the evaluation is done, the report is submitted. He may be summoned for his opinion based on his expertise. In general, an expert who has evaluated the victim may be asked to give his opinion regarding[1]:

- General information about harassment and discrimination
- Specific psychiatric conditions the victim has suffered in past if any
- Victim's credibility and any evidence of distortion on her part
- Factors related to work performance, evaluations of her work and termination if occurred
- The nature of the victim's current psychiatric condition
- Factors affecting the severity of the psychiatric condition she is suffering from
- Other concomitant or pre-existing possible causes of the victim's psychiatric condition
- Relevant medical conditions she is suffering from
- The victim's treatment needs and the likely prognosis of her medical and psychiatric condition

Information gathering during the forensic evaluation may vary from clinician to clinician. Some forensic clinicians start with the most neutral information, such as past psychiatric history and family history. This allows the clinician, for some time, to develop an interviewing relationship and permits the victim to become more relaxed and comfortable with the interviewer and the surroundings. Others prefer to start with the victim's account of the events related to sexual harassment, feeling that the victim may fear that the background information is intrusive and unrelated to what she wishes to say. Both the approaches are correct to cull out relevant information for preparing the expert report.

For a credible interview, an expert should avoid any opinions regarding whether or not the discrimination occurred, a question to be decided only by the judge or the jury with whom the case is under review. Statements regarding the consistency of the view of events, the similarity of the victim's reactions to those of others victimized by discrimination and comments regarding whether or not the victim's symptoms are consistent with her pre-existing character may help establish credibility if such questions are permitted in the courtroom. Genuineness of the victim's claim needs to be established carefully avoiding sensitive questions which might possibly hurt her. If she feels offended, it may defeat the purpose of seeking information. Credibility testimony is often disallowed. The clinician should look for evidence of distortion and paranoia, which could be possibly due to:

- Axis I or II psychiatric diagnoses which the victim might be possibly suffering from.
- Revenge motivations could make the victim distort her narration.
- Monetary motivation could also lead to distortion of the information.

One should look for the above-mentioned possibilities to determine if there could be any element of distortion in what the victim says. History of past sexual assault and evidence of hypersensitivity based on previous bitter experiences may be elicited. This information may have clinical significance, but from the forensic point of view, it could be inadmissible in court.[3] During the history taking, the victim may provide additional information, which could be notably significant from the clinical point of view. This is common during the process of litigation because victims are often humiliated or traumatized by the events and therefore reluctant to reveal all details during the first interaction. If further details come out just prior to deposition, however, this would be more of an indication of attempts at embellishment.[1], [3]

Poor performance evaluations by the supervisors and mentors at the workplace or termination from employment on the grounds of incompetence by the employers also need to be evaluated from different angles in order to understand whether there was the discrimination of any kind. Are these poor evaluations and termination from service because of a poor relationship between student and mentor or employee and the employer or because of caste prejudice or minority status of the victim? Is the victim's poor performance secondary to the stress of discrimination or evidence of pre-existing difficulties and therefore alternative explanations for the victim's complaint?

For example, alcohol and drug use may be the cause of poor work performance or the result of the victim's attempt to manage anxiety, stress and depression caused by discrimination. Victims of sexual harassment who indulge in drug abuse behaviour, in turn, have poor work performance or failure in examination. Asking victims what they hope to gain from the litigation, what they feel they may have done to contribute to the situation, or what they would have liked to have done differently can be helpful in establishing honesty and credibility. Such questions provide the victim with an ample opportunity for introspection and resolution of misconceptions.

The expert clinician may be asked to evaluate the victim's current psychological status and to opine about its possible causes. This may include any related medical conditions, such as stress-related ulcers and headaches. In such cases, psychiatric history and medical history need to be reviewed, and a detailed mental state examination is conducted to provide a holistic picture of the case. The following possibilities should be kept in mind, which may occur due to the psychological impact of stress due to sexual harassment:

- Presence of psychiatric and psychosomatic symptoms and their relationship with the occurrence of sexual harassment.
- Damaged interpersonal relationships with the colleagues, seniors, mentors and the family members, including the husband.
- Damage to a sense of self may occur due to the stress of sexual harassment. The victim may develop a lack of confidence in herself.
- Diagnosable psychiatric conditions, such as PTSD and major depression.
- Grief reactions related to multiple losses in the workplace and beyond including the family.

These reactions could be the consequence of the original sexual harassment or discrimination or be the result of retaliative action by the harasser against the victimized individual for complaining against him. The expert clinician should avoid inappropriate or overuse of classificatory systems to label a person, such as *Diagnostic and Statistical Manual* or 'International Classification of Diseases'. If indeed the victim does not meet criteria for a full diagnosis, like PTSD, it is better to state the damages in terms of symptomatology and other psychological injuries, rather than to overdiagnose a condition such as PTSD or major depression.

Pre-existing psychiatric conditions, pre-existing life stressors, the presence or absence of supportive relationships, the trauma of the litigation process and the severity, duration and context of the original sexual harassment events may all contribute to the severity of the reactions. If, in some cases, the adverse reaction to the litigation process cannot be claimed as damages, then the expert clinician may be asked to differentiate between conditions due to original events of sexual harassment and conditions due to stress of litigation.[4]

The expert clinician could also be summoned to differentiate non-employment-related causes of the current psychological condition from the symptoms caused by sexual harassment. Life stressors concomitant with or occurring after the sexual harassment events, pre-existing psychiatric illness or related medical conditions with psychological symptoms will need to be documented clearly, for example, psychiatric symptoms caused by hypothyroidism.

The expert forensic clinician is sometimes called to comment on the victim's prognosis and treatment needs. This will depend upon many factors, such as the persistence of pre-existing psychiatric condition where treatment is required and the presence of current diagnosable illness that may also require treatment. If no psychiatric illness is present, the severity and the degree of the damage to the self, relationships and other related losses, as well as the difficulties faced by the victim due to the sexual harassment such as resuming her normal life at the workplace, all need to be assessed to determine the treatment needs.

During the evaluation, the clinician should also be on the alert for countertransference reactions. Involvement in sexual harassment cases elicits strong feelings and can exaggerate personal biases on the part of the evaluator. The expert clinician needs to remain aware of his own professional responsibility to remain objective and neutral. There are many factors that may skew his judgment; he has to stay cautious about those. Strong ideological biases for or against women's' rights and strong opinions regarding the significance of gender discrimination as a problem can interfere with honest clinical evaluation. The expert may be inadvertently pulled into the adversarial atmosphere of the litigation process and appear to be more of a 'hired gun' than an impartial expert. The expert may confuse the role of the forensic evaluator with the role of treating clinician and attempt to save the patient or align with her inappropriately in his approach.[3]

The forensic experts may make treatment recommendations but should not offer treatment or agree to be the treating clinician for the victim or for any family members of the victim after the case has closed. Positive or negative media attention toward the case may also skew the expert's judgment. If the expert has ever been victimized by abuse, he may overidentify with the victim's damages or, conversely, minimize the victim's distress if he himself had very little reaction to the abuse. The trained clinicians may view the allegations as fantasy or have a tendency to blame the victimized person. Clinicians overidentified with the 'victim culture' may see the victimized person as always right. The expert forensic clinician has to be above all these situations.

11.2. Clinician as an Expert Witness

When the case lands up in the court for trial, treatment records may be required to testify in a sexual harassment case if the victim has undergone any treatment for the same. Records may be required to determine the extent of the damage or the money spent on treatment of the condition due to sexual harassment. The role of the expert witness differs from that of the treating clinician. Mental health professionals should not attempt to combine the two situations as the aim of the two situations is different. Expert witnesses conduct clinical evaluations that address the pertinent legal questions involved in the case. The evaluations are not confidential as they are openly argued in the court. A doctor–patient relationship does not exist, and no treatment is offered by the expert witness. The process usually involves:

- A pre-examination meeting between the lawyer and the clinician serving as the expert witness.
- Clinical evaluation of the victim is done from the forensic point of view and not the treatment point of view.

ıse and strategies, expert witnessing or both. The clinician providing xpert testimony should not join the lawyer to furnish ongoing input s the trial progresses[3] as it could undermine the credibility of the xpert's testimony.

Forensic consultation should take place privately between the awyer and the forensic clinician outside the courtroom. The forensic linician should ask the lawyer to arrange for the clinical evaluation of the ictim and provide time in which she could be available in a professional ffice location for the interview. Any arrangement regarding necessary psychological testing should also be made. The forensic clinician should discuss whether a formal report will be required and, if so, whether a particular format is mandated by the court. Some lawyers prefer to discuss the expert's findings regarding the victim via a private conference prior to obtaining a written report. This provides the opportunity for the lawyer to terminate further services if the opinion is unfavourable to the case. The clinician should feel free to define areas where he does not feel he has expertise in which to testify and to limit the scope of his services in accordance with his areas of expertise and experience.

After the evaluation and review of the relevant material, the expert should report the findings to the lawyer. If this verbal report is unfavourable, the lawyer may wish to terminate the consultation at this point or ask the expert for advice regarding how to best present the unfavourable information. The written report should include:

- A list of the materials reviewed
- A summary of the victim's history and clinical evaluation, including the mental status examination
- Any relevant history
- Diagnosis
- Prognosis of the case and treatment recommendations
- Any conclusions regarding other relevant legal questions pertaining to the case
- The reasons for the prognosis and the treatment recommended

The lawyer will discuss potential dates and times for testimony in court or for depositions if this will be required. If a pretrial deposition is

- Post-evaluation conferencing with the lawyer may
- Preparation of a formal written report, a verbal re
  findings during deposition.
- Courtroom testimony and cross-examination.

An outlined of various aspects of a case of sexual har
follows.[5]

Meeting of the clinician with the lawyer before exami
case should include the lawyer asking the clinician to revi
related to the case, evaluate the victim and render various p
opinions related to the case. The clinician should discuss
issues with the lawyer before agreeing to evaluate the victir
Victims calling directly to request the services of an expert fo
cian should be advised to have their lawyer contact him for
of the legal issues. Any contact between the expert clinici
victim prior to the examination will diminish the expert's cred
fee for the clinician's services should be agreed upon in advan
payment should be unrelated to either the evaluation results o
successful outcome. The clinician should also discuss with th
which materials will be reviewed and ask for all materials he fe
be relevant to assure an unbiased opinion. The commonly
materials are medical records, employment records, school
psychological testing and past employment records and the de
and interrogatories. If the treating clinician is brought into the
his role should be defined whether he is going to provide a p
ric or psychological evaluation of the victim, whether he will
general information regarding psychiatric or psychological tre
or particular psychiatric or psychological conditions. Will the cl
provide information regarding the nature of psychiatric or psycho
reactions to abuse or the nature of harassment or gender discrimin
It should also be clear whether the clinician will serve as a cons
to the lawyer and provide scientific studies, case examples, and re
materials and advise the lawyer regarding case strategies, psychol
issues related to jury selection, or the defendant's character.

The clinical expert witness provides testimony regarding
relevant issues in the area of his expertise while the forensic ex
provides consultation to the lawyer regarding relevant aspects of

required, the lawyer will request potential times that the expert could be available. The lawyer is also responsible for making the deposition arrangements regarding time and place with the opposing lawyer, who is responsible for paying the expert for the deposition time. It is prudent for experts to have a pre-agreement regarding the length of time for depositions, as well as in regard to pre-payment. If no deposition is required, a similar discussion regarding potential trial dates, potential times the expert could be available for trial testimony, and payment of the expert's fee should be negotiated.

11.3. Expert Testimony

During the trial in the court, before the deposition or the trial of the case, the lawyer and the forensic expert witness in the case should:

- Review any additional information that may have been accumulated since the time of the evaluation
- Discuss the legal issues of the case and the lawyer's theory regarding the case
- Plan the deposition or the trial strategy

The lawyer should discuss the expected questions with the expert, which may be posed by the opposing lawyer. If the expert is deposed, he will be asked to review and sign a typed transcript of the deposition prior to the trial. Prior to trial, the lawyer will plan the sequence of questions for the expert, review the deposition, and anticipate opposing attorney questions that are likely to come up during cross-examination. Some review of the expert's curriculum vitae, qualifications and special expertise in the field may also be discussed prior to trial.

Clinicians who are unfamiliar with the court proceedings may choose to visit a courtroom or practice their answers to proposed questions via a mock trial before the actual court proceedings take place. This exercise will help to reduce anxiety for those experts who are not used to provide testimony and for those who are appearing in the court as an expert for the first time. The expert should be dressed neatly and conservatively for the courtroom appearance; it commands respect, as well as demonstrates respect for the legal process.[5]

During the initial stage of the courtroom testimony, the lawyer will ask the expert witness a standard series of questions regarding the expert's education, training and expertise in order to establish the individual's credibility (*voir dire*). Relevant information regarding research publications are often obtained from the expert's curriculum vitae, and these are made available to the lawyer prior to the trial. The opposing lawyer will then continue the interrogation, focusing on any areas in which the expert may be weak or found wanting in answering. This testimony can provide the expert with the opportunity to accustom himself to the courtroom, assess the attitude of the jury and the opposing lawyer and prepare for direct testimony. After qualifying, the expert will be asked to describe the clinical examination, including any psychological testing or laboratory test results conducted by the expert. He will testify on victim's credibility, plaintiff's current psychological condition or mental health status, factors contributing to the victim's current condition, other possible causes for the victim's condition, general questions regarding the common psychological reaction to sexual harassment and discrimination, general questions and psychiatric illnesses that are commonly associated with it. The treatment recommendation and prognosis, as well as the reasons for the recommendation, may be elicited in detail. The opposing lawyer may object to questions at any point during the testimony. The court will rule on the merit of any objection, after which testimony will resume. The expert should not take objection personally or feel offended to any question and should feel free to ask that question posed to him be repeated or clarified for a better understanding to answer.

After the completion of the direct testimony by the case lawyer, the opposing lawyer will cross-examine the expert and attempt to discredit the expert or any opinion that is unfavourable to his case. Lawyers may clarify materials previously introduced via the redirect process. Opposing lawyer may then cross-examine regarding any redirect testimony, and the redirect process can be repeated. If the testimony is lengthy, the witness may ask for a break, and it is usually permissible by the court. When the testimony is concluded, the witness is excused by the judge, and the expert usually leaves the courtroom. If the expert is also serving as a forensic consultant to the lawyer, he may remain in the courtroom to hear other testimony. Providing direct assistance to the lawyer during the courtroom process, sitting in the court, however, would undermine the expert's credibility as a witness. Preparing the lawyer before the courtroom proceedings or conferencing with the lawyer during recesses is more appropriate and dignified for both.

Expert should ask the lawyer to provide information regarding the outcome of the case and should feel free to contact the lawyer if this is not provided to him. It is appropriate and ethical for expert to make clear to the victim any treatment recommendations that are needed and to assist in making a referral, but it is not wise for the expert to actually provide the treatment to the victim, even after the case has been concluded. It should be left to the treating clinician to handle.

11.4. Clinician as a Material Witness

The treating clinician should avoid testifying for victims of sexual harassment and should insist on the use of forensic expert witnesses for the court proceedings. The treating clinician who is subpoenaed as a witness is often asked questions that cannot be answered because the nature of a forensic evaluation is different from the nature of a clinical evaluation process. He may also be asked to reveal clinical information regarding the patient's private life or other unrelated materials that are intrusive and an encroachment on the confidentiality which the treating clinician ought to maintain. He may be asked to answer questions that may undermine his therapeutic alliance with the patient (the victim). The patient may harbour unrealistic wishes to be saved by her therapist and is often deeply disappointed that her confidentiality could not be protected in the courtroom. Patient's records can be subpoenaed, however, even when an expert witness has been deployed. It is better to discuss these possibilities with the patient directly in order to avoid late-stage disappointment. The treating clinician is advised to keep records that are clear, concise, meticulous, medically oriented and devoid of fantasy material or extensive historical or speculative material that is not directly relevant to her clinical condition.[6] The expert forensic witness needs to play an effective and constructive role in his opinion making.

References

[1] Binder RL. Liability for the psychiatrist expert witness. *American Journal of Psychiatry.* 2002 Nov 1;159(11).

[2] Jensen EG. When 'hired guns' backfire: The witness immunity doctrine and the negligent expert witness. *University of Missouri at Kansas City Law Review.* 1993;62:185–210.

[3] Simon RI. The credible forensic psychiatric evaluation in sexual harassment litigation. *Psychiatric Annals.* 1996;26(3):139–148.

[4] Binder RL. Sexual harassment: Issues for forensic psychiatrists. *Bulletin of the American Academy of Psychiatry and the Law.* 1992;20(4):409–418.

[5] Benedek EP. Forensic aspects of sexual harassment: Serving as an expert witness, providing courtroom testimony, and preparing legal reports. In: Shrier DK, editor. *Sexual Harassment in the Workplace and Academia.* Washington D. C., WA: American Psychiatric Press, 1996; 113–132.

[6] Lenhart SA. Clinical aspects of sexual harassment and gender discrimination. Psychological consequences and treatment interventions. Abington: Routledge; 2004.

CHAPTER 12

Prevention of Sexual Harassment at Workplace

Prevention is the act[1] of stopping[2] something from happening[3] or of stopping someone from doing something. In terms of health, it is about helping people stay healthy, happy and independent by reducing the chances of problem to occur and, when it occurs, supporting people to manage it as effectively as possible. In the case of medical conditions, particularly the infectious diseases, there are preventive measures in the form of vaccines which do not allow the occurrence of diseases in people; for other medical conditions, there are other preventive measures such as adopting a prescribed lifestyle, abstinence from smoking, alcohol and drugs, social distancing to break the chain of the spread of infection and many other measures. For preventing certain offensive behaviours like sexual harassment, there are strategies which have been found to be effective in preventing such behaviours. Prevention of sexual harassment at the workplace is a challenging task and involves a series of procedures which will be discussed in the following pages.

[1] https://dictionary.cambridge.org/dictionary/english/act
[2] https://dictionary.cambridge.org/dictionary/english/stopping
[3] https://dictionary.cambridge.org/dictionary/english/happening

Non-discriminatory approach and equality of opportunity for all are the internationally recognized principles incorporated in various conventions.[1] At the workplace, unbiased attitude with the provision of equal opportunity and treatment for all employees fall under the ambit of social justice and sustainable development of the society. When sexual harassment prevails at a workplace, its impact causes far-reaching consequences not only for the victims but also for the organizations which have to suffer adversely in terms of productivity and economic gains.[2] For victims, it is an exploitative and discriminatory experience affecting their right to life and livelihood, while for workplaces, it has a direct bearing on the working environment. It creates a hostile work environment for the employees, in general, and the victims, in particular.

For every workplace, value-based work culture is important for healthy and reliable interaction among its employees. With this, the workplace ensures enhanced work productivity and overall progress of the organization.[3] To achieve this goal at the workplace, discrimination of any sort, including sexual harassment, should be prevented.

To draw strategies for prevention, understanding recent developments related to sexual harassment is necessary and remedial measures need to be understood in a right perspective.[4]

In many countries, the law mandates for a mechanism with the accountability invested with the management. In the USA, the Title VII of the Civil Rights Act of 1964 holds managers liable for sexual harassment.[5] Under the law, the employer has the affirmative duty to rid the workplace of sexual harassment and discrimination.

12.1. Strategies for Prevention

The following strategies are generally adopted by an establishment to prevent sexual harassment.

12.1.1. Adoption of a Policy against Sexual Harassment

A policy is the basic document every organization must have with clear, precise and appropriately defined guidelines. Policy against sexual harassment is a mandatory requirement for every organization which explicitly conveys its approach that sexual harassment is not tolerated within the organization at any cost, explains the consequences of violation of the policy and sets forth a process for reporting and investigating complaints along with the punitive provisions.

The employer has obligation to get the policy drafted by experienced employment and labour lawyer or an employee of the establishment entrusted with this responsibility. A policy copy is made available online within the reach of every employee. The employer must exhibit the penal provisions of sexual harassment and the order of the constitution of ICC at a clearly visible site at the place of employment.

Under the Sexual Harassment of Women at Workplace Act, 2013, only the women are protected but sexual harassment has similar psychological and physical effects for all individuals, and in their greater interest, an anti-sexual harassment policy must cater to all employees regardless of their gender. It can also be mentioned in the communication material, sensitization sessions and activities planned out for raising awareness on this issue in the organization.

All stakeholders working in the organization must be covered under this policy, which must be extendable to all employees, workers, volunteers, probationers and trainees of the establishment or extended workplace, irrespective of whether they are on deputation or are part-time, contract, consulting or full-time employees. Every individual present on the establishment's campus is covered under the policy.

The policy should also cover the redressal of sexual harassment complaints made by the employees against the clients, partners and associated vendors or other visitors.

'An organization may modify the scope of its policy in accordance with the type of work it carries out and the sort of stakeholders its employees are likely to come in contact with.' To have a policy without the employees being aware of it is meaningless without serving its purpose. To make sure that employees have consistent knowledge of their rights under this policy, it may be mandated that all employees attend an awareness course on the policy every six months or a similar short duration. The policy may include an indicative list of basic instructions. It may include information on the dissemination of the information about this policy and may carry the format of the complaint to make it user friendly and easier for aggrieved employees to file a complaint.

The proceedings under the policy are not liable to be stalled, delayed or postponed merely because the complainant is proceeding against the accused under any other provision of law under IPC:

1. The policy provisions shall not restrict the powers of the employer or the complainant to proceed against the alleged offender for any other misconduct or other legal remedies.
2. The policy is periodically reviewed and revised to keep it up to date with changes in state laws, employment policies and experiences in consultation with all stakeholders.

To a new staff member, as a standard part of induction, a copy of the policy should be given so that he/she is aware of the institutional policy right from the beginning. The policy should be translated into relevant community languages, where required, so that it is accessible to employees from culturally and linguistically diverse backgrounds. The employer should also ensure that the policy is accessible to staff members with a disability. It should also be ensured that managers and supervisors discuss and reinforce the policy at staff meetings. Verbal communication of the policy is particularly important in workplaces where the literacy of staff may be an issue. Periodic review of the policy to ensure its effective operation and up-to-date information is essential.

12.1.2. Training of Employees

Awareness about a problem empowers a person to deal with it effectively by taking appropriate measures at an appropriate time. A prepared mind is in a better position to deal with the problem effectively than facing unprepared. For the awareness of the employees, an effective communication of the policy that prohibits sexual harassment, and its redressal mechanism is very important to deal with the situation when it arises. Periodic awareness and orientation programmes for all employees should be conducted so that all the employees know the provisions of the Act. They should receive awareness training periodically with a focus on common situations which, actually maybe sexual harassment that some employees might not be aware of and suffer silently. Names and contact details of complaints committee members, including their e-mail addresses, should be widely publicized names and displayed at prominent places in the establishment.

In India, the preventive measures are provided through the 'Sexual Harassment of Women at Workplace (Prevention, Prohibition and Redressal) Act, 2013.' Although there are other legal provisions in the country to deal with the problem,[6] the 2013 Act[7] specifically deals with the prevention of sexual harassment at the workplace. The Criminal Law (Amendment) Act, 2013,[8] deals with the sexual offences including rape and should be thoroughly understood for planning preventive strategies in accordance with the Sexual Harassment of Women at Workplace (Prevention, Prohibition and Redressal) Act, 2013, and the subsequent rules put to operations on 9 December 2013.[7] Section 19(c) of the Act requires the employer to organize workshops and awareness generation programmes at regular intervals for sensitizing the employees with the provisions of the Act. Setting up a sensitizing mechanism does not mean that there is a common occurrence of sexual harassment in the organization. Prevention is always better than cure, and being pro-active always helps. Along with performance, change in employees' behaviour patterns against sexual harassment also deserves the employer's close scrutiny.

Regular training sessions for all staff members and management personnel on a regular basis and the organizational policy are both important to keep everyone updated on the issue of sexual harassment. This training should be behaviourally based, which means it should increase knowledge and understanding of specific behaviours that may amount to sexual harassment under the Act and appreciation of their nature that they are unwanted and illegal acts. Regular refresher training is recommended to ensure no employee indulges into such unlawful conduct. All managers need to be trained on their role in ensuring that the workplace is free from sexual harassment. The Act should be given wide publicity by displaying anti-sexual harassment posters on notice boards.

There are different ways sexual harassment can be addressed, which should be known to the employees. This includes informal action such as confronting the harasser directly (but only if the victim feels confident enough to do so) or making a formal complaint using the organisation's internal complaints procedures. The way the complaints will be handled should be documented in the policy or a separate complaints procedure. Employees can also approach the commission or the relevant state or territory anti-discrimination agency for information and confidential advice.

In recent years, there has been an increasing number of lawsuits, settlements and hostility at the workplace. As a consequence, there are adverse effects on the working, the productivity and academic outputs which worries the employers. The legal battles not only bring a bad name to the organizations, but they also cause substantial embarrassment for the employers and financial losses to the organizations. These situations are alarming bells for the organizations to recognize occurrence and take appropriate preventive measures.[9]

Countries such as the USA, Canada and the UK have come up with several training programmes focusing their attention on identification and prevention of sexual harassment at workplace in order to avoid prolonged litigations and preventable burden on the organisations.[10] These training programmes are provided by independent consultants who also include retaliation prevention strategies in their programmes, educate employers and employees to identify sexual harassment and provide step-by-step guidance on how to deal with complaints, offer support to victims and provide information to alleged harassers.

Vishaka Guidelines judgment[11] on prevention to tackle sexual harassment, way back in 1997, was the first attempt in India. Its spirit has found its way into the 2013 Act,[7] which promotes the rights of women at the workplace free from sexual harassment and emphasizes prevention. The effective use of this legislation is possible only through awareness generation among the employees, employers, students, teachers and all those involved in the implementation of this Act. Majority of the workforce in the government sector is still unaware of the provisions and effectiveness of the Act because of poor exposure. Many of the private organizations are not even aware of the existence of such an Act in the country. They all need to be made aware through regular orientation workshops so that the Act is in effective use.[12]

Many private companies refrain from investing funds in such an activity which they consider is not relevant to their organizations. There is a general belief among most of the organizations that their organization is free from sexual harassment hence they need no complaints committee or awareness training programmes or even a policy as such.

Training empowers people to deal with the situation. However, in India, there are not many organizations capable to conduct quality training programmes. Sensitizing the employees about the fine line between healthy mixing of colleagues of different sexes and behaviours amounting to sexual harassment is a task only the skilled trainers can impart.

The Institute of Secretariat Training and Management[13] in India has been conducting gender sensitization training programmes since long, and currently, its focus is on the specific issue of prevention and the redressal of complaints of sexual harassment at workplaces. The Institute of Secretariat Training and Management invites all the stakeholders in the government to get their officials trained by this institute. A two-day workshop to equip the trainees with the skills to develop professional competence and prevent sexual harassment is carried out.

12.2. Authorities Responsible for Prevention

The following are the authorities responsible for the prevention of sexual harassment at the workplace.

12.2.1. Government

State governments are ultimately responsible to provide a safe and protected environment to their subjects whether at the workplace or otherwise. It is the overall duty of the government to provide a safe and conducive workplace environment so that the employees carry out their work without fear, free from any kind of intimidation.

12.2.2. District Officer (DO)

The government appoints District Officer (DO) for every district to exercise powers or discharge functions at the district levels (including every block, taluka, tehsil, ward and municipality). DO monitors the functioning of complaints committee and the training programmes dealing with the preventive aspects. He/she is bound to create forums for dialogue, that is, Panchayati Raj institutions, *gram sabhas*, women's groups, urban local bodies or like bodies to resolve the issue at the local level. He/she ensures the capacity and skill building of complaints committees through orientation workshops and other awareness programmes. Under the law, the employer or DO is obliged to create a workplace free of sexual harassment.

12.2.3. Employer

The employer of a workplace is responsible for all the activities taking place at his establishment. He/she is the key person for his work establishment as a leader of the team of employees to protect their interests and to provide them safety. He/she is legally bound to provide them a healthy work environment with no discrimination on the basis of gender. He/she should make it clear that any instance of sexual harassment is treated as misconduct. The employment agreements, service rules, policies and procedures and standing orders must clearly state that sexual harassment will be treated as misconduct. The repercussions of sexual harassment must also be clearly stated.

The companies registered in India need to file this annual report with the Registrar of Companies; societies and trusts need to file this report with the charity commissioner or registrar of societies. However, sole proprietorships, partnership firms do not need to file this annual report, rather, they need to inform DO about the sexual harassment cases filed with the organization and their status.

Employers are primarily responsible for all activities taking place in their organizations and they should be aware of all those activities. There should be a healthy communication between the employer and the employees regarding the difficulties faced by the employees at the workplace to make sure no one is bullied or intimidated on account of gender. For the fear of retaliation and further harassment, many of the victims do not come forward to report and suffer silently. An environment of trust needs to be created by the employer where confidentiality is ensured, and the victim comes forward with the complaint

without hesitation and fear. This should be clearly conveyed to the employees that making a complaint will have no bearing on their job or career prospects. They should be encouraged to open up with their grievances for appropriate redressal. The employer is also responsible to aid the employees in filing a complaint against the accused and help the victim in taking legal action, including a criminal measure. The employer may also choose to initiate a complaint against the accused if the woman employer desires so.

12.3. Preventing Online Harassment

Employers play a pivotal role in prevention, provided that they emphasize preventive mechanism in position descriptions and demonstrate their ability to deal with discrimination and harassment issues as part of their overall responsibility. It is essential for them to know the model appropriate standards of professional conduct and ethics related to the use of computer and the internet since most of the office work, in the current times, is done on a computer. There are certain responsibilities on the part of the user of the computer and monitoring of the employer to prevent the misuse of the device. As technology advances, computers have a greater role in workplace functioning, and correspondingly, the chances of its misuse also escalate.[14], [15]

The internet as a device can be used to pursue both healthy and pathological behaviours; it can be used for constructive and positive advancement and joy and also for negative purposes to humiliate, terrorize and block social progress. The use of the internet and email to access or communicate sexual material contributes to hostility in the working environment. It is generally believed that an email is a private form of communication, but once it is sent, it can be shared with any number of people, all with the person's or organization's name attached. With the increase in social networking[4] sites, more and more people are allowing their private information to be shared publicly. Social media platforms become fertile grounds for online harassment. Those who experience online harassment directly can have profound

---

[4] https://en.wikipedia.org/wiki/Social_networking_service

real-world consequences, ranging from mental or emotional stress to reputational damage or even fear for one's personal safety.

Emotional stress caused in such a way may cause adverse mental health effects on the victim, it prevents the genuine users from legitimate use of the internet for the fear of getting implicated into sexual intimidation by some harassers.

Again, employers have a big role in prevention. They should clarify to employees through an internet policy that inappropriate use of the internet and email will not be tolerated. The office policy should prohibit inappropriate use of computer technology. Employees should be directed not to forward offensive emails received from another source; if they do so, they make themselves responsible for the material and liable for punitive action.[16] There should be regular audits to monitor the incidence of sexual harassment and the use and effectiveness of the complaints procedure, policies, in order to provide a safe, healthy and conducive work environment to the employees.

Online guidelines containing explanations, recommendations, tips and instructions should be posted on various sites in addition to the training for proper internet use. It is likely that just educational attempts will not prevent people with high proclivities to misuse the internet, regular monitoring will help. It is possible that for some of these people, educational intervention might change their perceptions, attitudes and values. They should be made aware of considerations new to them, and that will be a contribution to changing their potential problematic behaviours.

Prevention of online sexual harassment generally involves three parallel ways.

12.3.1. Legislation and Law Enforcement

The legislation is required to draw well-defined boundaries for interpersonal sex-related behaviours. The legislation also plays an important social role in communicating the social context of what is accepted in a given society and thus serves as a clear sign of values and morals. Implementation of laws is necessary so that they do not just remain theoretical declarations.[16], [17]

In India, the Information Technology Act, 2000, deals with cyber-crime against women and children. Sections 66E, 67 and 67A of the Act provide for the punishment for voyeurism, publishing or transmitting of obscene/sexually explicit material in electronic form. Sections 354A and 354D of IPC provides punishment for cyberbullying and cyberstalk-ing. Section 79 of the Information Technology Act, 2000, provides for certain due diligence to be followed by intermediaries failing which they would be liable. No intermediaries users of computer resource should host, upload, display, modify, publish, transmit, update or share any information on that is grossly defamatory, paedophilic, harmful, obscene, pornographic, harmful to minor, in any way, or violates such other law.

12.3.2. Changing the Organizational Social Culture

Although the legal guidelines for internet use are important, they have a limited role in preventing sexual harassment. To control sexual harassment online effectively, there should be a change in the cultural norms in which sexual harassment occurs. Change in cultural norms should include the clear and consistent messages of zero tolerance for sexual harassment without laxity. Awareness should be created among people by conducting training workshops for potential victims, the harassers and the people in general.

The inherent culture of the internet with limitless space and mul-ticultural users makes it difficult to create awareness among its users. It may be possible in local online communities through the exercise of responsible, dedicated leadership armed with a firm anti-sexual harassment policy.

12.3.3. Education and Training of Potential Harassers

Educating the potential victims and harassers regarding ethics and cultural values will help preventing sexual harassment online.

The harmful impact of internet-related harassment should be taught in schools devoted to smart and safe internet use for beneficial purposes. Educational intervention helps the children and the potential victims and the harassers to review standards of behaviour, together with the identification of hostile and malicious communications.

12.4. Encouraging Employees and Trade Unions

The sole purpose of the preventive mechanism is not to ignore the initial symptom which can possibly enfold into full-blown sexual harassment. If the workplace culture discourages any kind of dissent and labels a complainant a 'troublemaker', the victim chooses to keep quiet and suffer silently and the purpose of preventive mechanism gets entirely defeated. Employees unions should come forward to encourage and help potential victims in their effort. The employer should encourage the employees for the followings.

12.4.1. Speak out Fearlessly

The potential victim should be encouraged to speak out and be told not to tolerated harassment silently. Speaking out helps to acknowledge and pushes the management to take effective measures in order to prevent a potential incident. Speaking out also helps in changing the attitudes of people towards the issue as they come to know that such a problem may occur at their workplace.

12.4.2. Not to Ignore Subtle Signs

There could be certain subtle signs and developments, which possibly culminate into harassing behaviour; therefore, an employee should not ignore others' warning about a particular employee or a social setting, which could cause her sexual harassment. Often such a warning is laughed away as an unfounded fear and doubt about some person and not taken seriously by the potential victim. There is no harm in acknowledging such a concern of a friend and adopt safety measures to prevent or avert a possible mishap. A prepared mind can deal effectively with the situation than when it comes as an unexpected shock.

12.4.3. Keeping Record of Events

Keeping a record of the event is useful in the long run, and the employer should encourage the employees to have them as documentary proof. The victim should keep track of what happens with her in a diary, and she should also keep any letters or notes or other documents like e-mails, pornographic material sent to her or restaurant bill received by her; such documentary evidence are helpful in proving her point during the inquiry process. She should write down the dates, times, places and an account of what exactly happened along with the names of the witnesses if present. The employer should encourage all the employees to follow these instructions.

All employees are responsible to comply with the organization's sexual harassment policy, offer support to anyone who is being harassed and let them know where they can get help and advice (they should not, however, approach the harasser themselves), maintain complete confidentiality if they provide information during the investigation of a complaint. Staff should be warned that spreading gossip or rumours may expose them to a defamation action.

12.5. Recommendations

The EEOC[18] recommends the interventions to help preventing sexual harassment and assault in the workplace; it provides resources and training and the development of new tools to prevent and address workplace sexual harassment. To make workplaces safer for all workers and capture resulting productivity gains, EEOC's recommendations are as follows:

1. Employers should conduct surveys to assess the extent to which harassment is a problem within their organization even in the absence of reported cases.
2. They should adopt, maintain and communicate comprehensive anti-harassment policy.
3. They should ensure prompt disciplinary action for perpetrators, consistent and proportionate to the severity of the circumstances.
4. Employers should train middle-management and supervisors on how to respond effectively to observed instances of sexual harassment.
5. Employers should include workplace civility training and bystander intervention training.

6. Labour unions should ensure that their own policies and reporting systems meet the same standards as employer systems.
7. Researchers should assess the impact of workplace training on reducing the level of sexual harassment in the workplace.
8. The government should conduct additional research, including developing and fielding new polls, adding questions to existing surveys on sexual harassment and assault through agencies such as women's commission.

12.6. Future Directions

Over the past few years, sexual harassment as a concept has gained considerably positive research attention, which reveals that sexual harassment comes either from an organizational or sociocultural standpoint or from a victim-based perspective. These studies have not only resulted in positive knowledge gains, but they also have made us aware of some important knowledge gaps that exist in our understanding and require attention for further research to fill up these gaps.

The main gaps and limitations evident in the field direct the possibility for future research in the concerned areas to deal with the issue more effectively and prevent its occurrence.

Although there has been one main valuable effort to develop an instrument that measures the likelihood of someone to sexually harass,[19] more such instruments are needed to be developed to authenticate the findings. The next necessary step forward in this direction is the integration of sociocultural and organizational issues with focused and rigorous research on the individual characteristics of sexual harassers, which is grossly inadequate at present.

The majority of researchers now view sexual harassment as an act along a continuum of behaviours that could result in sexual violence such as rape.[20] Longitudinal studies to follow young sexual harassers for long periods are required to examine their individual characteristics to determine who goes on to commit more serious sexual aggression and who does not. Once we are able to identify the types of sexual harassers who may go on to commit other forms of sexual aggression would increase our ability to devise effective preventative and treatment programmes for use with first time sexual harassers. This is essential for the reduction of sexual harassment, and possibly more severe sexual crimes as well. This could be possibly understood only when we consider sexual harassment as an act that is viewed along a continuum of behaviours that could result in sexual violence.[10]

For our understanding, research is required to know the basic typologies of men who sexually harass and other related areas. Most of the research is victim-focused, and rarely it is incumbent on sexual harassers themselves to obtain information as to the key factors facilitating sexual harassment. In comparison to other fields of related research (e.g., rape), current typologies of sexual harassers are very simplistic and offer no useful guidance about the key characteristics of harassers. The future avenue of research would be for researchers to develop more sophisticated typologies that may be tested empirically using self-report data for sexual harassers and or victims.

Currently, the most accepted theory of sexual harassment is only the multifactorial theory that has been adapted from an ageing theory of child molestation developed over 20 years ago. A comprehensive theory of sexual harassment needs to be developed. A more sophisticated multi-factorial theory, which could integrate individual, socio-cultural, biological and organizational factors convincingly, needs to be developed if this field is to grow meaningfully for better understanding and effective prevention of sexual harassment. Researchers also need to develop more convincing single-factor theories that focus only on the sexual harassers' characteristics and their proclivity to harassment.

There are well-established theories in other areas of sexual aggression which describe the cognitions of sexual offenders (socio-cognitive theories), their empathy deficits and also their intimacy problems and attachment styles.[21], [22] Concepts of these theories could be utilized in the research of sexual harassment to know the characteristics of sexual harassers in more detail.

Sexual harassment is more commonly prevalent than any other sexual crime and affects a significant proportion of working women impacting their personal lives, professional functioning and preventing them from advancing in their career at the workplace. It encroaches upon the fundamental human rights of the victims and the right to work with dignity.[23]-[27] It is recognized that both employers and employees need to know what the acceptable behaviour at the workplace is, how sexual harassment starts, what it is, how it works, what the personal and organizational consequences are and how to effectively deal with these consequences.[28]

Research over the past three decades has enabled sexual harassment to be put on the social map and has made people aware of it as an everyday problem potentially affecting anyone. Understanding sexual harassment is the very first step in dealing with it, and the ongoing research needs to focus on how to effectively deal with and treat the sexual harasser in order to prevent and control unwanted sexualized behaviour to improve the work experience of millions of women world-wide and maintain an all-important organizational balance.

References

[1]   United Nations Human Rights. The UN Convention on the Elimination of all Forms of Discrimination against Women. Available at: https://www.ohchr.org/en/professionalinterest/pages/cedaw.aspx (accessed on 8 January 2021).

[2]   Gutek BA. Sexual harassment: Rights and responsibilities. *Employee Responsibilities and Rights Journal.* 1993;6(4):325–340.

[3]   Fitzgerald LF. Sexual harassment: Violence against women in the workplace. *American Psychology.* 1993;48:1070–1076.

[4]   Lenhart SA. *Clinical Aspects of Sexual Harassment and Gender Discrimination.* Abington: Routledge; 2004.

[5]   AAUW. Know Your Rights: Title VII of the Civil Rights Act of 1964. Available at: https://ww3.aauw.org/what-we-do/legal-resources/know-your-rights-at-work/title-vii/ (accessed on 8 January 2021).

[6]   Wikipedia. The Indian Penal Code 1860. Available at: https://en.wikipedia.org/wiki/Indian_Penal_Code (accessed on 8 January 2021).

[7]   Ministry of Law and Justice. The Sexual Harassment of Women at Workplace (Prevention, Prohibition and Redressal) Act, 2013. The Gazette of India. Available at: http://www.nitc.ac.in/app/webroot/img/upload/77331401.pdf (accessed on 8 January 2021).

[8]   Mehta S. Rape law in India: Problems in prosecution due to loopholes in the law. *SSRN Electronic Journal.* 2013 Apr. Available at: https://papers.ssrn.com/sol3/papers.cfm?abstract_id=2250448 (accessed on 8 January 2021).

[9] Burnham L, Theodore N. *Home Economics: The Invisible and Unregulated World of Domestic Work.* National Domestic Workers Alliance Centre for Urban Economic Development: University of Illinois at Chicago Data Centre, 2012. Available at: http://www.idwfed.org/en/resources/home-economics-the-invisible-and-unregulated-world-of-domestic-work/@@ display-file/attachment_1 (accessed on 8 January 2021).

[10] Chan DKS, Chow SY, Lam CB, Cheung SF. Examining the job-related, psychological and physical outcomes of workplace sexual harassment: A meta-analytic review. *Psychology of Women Quarterly.* 2008;32(4):362–376.

[11] *Wikipedia. Vishakha and Others v State of Rajasthan.* Available at: https://en.wikipedia.org/wiki/Vishakha_and_others_v_State_of_ Rajasthan#:~:text=Vishaka%20and%20others%20v%20State,19%20and%20 21%20of%20the (accessed on 8 January 2021).

[12] Ministry of Women and Child Development. Handbook on Sexual Harassment of Women at Workplace (Prevention, Prohibition and Redressal) Act 2015. Available at: https://www.iitk.ac.in/wc/data/ Handbook%20on%20Sexual%20Harassment%20of%20Women%20at%20 Workplace.pdf (accessed on 8 January 2021).

[13] Ministry of Personnel Public Grievances and Pension. Institute of Secretariat Training and Management (ISTM). Government of India, New Delhi. Available at: https://www.istm.gov.in/home/view_course_template/205 (accessed on 8 January 2021).

[14] EEOC. Facts about Sexual Harassment. Available at: https://www.eeoc. gov/eeoc/publications/fs-sex.cfm (accessed on 8 January 2021).

[15] The United States Department of Justice. Sexual Assault. 2018. Available at: https://www.justice.gov/ovw/sexual-assault#sa (accessed on 8 January 2021).

[16] Barak A, Fisher WA, Belfry S, Lashambe DR. Sex, guys, and cyberspace: Effects of internet pornography and individual differences on men's attitudes towards women. *Journal of Psychology and Human Sexuality.* 1999 Jul 15;11(1):63–91.

[17] Thomas AM, Kitzinger C. *Sexual Harassment: Contemporary Feminist Perspectives.* Buckingham: Open University Press; 1997.

[18] EEOC. Policy guidance on current issues of sexual harassment. 1990. Available at: https://www.eeoc.gov/laws/guidance/policy-guidance-current-issues-sexual-harassment (accessed on 8 January 2021).

[19] Pryor JB. Sexual harassment proclivities in men. *Sex Roles.* 1987 Sep 1;17(5-6):269–290.

[20] Lucero MA, Allen RE, Middleton KL. Sexual harassers: Behaviours, motives and change over time. *Sex Role.* 2006 Sep 1;55(5-6):331–343.

[21] Ward T, Polaschek DLL, Beech AR. *Theories of Sexual Offending.* Hoboken, NJ: Wiley; 2006.

[22] Alieza D, Lenhart A, Miller R, Schulte B, Weingarten E. *Sexual Harassment: A Severe and Pervasive Problem.* Washington DC, WA: New America

Foundation; 2018. Available at: https://www.newamerica.org/better-life-lab/reports/sexual-harassment-severe-and-pervasive-problem/summary-of-findings (accessed on 8 January 2021).

[23] Campbell AF. Housekeepers and Nannies Have No Protection from Sexual Harassment under Federal Law 2018. Available at: https://www.vox.com/2018/4/26/17275708/housekeepers-nannies-sexual-harassment-laws (accessed on 8 January 2021).

[24] Faber M. Fox News Has Spent $45 Million on Sexual Harassment Settlements Since Mid-2016. *Fortune*; 2017. Available at: http://fortune.com/2017/05/11/fox-news-45-million-sexual-harassment/ (accessed on 8 January 2021).

[25] Frye J. Not Just the Rich and Famous: The Pervasiveness of Sexual Harassment Across Industries Affects All Workers. Centre for American Progress, 2017. Available at: https://www.americanprogress.org/issues/women/news/2017/11/20/443139/not-just-rich-famous/ (accessed on 8 January 2021).

[26] Hegewisch A, Deitch C, Murphy E. Sexual Harassment against Female Immigrant Workers and EEOC. In: *Ending Sex and Race Discrimination in the Workplace: Legal Interventions that Push the Envelope*. Washington DC, WA: Institute for Women's Policy Research; 2011. Available at: https://iwpr.org/iwpr-publications/report/ending-sex-and-race-discrimination-in-the-workplace-legal-interventions-that-push-the-envelope/ (accessed on 8 January 2021).

[27] Rodriguez M, Teofilo R. The Glass Floor: Sexual Harassment in the Restaurant Industry Report. ROC United, 2014. Available at: https://forwomen.org/wp-content/uploads/2015/09/The-Glass-Floor-Sexual-Harassment-in-the-Restaurant-Industry.pdf (accessed on 8 January 2021).

[28] Rossie A, Tucker J, Patrick K. Out of the Shadows: An Analysis of Sexual Harassment Charges Filed by Working Women. National Women's Law Centre, 2018. Available at: https://nwlc.org/resources/out-of-the-shadows-an-analysis-of-sexual-harassment-charges-filed-by-working-women/ (accessed on 8 January 2021).

About the Author

R. C. Jiloha is a visiting professor of psychiatry, All India Institute of Medical Sciences, Rishikesh (Uttatakhand). Currently, he is a professor of psychiatry at Hamdard Institute of Medical Sciences & Research, New Delhi. Formerly, he was the head of psychiatry at Faculty of Medical Sciences, University of Delhi.

After completing his MBBS from a medical college in Rohtak, Dr Jiloha completed his postgraduation (MD) in psychiatry from Postgraduate Institute of Medical Education and Research, Chandigarh, and obtained his postdoctoral fellowship from the University of California, Los Angeles (USA). He worked at Maulana Azad Medical College and Govind Ballabh Pant Hospital for 32 years in various capacities and retired as director professor in 2015. He was associated with several governmental programmes like the National Mental Health Programme. Dr Jiloha was resource person to Indian Council of Medical Research and Medical Council of India and served as the member of the Academic Councils of Aligarh Muslim University and Banaras Hindu University. Winner of several national and international awards, Dr Jiloha is the former president of many professional bodies. He has published 200 research papers and six books. His main areas of interest are social psychiatry, forensic psychiatry and drug addiction.

Index